Fodor's

E X P L O R I N G

COSTA RICA

FODOR'S TRAVEL PUBLICATIONS, INC.

NEW YORK • TORONTO • LONDON • SYDNEY • AUCKLAND

HTTP://WWW.FODORS.COM/

Published in the United States by Fodor's Travel Publications, Inc.
Published in the United Kingdom by AA Publishing.

ISBN 0–679–03204–5
First Edition

Fodor's Exploring Costa Rica

Author: **Fiona Dunlop**
Original photography: **Clive Sawyer**
Joint Series Editor: **Josephine Perry**
Cartography: **The Automobile Association**
Copy Editor: **Susi Bailey**
Cover Design: **Louise Fili, Fabrizio La Rocca**
Front Cover Silhouette: **Schafer & Hill/Tony Stone Images**

Special Sales

PRINTED IN ITALY by Printer Trento srl
10 9 8 7 6 5 4 3 2 1

How to use this book

This book is divided into five main sections:

❏ Section 1
Costa Rica Is
discusses aspects of life and living today, from ecotourism to pacifism

❏ Section 2
Costa Rica Was
places the nation in its historical context and explores those past events whose influences are felt to this day

❏ Section 3
A to Z Section
covers places to visit, arranged by region, with suggested drives. Within this section fall the Focus On articles, that consider a variety of topics in greater detail

❏ Section 4
Travel Facts
contains the strictly practical information that is vital for a successful trip

❏ Section 5:
Hotels and Restaurants
lists recommended establishments in Costa Rica, giving a brief résumé of what they offer

How to use the star rating
Most places described in this book have been given a separate rating:

▶▶▶ **Do not miss**

▶▶ **Highly recommended**

▶ **Worth seeing**

Not essential viewing

Map references
To make the location of a particular place easier to find, every main entry in this book is given a map reference, such as 66B3. The first number (66) indicates the page on which the map can be found; the letter (B) and the second number (3) pinpoint the square in which the main entry is located. The maps on the inside front cover and inside back cover are referred to as IFC and IBC respectively.

Contents

5

Quick reference

This quick-reference guide high-lights the elements of the book you will use most often: the maps; the introductory features; the Focus-on articles; the walk and the drives.

My Costa Rica by Fiona Dunlop

As the light faded and the jungle chorus moved into top gear, water started seeping into the van and the engine eventually cut off. This was Costa Rica, in the depths of the Península de Osa, and we'd forded just one river too many. Half an hour earlier, an uninspiring-looking man had appeared, wading through the river, machete tucked into his belt, cigarette stuck firmly to his bottom lip, hat low over his eyes. Two Western women confronted by a Tico gold-digger in the middle of nowhere... "You'll need a tractor," he stated laconically after surveying the van, which sat firmly entrenched in the riverbed, then wished us luck and strolled off down the dirt road. Meanwhile, unknown to us, our enterprising driver had borrowed a bicycle from a Guaymi Indian settlement and luckily had found just thatthing at a distant farm. Our trauma ended in the glare of tractor headlights as we bounced back onto the potholed road.

Encounters with the unexpected are the norm in Costa Rica, but so is survival. Ticos are always at the ready. Equally open are the expatriates involved in ecotourism ventures, often motivated by idealism and a taste for tropical nature. Less clear cut is the nonchalant Talamancan style on the Caribbean coast. When a bridge collapsed during torrential rain in Puerto Viejo, nobody quite knew where, when or how the morning bus would arrive... Meanwhile, 60miles away, a boat was awaiting me to explore Tortuguero. My tight, very Western-style schedule was shrieking, but Talamanca was not responding. The bus did eventually materialize – at a distance and necessitating a quick sprint down the beach – and I made it to my riverine appointment.

Kayaking at sunset on mercurial Pacific waves, sleeping (or not) to the background booms of Volcán Arenal, diving under a waterfall in Corcovado after a muddy, insect-infested trek, being winched 120 vertiginous feet up onto a jungle observation platform, cycling along a dirt road in the scorching midday sun to check out hotels on the Caribbean coast, having the intricacies of rainforest eco-systems explained by a botanist, sharing a drink and some tall stories with a San José con man and Clive Sawyer, the photographer, glimpsing the ethereal resplendent quetzal in flight, or FINALLY spotting the elusive residential sloth of a town square: researching *Explorer Costa Rica* certainly kept all my senses alive.

So, *buen viaje y pura vida*!

COSTA RICA IS

■ **A biodiversity of inspiring richness is squeezed into this tiny country of 19,600 square miles, offering an intoxicating cocktail of nature that has now been opened up to tourism. Volcanoes, rivers, rain forest, cloud forest, beaches, and two oceans are all in the mix, with an often-minimal infrastructure that makes access part of the adventure.** ■

Costa Rica's top generator of foreign revenue is now tourism. This may sound daunting, but do not be deterred: the industry is still in its infancy. Travel to Costa Rica and you are offered the extremes, from cosseted guided tours and comfortable luxury hotels to trekking through the wilds and sleeping in basic huts. Around 700,000 visitors crossed the borders in 1994 to visit the birthplace of the term "ecotourism," ready to birdwatch, wrestle with sailfish, snorkel around coral reefs, surf, trek up the cold slopes of Chirripó, pump adrenalin while whitewater rafting, watch a nesting turtle, or slap mosquitoes in the jungles of the south. One thing these diverse activities all have in common, and which is essential to appreciate if you visit Costa Rica, is nature.

National parks This foresighted nation first took formal measures to protect its natural assets in 1955 when a 2km (1.2 mile)-band around every volcanic crater was declared a national park. Foreigners have always played a significant role in Costa Rica's environmental issues (for better and worse). It was a Swedish naturalist who instigated the first nature reserve, of Cabo Blanco, in 1963, then an American biologist who lobbied for Tortuguero's turtle nesting grounds, in 1975. Today, Costa Rica's network of national parks and biological reserves covers 1.3 million acres, just over 10 percent of the entire country, making an enticing proposition for ecologically motivated visitors.

However, in a sensational step in 1994, park entrance fees for foreigners were suddenly hiked from a ridiculous low ($1) to an unrealistic high ($15), so spot-lighting the "ecotourism" issue in dramatic fashion. Arguments for and against continue to rage as, on the one hand, parks need to be protected from tourist damage and have their infrastructures improved, while on the other, they need paying visitors but few foreigners are willing to pay this amount. Costa Rica's greatest attraction for tourists thus wavered on the brink, before moderation finally prevailed and the "Green Pass" was produced.

Rural pleasures Not all Costa Rica's delights lie within the boundaries of its protected areas. Oceans, white sandy beaches, bucolic valleys, open pastures, torrential rivers, tropical vegetation, wildlife, and, not least, charming people, are the norm. Roads may be appalling but

10

Lower left and above: exceptionally rich wildlife draws many visitors to Costa Rica—despite the tropical downpours. Right: buggies are a new option for those wishing to explore the rough backroads

small planes can be used. Add to these attractions a high consciousness of ecotourism issues reflected in carefully planned, small-scale lodges, private nature reserves, and biological research stations, and you have a compelling mix. The only deterrent is cost. Many operators have used the eco-bandwagon to hike prices to unacceptable levels, with services that do not match, but the current surfeit of hotels and tour agencies should restore the balance.

Where to go Costa Rica's small size allows tourists to zigzag between beach, jungle, and mountains, all in one day and despite the atrocious roads. Although it is targeted for increasing beach development, Guanacaste still offers the best in beach facilities as well as extensive parks and reserves. In contrast, the Caribbean coast has a low-key, laid-back atmosphere, boosted by an intriguing local culture—and frequent

downpours. Head north to witness Volcán Arenal spitting fire, experience cloud forests, or take a boat trip along the Sarapiquí, then veer east to Tortuguero's Amazonian-style waterways or fish at Barra del Colorado. Don't miss Costa Rica's most beautiful beaches at Manuel Antonio, but, to escape the crowds, go south as well to where Costa Rica's highest peaks loom and densest rain forests flourish. In this region, Dominical, the Península de Osa and adjacent Golfo Dulce provide endless wildlife, rainforest and watersports options through small enterprises whose owners' pioneering enthusiasm is perhaps the most promising sign for Costa Rica's future.

■ **Elections are fiestas in Costa Rica, but political awareness is high, and so is pride in democratic and pacifist traditions. This has not, however, shielded the country from the economic ills of the rest of the world, nor can it prevent social tensions. Economic conditions attached to international loans also irritate the independent spirit of the Ticos, as Costa Ricans are known.** ■

In 1949, Costa Rica became "the country with no army." Ever since the army was abolished in that year, this has been the nation's hallmark, a tradition that has been reinforced by Costa Rica's recurring role as mediator and pacifier in Central American conflicts. International recognition of this came in 1987 when President Oscar Arias was presented with the Nobel Peace Prize, while Ticos proudly point out that what would have been defense budgets are channeled into schools and health services. Yet no system is perfect, and behind Costa Rica's apparent moral dignity lurk mounting socioeconomic problems that, although less severe than those of its neighbors, are creating increasing discontent.

Ideals and reality The new constitution of 1949 not only abolished the army but also aimed to eradicate police corruption by allowing senior officers four-year terms only. Since then, this idealistic move has produced short-term corruption among police chiefs making money as fast as they can. Nor is it true to say that Costa Rica is a country without arms. Khaki-clad *guardia civil* (police) manning roadblocks near the Panamanian and Nicaraguan borders brandish submachine guns, while armed civilian assaults from San José to Limón sporadically interrupt the tourists' idyll. Once a civilized haven of tranquillity, Costa Rica is now confronting the same problems of rising insecurity as the rest of the world.

❑ Costa Rica's relaxed attitude toward arms is best illustrated by a 1995 General Auditor's report. This revealed that over 1,000 weapons, including a bazooka and four cannons, were missing, presumed stolen, from the National Arsenal and the Public Security Ministry. ❑

Austerity After several decades of progress aided by loans from the World Bank, the International Monetary Fund and the Inter-American Development Bank, often totaling sums of over $350 million per year, Costa Rica is entering recession. Economic growth dropped from over 7 percent in 1992 to 3 percent in 1995, while inflation rocketed to 23 percent. Government responses included increasing sales taxes, raising import tariffs, and implementing a public-sector austerity package that made massive cuts in personnel, and limited top monthly salaries to $2,600. This last measure was typically Tico in its detail: any monies earned over that amount were to be donated to the Child Welfare Office.

Numbers One of Costa Rica's problems is the size of its population. In the 1930s there were about 400,000 inhabitants, today there are 3.4 million and in the year 2000 there will probably be 4 million. These modest figures unleash a string of problems, from unemployment (still under 5 percent) to financing the extensive welfare system and dealing with squatters, who can claim abandoned

Opposite top: election fever
Right: President Figueres
Above: Oscar Arias receives his
Nobel Peace Prize in 1987

land by proving they have farmed it.
North Americans and Europeans
pour in to retire or set up hotels and
restaurants, so creating new social
categories. Cheap labor from
Nicaragua deepens Tico
dissatisfaction and makes law
enforcement difficult, as about 90

❏   Presidency runs in the
family. Of Costa Rica's
presidents prior to 1970, 75
percent were descended from
three families of original settlers.
President José María Figueres
(term of office 1994–8) of the
Partido Liberacion Nacional
(PLN) is the son of Don Pepe,
who ignited the 1948 Civil War,
while his PUSC predecessor,
Rafael Angel Calderón, is the
son of Don Pepe's arch rival.   ❏

percent of immigrant workers are
undocumented. Yet Costa Rican
tolerance and finesse prevail, and in
the early 1990s, under President
Calderón, thousands of impoverished
Nicaraguans were given the right to
free medical care and public school-
ing through a general amnesty. This
type of altruism, combined with fore-
sight in advocating sustainable
development as the only hope for
future prosperity, reaffirms Costa
Rica's unique role in Latin America.

■ **The classic Costa Rican physique is as difficult to define as the Costa Rican character. Predominantly of Spanish descent, the population has been injected with numerous other nationalities over the years and encompasses three important minority groups: the Afro-Caribbeans, the Chinese, and the indigenous people.** ■

Tico, the self-appointed national nickname, derives from the Costa Rican habit of forming diminutives—a habit that, for example, euphemistically transforms *momento* ("moment") into *momentico* ("little moment"). Ticos (or Ticas for women) are mainly direct descendants of Spanish settlers, who first arrived in the 16th century but came in far greater numbers in the early 19th century to grow coffee on free land. *Mestizos* (Spanish-Indian half-castes) are seen particularly in Guanacaste, while indigenous people remain virtually invisible in their reserves. Since the 1870s, Costa Rica has also absorbed Chinese, Italians, Afro-Caribbeans, and smaller numbers of German, English, French, and Lebanese traders. Today the population is diversifying yet again with a notable influx of *gringos* and *gringas* (foreigners, but especially Anglo-

Americans) following in the footsteps of the Quakers of Monteverde (see panel on page 77).

❑ Costa Rica's inhabitants boast Central America's highest literacy rate (93 percent) and life expectancy (75.2 years). Over 88 percent are officially Catholic but religious fervor is not a Tico characteristic—perhaps because Costa Rica's early settlers were too busy with earthly survival. ❑

The lie of the land The Central Valley still holds some 60 percent of the total population of 3.4 million, with 36 percent living in San José's metropolitan sprawl. Move out to the edges of Costa Rica, to Guanacaste in the north, Limón in the east or to the southern zone, and you come to the least populated, most impoverished areas. Indians are concentrated in often-inaccessible mountain reserves, while in contrast the Afro-Caribbean and Chinese populations are highly visible, particularly in Limón. Guanacaste presents yet another picture as many of the inhabitants are *mestizo* descendants of Chorotega Indians, with a more outgoing character and with a history of close links to Nicaragua. In general, Ticos are friendly,

courteous, and often discreet, with a sure sense of their distinctness from the rest of Latin America. Tolerance is their overriding feature.

Jamaica's legacy Before the 1880s, a small community of Afro-Caribbeans had for decades been fishing and turtle-hunting off the Talamanca coast, between seasonal work in Nicaragua or Panama (see pages 138–139). Then, suddenly, this population was boosted by 10,000 Jamaican laborers brought in by Minor Keith to build the Atlantic railroad (see page 132). Many chose to settle in Costa Rica, working on the banana plantations or their own smallholdings but proudly maintaining their Jamaican English language, Protestantism, and countless traditions. Until 1949 they had no rights, nor were they allowed outside their isolated coastal region, but today they are full Tico citizens, forming 5 percent of the population.

Chinese Before Keith turned to the Caribbean for labor, he had tried out 1,000 Chinese, who, although "addicted to work," suffered greatly from the climate and tropical diseases. Despite this they soon began to run small grocery stores and restaurants, established strong community groups and sponsored the immigration of relatives from China. Some have intermarried with Ticos, but Chinese identity remains strong and clannish solidarity is

always a priority. There are hundreds of Chinese restaurants and shops scattered across the country.

Indigenous groups High in the Talamanca mountains and deep in the jungle of the south are the last descendants of Costa Rica's original inhabitants, now numbering barely 15,000 (see pages 158–159). Visitors who do not make a specific effort to visit their reserves could be quite unaware of the indigenous peoples' existence. Apart from the Guaymi, most have adopted Western-style clothes and housing. Their story is a classic one of colonial cause and effect, with disease, war, and slavery playing significant roles. Today they find themselves torn between a growing consciousness of their traditions and the attractions of integration into Costa Rican society.

Indian, Spanish, Talamancan— some Costa Rican faces. The people of the Talamancan coast (right) are strongly Caribbean in spirit

■ **Few Central or South American countries can rival Costa Rica for the sheer quantity and range of plants and animals found within its boundaries. For the visitor who is interested in wildlife, the relative ease with which the country can be explored is a wonderful bonus.** ■

Sandwiched between Nicaragua to the north and Panama to the south, Costa Rica forms part of the land bridge between the Americas, and contains flora and fauna from both land masses. By American standards, it is a tiny country, barely more than 90 miles wide in places and only 180 miles long. What it lacks in size, however, it more than makes up for in altitudinal range. Between the Pacific west coast and the Caribbean east coast, the land rises to a central spine more than 10,000 feet high. This continental divide runs the length of the country.

Paradise for naturalists Without its altitudinal range and the juxtaposition of two oceans, a tropical country the size of Costa Rica would have rather uniform vegetation. As it is, the country's altitude has had a profound influence on the climate and, in particular, the temperature and rainfall. This climatic variation ensures that almost all types of tropical

habitat can be found within the country's borders, with the added advantage that many can be visited in a single day. From the coasts, with their mixture of sandy beaches, coral reefs, mangrove forests, and dry tropical forests, the land rises through rain forests and cleared agricultural land to cloud forests, cloaked in mist for much of the day. At the highest altitudes, there are even small areas of "paramo," a kind of bleak plateau landscape associated with South America. The one habitat that you might expect at this latitude, and do not find, is true desert.

Wealth of wildlife The diversity of Costa Rica's habitats is reflected in the wealth and range of its wildlife. Around 9,000 plant species have been found here (just under 5 percent of the total world plant list) and a staggering 1,200 of these are orchids. Insect life abounds, ranging from army and leaf-cutter ants, mantids and katydids to stunning

❑ Hummingbirds are referred to collectively as *gurrion*. For certain species, hovering is essential since the nectar-producing flowers upon which they feed can only be exploited from the air. Many plants have these tiny birds as sole pollinators, and some have even evolved flower shapes to suit the bill shape of a particular species. Male hummingbirds are often highly territorial and have brightly colored feathers. In some species, the plumage has a startling iridescence in certain lights. ❑

blue morpho butterflies and giant hawk moths. Tropical mammals such as sloths and monkeys are locally common and birdlife is prolific, with more than 800 species. Of these, 600 or so are resident, the rest migrant visitors. Like its neighbors, Costa Rica is very important for migrant breeding birds from North America. Each autumn, countless millions head south to northern South America for the winter, the vast majority following the course of the Central American land bridge. Over 50 species of hummingbird alone have been recorded in Costa Rica. Wherever you go, from gardens in San José to the cloud forests of Monteverde, you will come across these amazing birds whose best-known trait is the ability to hover in mid-air.

Corridors for life

Sadly, having the right climate and terrain for tropical habitats and wildlife is not enough these days. Many other countries in the region have lost or at least degraded important areas for wildlife through commercial exploitation or simply the pressure of a growing human population. In this respect, Costa Rica has fared surprisingly well. Although it has experienced its fair share of forest clearance in lowland regions for agriculture and dwellings, and although logging and the persistent use of pesticides are still a problem, something like 10 percent of the total land area is now given

Watch for beetles bigger than small mammals—and (clockwise from bottom left) the rufous-tailed hummingbird, processionary caterpillars, cayman, and spider monkey

over to national parks and 25 percent to protected areas of some sort. These areas are important in their own right, and a new awareness of the need to preserve land corridors between prime habitat sites is developing. This is needed for a genetic mix to occur, and perhaps more significantly because many of the resident tropical bird species are altitudinal migrants. They change altitude according to season and are reluctant to cross cleared land on their travels.

■ **Paradoxes abound in this country that is regarded as a pioneering environmental force in Latin America. Much of Costa Rica's natural forest has disappeared and even the label "conservation" often conceals commercial aims. Yet most Ticos recognize that long-term prosperity lies in protecting the environment.** ■

Few countries can claim such a high environmental consciousness as Costa Rica. No fewer than 450 environmental organizations keep their watchful eyes on both the public and private sectors, while the government itself preaches the merits of sustainable development— that is, investing in long-term, non-destructive projects that benefit the population. Private reserves, aimed at ecotourism or biological research, spring up yearly, national parks cover over 10 percent of the territory, and future projects include the *Paseo Pantera*, a protected corridor linking protected areas throughout Central America. The other side of this apparently rosy picture is one of large companies, often multinationals, carving up rain forest or dumping noxious chemicals, and buoyant real-estate and tourist industries spawning developments that violate conservation laws.

Pesticide-spraying of bananas—a major environmental problem

Black spots Since the 1950s forest cover has been reduced from over 70 percent to about 23 percent of Costa Rica. Guanacaste was one of the first regions to suffer when forest was cleared for cattle-raising on huge haciendas. An African grass (*Hyparrhenia rufa*) was planted, and is now destroying the natural savannah. Environmental groups are also warily monitoring Guanacaste's hotel developments, such as the Papagayo mega-resort that, however conscientiously completed, would set a dangerous precedent. The tropical rain forests of Sarapiquí and Osa have long been favored by logging companies for their precious hardwoods, while much of Talamanca's forest disappeared earlier this century to make way for the ubiquitous banana plantations.

❑ Apart from their ecological shortcomings (fertilizers, loss of topsoil leading to sedimentation in rivers and eventually coral reefs), monocultures such as cacao, bananas, and the more recent oil palms are highly vulnerable to parasites. These have already destroyed the source of income of thousands of Talamancans who depended on cacao, and prompted United Fruit Company's transfer of operations from Talamanca to Osa in the 1930s. ❑

Abuse Even when land is protected by government decree, its problems are far from over. Shortage of funds is a perennial difficulty that engenders massive abuse. Some

20 percent of national park land is still privately owned, rising to 46 percent at the popular Manuel Antonio park, and the limited number of guards leaves plenty of space for poachers, illegal loggers, and squatters.

Nor does Costa Rica's diminutive size help. A proposed road link between the Pacific and the Atlantic coasts would almost inevitably pass through a Talamancan indigenous reserve, a wild region that is also targeted by mining companies, a hydroelectric project, and an oil pipeline. Elsewhere, real-estate investors buy huge tracts of forested land that they sell off as small lots under the alluring catchphrase "save the rain forest."

Hope for the future Fortunately, environmental watchdogs raise the alarm when companies are found to contaminate rivers, or when a hotel's waste-treatment is inadequate, or when a foreign-owned paper-manufacturing giant proposes to build a chip mill and dock in an ecologically

Northern Costa Rica's landscapes show the ravages of logging. Meanwhile, sawmills flourish

vulnerable zone. Between Costa Rican laws and other vigilance, investors must watch their step and, as a result, many choose to bypass Costa Rica for more malleable systems elsewhere.

Meanwhile, the country has attracted numerous alternative lifestyle groups, and is seen as an asylum by both idealists and those wanting to start afresh. The economy needs more than idealism, however, and at Berlin's 1995 Climate Change Summit (the follow-up to Rio's Earth Summit in 1992), President Figueres and the USA proposed that industrialized countries should pay for their pollution by financing energy conversion projects (notably reforestation) in developing countries. However, once again, Costa Rica's pioneering voice went unheard and the proposal was shelved. The battle between short-term commercial interests and long-term survival is far from over.

COSTA RICA IS *Coffee and bananas*

■ **Far from being a new diet-plan, these two products form the backbone of the Costa Rican economy, together representing over 80 percent of Costa Rica's agricultural exports. Blanketing the slopes of the Central Valley are row upon row of lustrous green coffee bushes, while in the coastal lowlands the view is of acres of banana palms.** ■

For over one-and-a-half centuries, Costa Rican coffee has been recognized as some of the finest in the world, but it is by no means a natural Tico product. Arabica seeds were brought by the Spanish from Africa and the Middle East via Cuba at the turn of the 19th century, when free land and seedlings were offered to anyone willing to cultivate the new plant. The natural nurturing qualities of the Central Valley's cool climate and fertile volcanic soil soon repaid the labor. Coffee bushes bore fruit so easily that by the mid-1840s coffee had become the country's main export, transported on muleback to Puntarenas and then to Chile and Europe. This was the time of the rise of the coffee barons, a new class with a new prosperity. Then, in 1878, along came bananas.

❑ An English sea merchant, William Le Lacheur, was partly responsible for the meteoric rise of the coffee industry. In 1843 he docked at Puntarenas looking for a suitable cargo to fill his empty ship on its return from North America to England. That year's surplus coffee production soon filled his hold—but he had no money to pay for it. The trusting Ticos gave him credit, and two years later were repaid. From then on, they never looked back. Coffee was launched on the European market. ❑

Not competely bananas Although bananas overtook coffee in economic importance in the early 20th century and today account for over twice as much revenue (one third of total exports), the history and reality of their plantations is less glorious. It was above all the completion of the Atlantic railroad in 1890 (see page 132) and the associated founding of the American company, United Fruit, that propelled this fruit to importance in the Costa Rican economy.

Arabica coffee relishes rain and fertile volcanic soil, and thrives at altitudes of 3,000—7,000 feet

The exploitation of immigrant labor and independent planters is well documented, and banana plantations continue to have a destructive effect on the environment, through pesticide-spraying, soil-erosion, and the chemical-impregnated protective plastic bags that pollute rivers and land—a negative side-effect not shared by "cleaner" coffee plantations. The living conditions of banana workers have improved—wages exceed by 25 percent the minimum legal amount, and they enjoy extensive social benefits—but they also suffer from pesticide poisoning.

After a brief dalliance with oil palm plantations on the Pacific coast, businesses such as the Standard Fruit Company, Chiquita, and Dole are now expanding their banana plantations as well as controlling overseas shipment, marketing and pricing for the 57 percent of plantations owned by Tico. Conservation groups, ever alert, have recently devised a label to identify banana companies that have cleaned up their act—it says "ECO-OK."

A cup of Costa? Costa Rica's best coffee is said to be from the Central and Coto Brus valleys, although the Cartago and San Isidro regions are strong contenders in the stakes. Ticos claim that of the world's 1,200 varieties of coffee bean, theirs make coffee that "tastes as it smells." One of the country's most beautiful sights is when plants are in bloom, producing a fragrant white haze (engagingly called "snow"). Today planters are reverting to the former system of interspersing coffee-bushes with taller plants for shade, often *poro* trees, whose deep roots prevent erosion and also attract insects away from the plants.

Harvesting takes place in December–February, when the reddest berries are handpicked, loaded into baskets and then into sacks, and taken to a receiver who pays the coffee-pickers. The next stage is at a mill, where washing, sun-drying, filtering, and separating is carried out before the final roasting. Decaffeinated coffee is processed by steaming in Germany, although the best is low in caffeine already.

Plantains—the banana's useful cousins

■ **Tico cuisine follows the contours and elevations of the country's varied terrain. From Pacific lobster to Monteverde cheese, Guanacaste *tamales* and Caribbean "run-down," the menu changes radically. But two dishes crop up again and again— *casado* and *gallo pinto*. Develop a taste for these and you won't go hungry.** ■

22

Keeping the body firing on all cylinders is not a problem in Costa Rica. Roadside *sodas* (small family-run restaurants) abound, offering the full gamut of the day's sustenance from breakfast through *bocas* or *bocadillos* (snacks and starters), which accompany drinks, to the main meal. These simple eating-places are the stalwarts of Tico rural society, but visitors seeking more sophisticated fare should head for upscale hotels, which usually take full advantage of the cornucopia of produce that Costa Rica's fertile valleys, pastures, and oceans nurture.

Rice? beans? Apart from an enticing range of tropical fruit, vegetables, and ultra-fresh seafood, Costa Rica offers

Kitchens in sodas *may be basic, but the ingredients are always fresh*

❑ Typical Tico vegetables include: plantains, longer and thicker than bananas and only edible when cooked; yucca tubers also known as cassava or manioc and used for centuries by the Indians; *palmito*, palm-heart; and *chayote*, a pear-shaped vegetable whose flavor resembles squash. ❑

endless variants on the rice and beans theme, the staple diet of Latin America. The classic *casado* (literally meaning "married man") offers a perfect nutritional balance of rice, black beans, meat or fish, and carrot and cabbage salad, all topped by a fried plantain. A budget alternative on *soda* menus is *arroz con pollo* or *gambas* (fried rice with chicken or shrimp). *Gallo pinto*, the substantial national breakfast, consists of rice and black beans seasoned with onions and peppers, accompanied by fried eggs and sour cream, and mopped up with a corn tortilla. Start the day with this and you will feel fit to climb the slopes of Chirripó.

Olla de carne, a beef stew or soup made with potatoes, carrots, *chayote* (vegetable pear), yucca, and plantain, is sometimes on the menu, as is *sopa*

Rice fields near the Río Tempisque

negra, a reincarnation of black beans in soup form. Another filling soup is *sopa de mondongo,* which is made from tripe and vegetables. A common side dish is *patacones*: fried mashed plantains eaten with liberal sprinklings of salt. Starters include delicious ceviche, raw fish marinated in lemon juice with parsley and onions. Empanadas are savory pies.

Caribbean goodies A distinctive, highly flavored cuisine is concocted by the Afro-Caribbeans who, over the centuries, have found ways to combine typical Caribbean ingredients with odd reminders of their days of enslavement to the English. The main ingredient here is the coconut, its milk used to bind any number of ingredients, whether rice and beans or the popular "rundown," consisting of fish or meat with yams, plantains, breadfruit, peppers, and spices. Grated coconut is used in countless desserts and cakes. The spongy yellow fruit ackee, a plant native to Africa and brought to the Caribbean by the English, is boiled to produce a likeness of scrambled eggs, then sautéed with salted cod. *Patti* (similar to the Tico empanada) is a spicy meat pie that resembles a large turnover.

Refrescos *and ices cannot beat a fresh coconut*

Sweet tooth Ticos are renowned for their love of sugary drinks and dishes, a taste shared by the Afro-Caribbeans, who acquired numerous cake recipes from the English. *Tapa dulce*, a local brown sugar sold in solid form, is used to sweeten *tres leches*, a Nicaraguan import consisting of a rich cake of whipped cream, condensed milk, and evaporated milk. Dieters should abstain, but need not go hungry—Ticos also whip up an excellent *ensalada de frutas* (fresh fruit salad) with seasonal tropical fruits. *Cajeta* (fudge) is ubiquitous, even better as *cajeta de coco* (coconut fudge), while in mountain regions, *natilla*, a bowl of thick sour cream, is the energy-giver. Sugar is poured into *refrescos*, natural or bottled fruit drinks, while sugarcane is distilled into *guaro*, the national, potent alcoholic drink, which will finish off any meal—and anyone.

23

■ It is not just for its mountain pastures that Costa Rica is often called the Switzerland of Latin America. The lure of tax-free investment and the less-than-transparent banking systems has combined with Costa Rica's geographical position to attract a swarm of financial dealers on all scales. ■

By the 1970s San José claimed the highest concentration of foreigners in Central America after Panama. Pleasant living conditions and tolerance had long attracted political refugees from more radical Latin American regimes. On top of this, Costa Rican law permits foreign ownership of property with no restrictions and, until recent changes in regulations, rights to duty-free goods drew North American retirees. Along with such respectable folk came shadier citizens, including drug-traffickers and con men who reveled in Costa Rica's easy system.

❑ Private offshore banks are booming in Costa Rica. Although technically they are branches of national banks, offshores are not audited or taxed by the government. This leaves many options open... ❑

The trade in Colombian cocaine (top) is inadvertently aided by Costa Rica's liberal banking laws

Staging post Costa Rica's strategic site makes it a perfect staging post for drug consignments *en route* from Columbia to Europe or the United States. On the Caribbean coast this has produced social problems and a proliferation of drug-related crimes. Court wranglings continue over expropriations of US-owned property in Pavones, which was used for narcotics operations in the 1980s. Protagonists included the infamous Robert Vesco, who inhabited a heavily guarded San José property after allegedly embezzling half a billion dollars, and U.S. citizen Danny Fowlie, now serving a 30-year jail sentence in the States. In 1995, homegrown Ricardo Alem, a government representative under Arias' regime, was convicted of money-laundering and drug-smuggling after seven years of legal tussles. In 1986, Oliver North came to prominence when it was revealed that he was supplying Nicaragua's Contras with arms (see panel, page 50) from a remote hacienda. Today, the Italian mafia is reportedly laundering money by investing in Tico hotels.

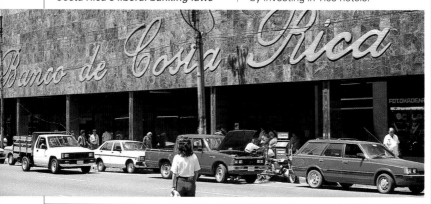

COSTA RICA WAS

■ The distant past of Costa Rica is still a matter of conjecture, but a picture is gradually emerging of agrarian societies steeped in ritual, who developed highly sophisticated craft techniques. Their strategic geographical location on the land bridge between Mesoamerica and South America was to fashion their culture. ■

The mysteries of Costa Rica's pre-Columbian inhabitants have been significantly researched only in the last 20 years, although some excavations started in 1861. This lack of research, combined with the absence of reliable records by conquistadors, means that the picture is nebulous. Even the names of the original tribes have been lost, replaced by Spanish identifications that probably derived from the names of local *caciques* (chiefs). As a result, archaeologists resort to a geographical definition, breaking the country down into three main indigenous regions: Greater Nicoya (Guanacaste), the Atlantic watershed (Talamanca), and the southern Pacific zone (Térraba and Península de Osa). Each developed its own craft forms and trade contacts, in effect making pre-Columbian Costa Rica a cultural crossroads for the "high" civilizations of Mesoamerica to the north and the Andes to the south.

Early days Although nomadic inhabitants roamed the region from about 20,000 BC, it was around 1000 BC that small settlements took shape, marked by settled agriculture and the creation of ceramic pots. Root crops and *pejibaye* (palm fruit) were cultivated, later joined by corn and cacao (cocoa), both Mesoamerican imports. Cocoa beans were also used as currency among the Indians

❑ Mesoamerica was a vast multicultural zone extending from central Mexico down through Guatemala, Belize, western Honduras, and El Salvador. Over the centuries, this area was home to major civilizations such as the Olmecs, Teotihuacan, Zapotecs, Mayas, and Aztecs. ❑

of Nicoya. All peoples continued to gather wild fruits, fish, and hunt monkeys, tapirs, and armadillos with bows and arrows. By AD 500, ranked societies had become established, with political and religious leaders in each community.

Growing sophistication Jade-carving skills can be traced back to around 500 BC. By AD 700, jade was replaced for mortuary work by gold. The origins of metallurgy are typical of Costa Rica's frontier role: gold techniques came from South America and copper techniques from Mesoamerica, together leading to the creation of the alloy tumbaga. The Diquis of the southern Pacific zone became masters of metalcraft, producing thousands of zoomorphic ornaments from gold nuggets found in local rivers. More perplexing is the source of jade: none has ever been found in Costa Rica, yet Greater Nicoya and the Atlantic watershed have yielded thousands of exquisitely carved pieces. This stone could have been brought directly by the Olmecs or by the Mayas, or traded through intermediaries. Olmec influence has also been traced in "baby-face" sculptures that possibly followed the same route.

Pre-Columbian artifacts can be seen in San José's National and Jade museums

Lifestyles There were two main linguistic groups: Nahuat was spoken by the Chorotegas of Guanacaste, who are thought to have emigrated around AD 900 from southern Mexico, while the older Chibcha language was shared by ethnic groups of southern Costa Rica, Panama and Colombia. These were not peace-loving people. Tribal wars were fought to acquire slaves for human sacrifices or to hunt heads for trophies, and many excavated tombs have revealed that slaves were killed to accompany their masters into the afterworld, along with offerings of elaborate vases, gold ornaments, or semi-precious stones. Warrior cults and fertility rites appear to have held an important role, symbolized by countless sculptures and phallic images, while *chicha* (alcohol) drinking bouts and the ritual use of *coca* (cocaine) were both common.

Enigma By the time Columbus disembarked, Guanacaste's sheltered bays and the Tempisque Valley harbored extensive settlements producing highly sophisticated polychrome ceramics. In the Talamanca mountains the impressive city of Guayabo had flourished until about AD 1400, when it was mysteriously abandoned. Meanwhile, the Diquis in their fortified villages of the south had mastered the art of weaving fine cotton cloth as well as the technology for their perfect stone spheres—perhaps the most enigmatic emblems of early Costa Rican history.

■ **Compared with neighboring Nicaragua and Panama, this tiny but inhospitable corner of Central America proved difficult to conquer. From the day Christopher Columbus stepped onto Costa Rican soil, it was to take 60 years of death, disease, and destruction for a permanent Spanish colony to be founded.** ■

One fine day in 1502 Christopher Columbus—Cristobal Colón in Spanish—anchored off Puerto Limón to repair his storm-damaged ships and restore the spirits of his exhausted men. This was his fourth voyage across the Atlantic in search of a passage to the fabled riches of Asia, and to his growing list of Spanish territorial possessions he now added Costa Rica de Veragua (the rich coast of Veragua). It was called "rich" allegedly because of the dazzling gold ornaments worn by the Indians who greeted Columbus and his expedition, and unknowingly fanned the blaze of the Spanish lust for ingots. Veragua was the Indian name for the Panamanian coast.

A 16th-century portrayal of Columbus

resistance from the Indians foiled the conquistadors' ambitions again and again. In 1522 a second expedition led by Gil Gonzalez Davila succeeded in reaching Nicoya on foot from Panama, carrying out mass baptisms, amassing gold, and enslaving hundreds of Indians in the process. Frustrations grew, as did Indian attacks and avaricious in-fighting between the conquistadors themselves, and it was not until 1562 that Juan Vásquez de Coronado succeeded where the others had failed. Recognizing the potential of the Central Valley, he moved a nascent settlement up to the cooler air and fertile, volcanic soil of Cartago.

❑ "On Sunday, Sept 25th towards midday, we dropped anchor in an islet named Quiribiri off a coastal town named Cariay, which were the best people, country and places that we had so far discovered; this was because the high land was full of rivers, with abundant tall trees..." From *Life of the Admiral, Don Cristobal Colón* by his son, Hernando Colón. ❑

Hardship Dense jungle, rugged mountains, tropical diseases, extreme climatic conditions, food shortages, and, not least, aggressive

Slavery In contrast to previous leaders, Coronado was relatively respectful of the Indians and soon managed to gain the confidence of certain chiefs, and to obtain allies by siding with one tribe against another. *Encomienda* slavery had been officially abolished in 1542 thanks to various enlightened clergymen, but a replacement system called *repartimiento* allowed forced labor of one week per month. Coronado's successor, Perafán de Rivera, succumbed to the arguments of struggling settlers and in 1569 bent the rules to permit slavery again.

However, one of the problems the colonizers faced was lack of people to enslave. Where were the Indians?

Disease The near-destruction of the indigenous population had begun in waves, in some cases before any physical contact with the conquistadors had been established. It was caused by European illnesses against which the local population had no resistance: influenza, measles, smallpox, typhoid, and the bubonic plague. Terrible epidemics took place in 1519, then again in 1545–8, reducing an already small Indian population to next to nothing. No reliable figures exist of the number of Indians at the time of the Conquest, estimates varying from 27,000 to 500,000, but what is certain is that within a century of Columbus' disembarkation, the tiny surviving indigenous population had sunk into oppression.

Below: St. Blas, Nicoya, founded in 1522. Right: Indians were shipped off to the mines in South America

❑ The Spanish *encomienda* system lies at the basis of many unresolved sociopolitical problems in central America, especially Guatemala and Mexico—for example, it led to the 1994 Zapatistas rebellion in Chiapas. This system allowed early colonizers to enslave large numbers of Indians. Although it was later outlawed, it had meanwhile made thousands destitute, landless and chained by debt to their masters. ❑

■ **For most of the 17th century Costa Rica foundered in poverty, its lack of progress caused partly by its remoteness from central power and partly by its difficult terrain. Two centuries went by before the colony finally raised its head from ploughing fields and envisaged real development.** ■

Colonial Costa Rica was far from dynamic. The gold that had so inspired Columbus had been exhausted, and manpower was severely limited as the Indians had died of disease, been killed or enslaved, or fled to the mountains, their fine artistry reduced to distant memories. In their place came poor Spanish immigrants from Cataluña, Galicia, and Andalucia, who settled for the most part on isolated farms in the Central Valley, eking out an existence by subsistence farming.

Backwater The government of this newly subjugated colony was in distant Guatemala, from where the Spanish colonial governor ruled over San Salvador, Nicaragua, and Costa Rica, leaving Panama under the Spanish Columbian yoke. This meant that Costa Rica was a poor cousin at the end of a long line, three months on horseback from the "capital," with even its bishop based in Nicaragua. Once the Indian tombs had been looted (by royal decree of Charles V, in 1540) Costa Rica held no interest for the Spanish Crown, and the struggling farmers were left to their own limited resources. By the early 1700s, settlers were so poor that they had to revert to the old currency of the cocoa bean.

Social system Much has been said about how this period was also the key to the Tico character, producing self-reliant homesteaders with no caste system of powerful hacienda-owners like those of Guatemala or Mexico. *Mestizos* (descendants of Spaniards intermarried with Indians) are said not to have existed, and yet recent research has shown that the lack of Spanish women led early soldiers and settlers to take Indian women as mistresses, producing generations of mixed-race descendants. At the same time, traditional Indian hierarchies were disrupted by the subservient role imposed by the white men. This subjugation was emphasized in 1747 when the Indian resettlement policy relocated hundreds from the remote Talamanca mountains to the Central Valley, to provide desperately needed labor.

Pirates If life went on in relatively bucolic fashion in the fertile valleys of central Costa Rica, such was not the case over on the Caribbean coast. This became prey to swash-buckling pirates and privateers of the Spanish Main, above all the English: Morgan, Mansfield, and Owen, but also French and Dutch buccaneers. By the late 17th century the English had found faithful allies in the Miskito Indians of the coasts of Honduras and Nicaragua, whose looting targets included the extensive cacao plantations that had been developed

❑ The Miskitos' fidelity to their early English allies created an unsettling threat to Spanish supremacy in the Caribbean for almost two centuries. In 1783 England finally abandoned the Central American shore in return for receiving Gibraltar, but local Miskitos continued to reject Spanish colonization and favor the English language. ❑

Following in Drake's footsteps, Henry Morgan (c 1636–88; portrayed below left) was one of many buccaneers to lead expeditions from Europe to Central America in pursuit of Spanish merchantmen

in Limón. Raids were so successful that by 1779 the Miskitos were able to demand tribute from Costa Rica, a tradition that continued until 1841. A black market also flourished between the pirates and settlers.

Growth Costa Rica was gradually changing. Three new towns were founded: Heredia (1706), San José (1737), and Alajuela (1782), which joined the tiny capital of Cartago, virtually wiped out by an eruption of Irazú in 1723, but soon rebuilt. During the same period tobacco was being developed as a commercial crop and, in a vain attempt to stimulate the ailing colony, Costa Rica was given exclusive rights for its cultivation in the Spanish colonies. This was a limited success, but a new product was on the horizon that was to propel this backward colony to the forefront of Central America. In 1808 free land was offered as an incentive to anyone who would grow a new import from Cuba—coffee.

■ Costa Rica must be one of the few countries to have remained ignorant of its new state of independence for a full month, and to have achieved independence without even aspiring to it. For several decades the fledgling nation veered between democracy and military coups, on the climb to its economic zenith. ■

In October 1821 news came by special mule-courier from Guatemala that the Spanish Crown had relinquished control over Mexico and its Central American empire. Suddenly Costa Rica found itself propelled into a situation it had never envisaged, one that had been brought about by the more politically motivated and oppressed populations of the north.

Confusion Although the leaders of the four main towns rapidly agreed on a constitution (based on the Spanish one of 1812), confusion reigned. Two routes were open: total independence, or adhesion to the newly declared Mexican empire of General Iturbide. A split soon appeared, between San José's and Alajuela's supporters of independence on the one hand and, on the other, the more conservative, Catholic inhabitants of Heredia and Cartago. The independence movement won the day in typically small-scale Tico fashion, in a battle that left 20 dead. More democratically, the inhabitants of Guanacaste chose by referendum to join Costa Rica rather than Nicaragua.

Braulio Carrillo In their first try at democracy, Costa Ricans elected as head of state a modest schoolteacher, and adhered to the short-lived confederation of Central American states. Government became more structured in 1833 with the election of the authoritarian Braulio Carrillo, a San José lawyer with despotic leanings. The burgeoning coffee plantations were by then creating a prosperous middle class, but prosperity had side effects such as prostitution, gambling, and theft. Braulio Carrillo stepped in with a

strong hand, built new roads and ports, repaid national debts, introduced civil reforms, and, in 1837, moved the capital to San José. But he went a step too far and, after reclaiming power through a military coup in 1842, found himself deposed and exiled by a general with the coffee barons' backing.

National threat The next significant episode in Costa Rica's embryonic history took place under President Juan Rafael Mora, an astute representative of the coffee oligarchy who is perceived today as a hero, although his 10-year rule ended abruptly, like that of others before and after him, in front of a firing-squad. Mora's legendary status stems from

❑ William Walker *(above)*, a Tennessee goldminer, adventurer and hack journalist, had already considered Mexico's Baja California as a base for his infamous "ideal" state, where slavery would be institutionalized. His Nicaraguan incursion was sanctioned by the U.S. President and a group of American industrialists. ❑

his swift rebuttal of the first threat to Costa Rica's national sovereignty.

In June 1855 William Walker took control of Nicaragua, from where he aimed to implement his Central American territory of slavery, as well as constructing a canal linking the Atlantic and the Pacific. With 300 filibusters (adventurers), he advanced into Costa Rica as far as what is today Parque Nacional Santa Rosa, and prepared an attack on San José. President Mora rapidly organized a motley army, many of whom were farmers and traders, who, after dislodging Walker and his men, delivered a final *coup de grace* at Rivas, in Nicaragua. Here a heroic drummer-boy, Juan Santamaría, torched the invaders' hideout, but he lost his life in the process.

Walker's ambitions ended with his life in 1860, in Honduras, the same

year as the overconfident Mora was executed for an attempted *coup d'état*.

Prosperity By 1889, when Costa Rica's new constitution was drafted and four-yearly democratic elections were implemented (without giving the vote to women or Afro-Caribbeans), the nation was enjoying a new-found prosperity. European ideas, cosmopolitan lifestyles, a university (1844), free elementary education (1869), a rejection of Church domination (the Bishop was expelled in 1884), a major railroad under construction, and the potential profits of the new crop, bananas, all contributed to the confidence of a burgeoning young nation.

33

Coffee (top) came before banana plantations (right), which were first introduced by the builder of the Atlantic Railroad

■ **As Costa Rica's fortunes increased, so did social divisions and ambitions. The 20th century has been a period of tumultuous politics, a roller-coaster economy, and, despite the difficulties, important social reforms, finally culminating in civil war, a new constitution, and a reborn country.** ■

34

In 1890, the long-awaited Atlantic railroad was completed, 19 years after the contract was signed. Over 4,000 imported laborers had died building it, and 800,000 acres of trackside land had been given to its constructor, the American Minor Keith. After the trains started rolling, Keith concentrated on building up the United Fruit Company, an economic force that was to transform the country, economically, ecologically, and socially. By 1913, the Talamanca plantations were producing 11 million bunches of bananas annually, and Costa Rica was the world's top exporter. Then came banana disease and World War I, a double blow to production.

Polarization As the republic prospered, its interests became increasingly polarized between the conservatism of the plantation owners and the reforms demanded by a growing work force backed by intellectuals and even the Church. In 1917 the democratic tradition was interrupted by Federico Tinoco Granados, who imposed himself as dictator, but in 1919 he was toppled by a popular movement spearheaded by the extraordinary character Jorge Volio Jiménez, a former Catholic priest who was later made a general. For over a decade Volio campaigned for social improvements, even leading Nicaraguan revolutionaries in battle, and in 1923 he founded the Reformist Party, which advocated extensive agrarian

National symbols of resistance: above, statue of Juan Santamaría in Alajuela and, inset right, Don Pepe. Top right: government troops are flown into action, 1948

and social reforms. However, his vitriolic attacks on Costa Rica's ruling classes finally earned him psychiatric internment in Belgium.

Rising tension From that point on, reformist aims could not be ignored. Further advances came in 1931, when an intellectual follower of Volio, Manuel Mora, formed the Costa Rican Communist Party. This helped to organize strikes on the plantations and to legalize unions, and later supported President Rafael Angel Calderón Guardia, elected in 1940. Calderón's momentous presidency coincided with the foundering of the national economy, precipitated by the 1930s world depression and the outbreak of World War II. After declaring war on Germany and Japan, Calderón unwisely confiscated property owned by Germans (often longstanding immigrants and well positioned within the nation's economic élite), a move that sparked off xenophobic riots. He also implemented social reforms. Having antagonized both the upper classes and the conservatives, he allied

❑ Figueres worked in the United States but returned to Costa Rica in the 1920s to establish a community farm (*La Lucha sin Fin*, "The Endless Struggle"), but his outspoken criticism of Calderón's administration resulted in exile to Mexico, in 1942–4. Inspired by revolutionary idealism, he concluded that an armed uprising was the only solution to his nation's woes. After his victory he was twice elected President, in 1953–7 and 1970–4. He died in 1990. ❑

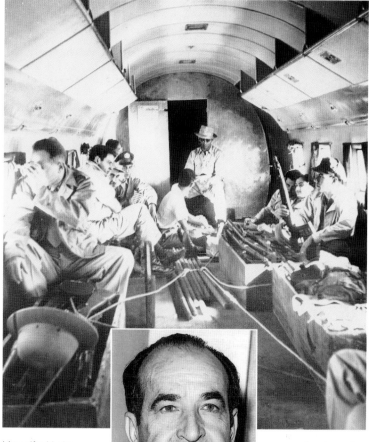

himself with the Church, so adding the intellectuals to his adversaries. After rigging the elections of 1944, Calderón's party annulled the opposition victory in 1948. Tension and distrust reigned. Then along came José Figueres, father of the nation, known as Don Pepe.

Civil war In March 1948, Figueres launched a well-planned offensive from his farm near Cerro La Muerte, where arms had been flown in from Guatemala. Forty days of civil war left 2,000 dead but culminated in the overthrow of Calderón's disciple, President Picado, and a triumphant procession through San José. For the next 18 months, Figueres wiped the slate clean with radical, often unpopular measures. He reformed the corrupt and inefficient public administration, expanded Calderón's social reforms, nationalized banks, and abolished the army. Not least, women and Afro-Caribbeans were given the vote, and the latter were at last given citizenship. Don Pepe's 1949 Constitution provided the foundation for a unique pacifist democracy, and his party, the Partido Liberacion Nacional (PLN), is a major force in Costa Rica today.

A to Z

GUANACASTE

GUANACASTE

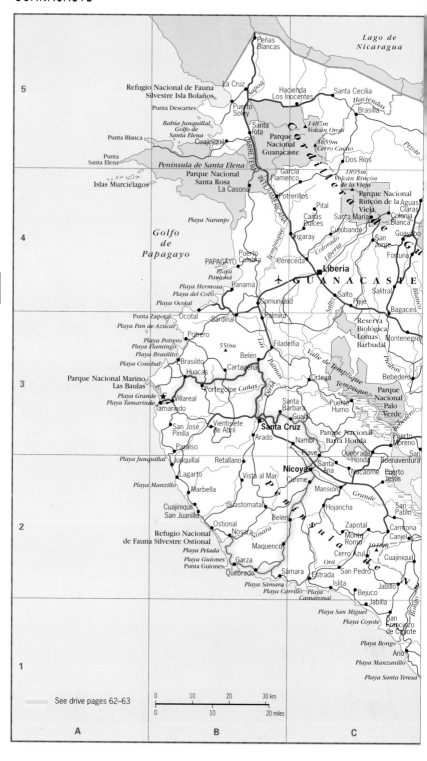

38

See drive pages 62–63

| 0 | 10 | 20 | 30 km |
| 0 | 10 | 20 miles | |

A   **B**   **C**

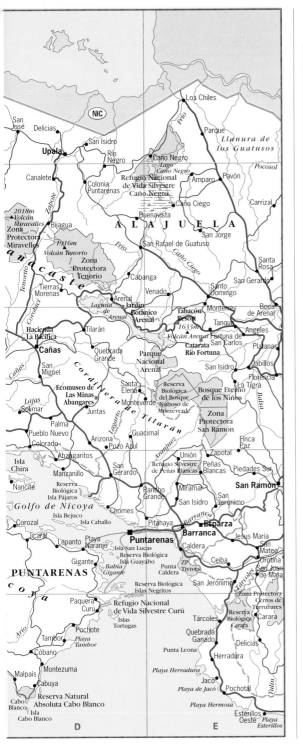

Cruising the gulf
The Golfo de Nicoya is dotted with little islands, many of which are protected as biological reserves (Isla Pájaros, Islas Negritos, Isla Guayabo) while others such as the Islas Tortugas have become popular and often overcrowded day-trip destinations. The easiest way to see these islands is by boat tours that can be arranged at Tambor, Montezuma, or Bahía Gigante, or directly with tour company offices in San José. Alternatively, paddle out there in a kayak (see panel on page 55).

Above: Guanacaste's upmarket resort of Playa Flamingo Pages 36–37: late afternoon sun illuminates the contours of volcanic Rincón de la Vieja

The unmistakable Guanacaste tree gives welcome shade in a tinder-dry landscape

Guanacaste tree
In English and Spanish this majestic tree (*Enterolobium cyclocarpum*) is also known as the elephant's ear, monkey ear, or mulatto ear. Often growing in complete isolation, it is easily identifiable by its thick gray trunk whose branches spread umbrella-style in a strikingly symmetrical fashion, and provide generous shade for cattle and people. Even more curious are its seed pods. These huge, ear-shaped pods (up to 4 inches wide) dangle from the tree in the dry season and are favorite cattle snacks. Guanacaste wood is used for making furniture and boats, and the bark for tannin, soap, and medicine.

Guanacaste Vast plains of savanna, rolling hills, exquisite beaches, and towering volcanoes form the northeastern corner of Costa Rica, most of which belongs to the province of Guanacaste. Notorious for its excruciating roads, proud cowboys, glorious sunsets, huge cattle-ranches, and oven-like temperatures, this formerly remote region is evolving fast. The transformation of Liberia airport into an international airport (mainly for charter flights) has given extra impetus to beach resorts due west of the provincial capital. Elsewhere, this sparsely inhabited region, harboring only 6.5 percent of the population, offers isolated pockets of development, for the most part pleasantly small-scale.

Into the heart This section of the book includes the entire Península de Nicoya and the national parks of the striking Cordillera de Guanacaste (a mountain range that creates a north-eastern barrier), but it excludes the Laguna de Arenal, more logically included in The North (see page 72). There are three main entry points to the region, two of which are off the Interamerican Highway: first, the Río Tempisque ferry arrives directly into the heart of the peninsula; second, some 40 miles farther north, the regional capital, Liberia, is the gateway to the far

north, volcanoes or burgeoning beach resorts; and the third access route is by sea from Puntarenas to Playa Naranjo, Paquera or Montezuma in the south.

Independent-minded Guanacaste's indigenous people were joined, probably around AD 900, by a major new influx, the Chorotegas from southern Mexico. Many of today's inhabitants are *mestizo* descendants, with swarthy complexions and dark wavy hair, although this Indian group suffered more than any other from colonial slavery. In the 15th century the Isla Chira in the Golfo de Nicoya was a buzzing marketplace for trading Nicoya pottery with the Aztecs; earlier still, the Chorotegas had traded with Mayas and Zapotecs. Countless jade, gold, and ceramic artifacts have been unearthed in the peninsula, and show a high level of artistry. Under Spanish rule, Guanacaste found itself tossed between Nicaragua and Costa Rica (both part of the Spanish Captaincy General of Guatemala). After independence in 1821, the Guanacastecos chose Costa Rica by referendum, but they maintain their independent streak, preserving their own flag and displaying signs inscribed *orgullosamente Guanacasteco* (proud to be Guanacastecan). This determined cast of character has also helped them fight off repeated invasions from Nicaragua over the years.

Into the oven Craft traditions continue in the kilns of Guaitíl but the tropical dry forest that once clad the peninsula has been mercilessly shorn. African grass has swept the plains and hillsides, providing sustenance for thousands of Brahma cattle but creating ecological and climatic havoc. When it's dry in Guanacaste, it's very dry indeed: rivers become waterless, animals head for the mountains and tourists for the breezy beaches. Fortunately, large tracts of land are now protected, above all the three neighboring national parks (Guanacaste, Rincón de la Vieja, and Santa Rosa), which, with some smaller spots, form the Área de Conservación Guanacaste, concerned for local people and wildlife alike.

To the beach
Hedonism is well catered for along the coastline, where Guanacaste's beaches offer some of the best sportfishing and watersports in Costa Rica, coupled with some remarkably designed, often isolated hotels. Swimming is not always safe (see panel page 55), but areas such as the Bahía de Culebra (Papagayo and Playa Hermosa), Playa Conchal, Playa Tamarindo, Playa Flamingo, Playa Sámara, Playa Tambor, and Montezuma all have sheltered beaches. Getting around the peninsula is more of a problem: public transport is limited and infrequent, and, unless you choose to fly directly into a beach resort from San José, the most convenient transport is a rented car. Most roads are rough and poorly marked—but that is part of the wild beauty of Guanacaste.

Playa Conchal, one of the region's safe swimming beaches

GUANACASTE

Pots

In pre-Columbian days, much-prized Chorotega pottery from Guanacaste was traded with the Aztecs. During Spanish occupation the craft died out, possibly because of the pagan images and symbols used for decoration, but the tradition was resuscitated so successfully earlier this century that many new pieces are indistinguishable from early artifacts. They are still handmade, without wheels, and are painted only with white, black and ocher pigments from the nearby mountains. After drying in the sun for a day and before firing, the objects are rubbed with a special stone dipped in water to produce a natural sheen.

A Guaitíl potter churns local clay in a huge pestle

► Cañas   39D3

The small agricultural town of Cañas lies in the hot plains of Guanacaste on the Interamerican Highway. It is only useful for some budget hotels but a few miles to the north are three organizations worth investigating. Safaris Corobicí (tel/fax: 669-1091) organizes half-day tours boating down the gentle Río Corobicí, with plenty of potential for birdwatching and swimming, or longer trips into the estuaries of Palo Verde, again with a strong likelihood of bird-sightings. Close by is **Las Pumas►** (tel: 669-0444. *Open* daily 8–5. *Admission free*, donations welcome), a private rehabilitation sanctuary for wild cats run by the dedicated Lily Hagnauer. Here, too, is **Hacienda La Pacífica►►** (tel: 669-0266), an interesting model of sustainable development that combines agriculture, forestry, conservation, and tourism. Its dry tropical forest offers horseriding, hiking and fantastic bird watching (225 species spotted so far), particularly along the banks of the Corobicí, with howler monkeys as common companions. A small museum and library, an organic farm, a cattle-ranch, comfortable accommodations, and a restaurant complete La Pacífica's attractions.

►► Guaitíl   38C3

Guanacaste's pottery-making center lies in scenic pasturelands east of Santa Cruz. This tiny village is composed of 85 houses, nearly all devoted to making pots, urns, vases or zoomorphic whistles whose design and technique date from pre-Columbian times. There is an ICT co-operative showroom on the northeastern corner of the playing field, and individual stalls front the numerous family workshops. Wander around, talk with the potters and watch clay creations being modeled, dried, then shovelled into igloo-shaped kilns before they are hand-painted with natural pigments to render the traditional polychrome designs. A few miles farther on, the even smaller village of San Vicente produces pottery that is marginally more intricate in modeling and painting, and is displayed at the cooperative showroom on the main road.

►► Juntas   39D3

This picturesque old mining town (also called Las Juntas de Abangares) offers some surprises—namely colorful, harmonious, and unspoilt old houses, hand paved streets, striking vegetation and a landmark statue in honor of gold miners in the main square. From 1884 to 1931 Juntas was a center for gold miners who flocked there from all over the world in search of a fortune. Mining still goes on near by and visitors can make an interesting side trip to **Las Minas de Abangares**, 2.5 miles northeast of Juntas on a little-used rough road to Tilarán. Here, what is bizarrely termed an Ecomuseo preserves old mining equipment, displayed beside photos and models (tel: 662-0129. *Open* daily 8–5. *Admission charge* inexpensive). Its rural riverside location and shady access road offer plenty of birdwatching, and across a suspension bridge lies the nature reserve of Aguas Claras.

▶ **La Cruz** *38B5*

Guanacaste's last outpost before the Nicaraguan border is a sleepy, hot, rather ramshackle town on the Interamerican Highway, which is only just opening up to tourists, thanks to a newly opened hotel. It makes a good base for exploring the untouched beaches of northern Guanacaste, although the dusty local roads are poor in quality. Road-checks are common due to the proximity of the Nicaraguan border, so always carry your passport.

Arriving from the south, turn left at the gas station to reach the main square, before continuing uphill to a windy lookout point, **El Mirador▶▶**, situated behind the Restaurante Ehecatl. This offers breathtaking vistas (spectacular at sunset) over the Bahía Salinas and the wildlife refuge of Isla Bolaños, as well as the fishing community of Puerto Soley 3.5 miles away down at the water's edge. This is where boats can be hired to take you near the 600-acre island refuge, and there is *cabinas* accommodation near by. For exquisite, protected waters and deserted white sand, drive on to **Playa Rajada▶▶**, just beyond the remote village of Jobo, or to **Playa Jobo▶** on the tip of the peninsula, which attracts a few locals. It is also possible to reach Bahía Junquillal (part of the Área de Conservación Guanacaste, see page 41) by cutting south across the headland along a testing road.

Frame houses line the few streets of La Cruz, near the Nicaraguan border

Isla Bolaños
This windswept little island rising 260 feet out of the magnificent Bahía Salinas was declared a wildlife refuge in 1981 in order to protect its nesting colonies of brown pelicans, American oystercatchers, and magnificent frigate birds. The latter build their nests in the frangipani and alfaje trees that make up much of the island's dry tropical forest. Other species that can be spotted are magpie jays and black vultures, although landing on the island is not allowed.

GUANACASTE

Puertas del sol
Common features of
Liberia's traditional adobe
houses are the *puertas del
sol* ("doorways of the
sun"), diagonal doorways
which let both morning and
afternoon sun into north-
facing corner houses.
Terracotta tiled roofs are
also common, but enter
any of the more elaborate
mansions on Calle Central
and you are plunged into
pure 19th-century colonial
style. Grandiose rooms
with high ceilings are
sometimes decorated with
cherubim-enhanced
murals, while kitchen quarters are relegated to the
rear beside a courtyard
used for drying grain.

44

► **Liberia** *38C4*

The historic capital of Guanacaste, founded in 1769, will
no doubt expand as a result of its airport becoming international, but for the moment it remains a tranquil place. It
is built on a grid system but finding your way round is
made tricky by the lack of street-signs. Liberia's strategic
position on the Interamerican Highway has endowed it
with a pleasant straggle of hotels, bars, and restaurants.
Often dubbed the "White City," it is renowned for its old
adobe houses constructed from the white volcanic soil of
Rincón de la Vieja: some lovely examples remain in **Calle
Central►►**, which runs south off the main square. Many
have been restored, and owners leave their front doors
wide open to allow visitors to peep inside. Back on the
main square, follow Avenida Central (which becomes
Avenida Julio 25) to its eastern end to reach **La
Agonía►►**, a simple 19th-century adobe church that
replaced a 1769 chapel. The bare, raftered interior
functions partly as a museum, with displays of religious
statuary. It is usually open after midday.

Cultura The helpful local tourist office (tel: 661-1069.
Open Mon–Sat 8–noon, 1–4) is at the Casa de Cultura, a
19th-century adobe house signposted from the main
square. It doubles as the small
Museo del Sabañero►, which
pays tribute to Guanacaste's
great cowboy tradition with
displays of saddles, costumes,
and other related objects. The
tourist office will advise on local
tour agencies that organize day
trips to the nearby national parks
and volcanoes, or you can set off
on a rented mountain bike.

*A remnant of
Liberia's golden
age in one of the
Calle Central's
19th-century houses*

►►► **Montezuma** *39D1*
Costa Rica's New Age hippy
resort has been raising its
standards and now offers some
good accommodations, upscale
dining, and clean beaches. Its
fabulous, though isolated location
at the southern tip of the
Península de Nicoya means that
road access is slow, bumpy and
dusty, though things are changing
with the growing tourist influx to Tambor and a new
motor-yacht service (Simba) linking Montezuma directly
with Puntarenas. The laid-back atmosphere still hovers
between a remake of the Greek islands or Bali, *circa*
1970, and vegetarian food is ubiquitous.

The hub Shops, bars, hotels, and restaurants are clustered around the main junction, which borders a small fishing beach to the south (not good for swimming) and, five
minutes' walk north past a pretty, green, timber church, a
magnificent stretch of white sand edged with gentle surf.
Money exchange, ticketing, rafting, fishing, scuba-diving,
and horse riding tours can be organized through Monte-
Aventuras (tel/fax: 642-0272), by El Jardín restaurant.

Peace and quiet Follow the main road south from the junction and round the point to reach a string of small hotels overlooking more beaches, as well as a river with a 20-minute trail leading to La Catarata (waterfall). Those in search of more complete tranquillity should drive some 6 miles south past a string of sandy coves along a rough road (necessitating four-wheel drive during the wet season) to Cabuya►, a lush, straggling coastal village practically at the entrance to the Cabo Blanco reserve (see page 60). Although Cabuya's beaches cannot compete with those of Montezuma, a handful of hotels offer a variety of fishing, biking, and horse riding tours, including as a destination the stunningly beautiful surfing beach of Malpaís►►, just across the tip of the peninsula.

►► **Nicoya**   *38C2*

The crossroads position of this pretty little town makes it useful for changing money or stocking up on necessities. As the accommodations are nothing special, try to make a daytime visit between beach-hopping or visiting Palo Verde. The obvious focal point is the lively Parque Central, dominated by the historic church of San Blas►►►, founded in 1522, rebuilt in 1644, subsequently damaged by an earthquake, restored and now a museum (*Open* 8–noon, 2–6, closed Sun, Wed. *Admission free*). Adjoining it is a lush, shady garden, while bordering the square are several decorative buildings, including a 1930s cinema converted into a café. Keep an eye out for the huge Guanacaste tree wreathed in philodendron in the southeast corner.

Isla Cabuya
Lying in the ocean just off Cabuya, this strange little island is accessible on foot at low tide. Although uninhabited by the living, the Isla Cabuya remains a cemetery for local villagers, a use dating from fishermen's customs earlier this century and continued by Cabuya's first settlers in the 1950s. For a few decades, before the Montezuma road was built, it was also the village lifeline, as all ferries from the mainland stopped there to unload supplies and passengers, who would cross to the shore on foot.

45

Bird's-eye view of a stretch of coast near Montezuma

GUANACASTE

Inventory of species
Parque Nacional Guanacaste is the site of a 10-year survey (INBITTA) which aims to analyze and list every living species, from the tiniest microorganism to fungi, birds, insects, mammals, and lofty tropical trees, which exists within the Guanacaste Conservation Area. This vast zone was created in 1989 when five adjoining conservation areas (Santa Rosa, Rincón de la Vieja, Guanacaste, Bahía de Junquillal, and Isla Bolaños) were amalgamated. It is hoped that analysis of some 300,000 species will provide essential data for medical, agricultural, and biotechnological advances.

Papagayo and a blowhole at Nosara

▶▶▶ Nosara 38B2

Understanding the confusing layout of Nosara and its beaches is not easy, but wrong turns only bring you into closer contact with the superb natural surroundings. These lush forested hills with sweeping views, cliffs, sandy beaches, and a rich birdlife have attracted extensive North American real-estate development, but conservation standards are high and the roads appalling, so scenic beauty survives intact. The rural village of Nosara itself, 3 miles inland, boasts no fewer than three restaurants, four bars, and two dance halls. Most visitors will arrive from the south via Sámara and Garza, passing the wide sweep of Playa Guiones and Playa Pelada, home to several hotels and the popular beachfront Olga's Bar. From Nosara it is a short drive northwest to Ostional, through the wilds of the nature reserve (see page 58). Scuba divers can explore reefs and shipwrecks with Pacific Aquatic (fax: 238-0378).

▶▶ Papagayo 38B4

Costa Rica's most controversial beach development covers 5,000 acres of an idyllic peninsula of sheltered coves curling around the beautiful Bahía Culebra. This mega-development, dominated by the Mexican group SITUR, is intended to be an upscale resort zone with hotels, condominiums, and a 300-boat marina, all of which, if actually completed, will definitely tilt Costa Rica's balance of tourists in favor of Guanacaste. Only a few hotels have so far been finished, bringing improvements to the previously very meager infrastructure, and SITUR claims that it will preserve some impressive mangrove forests and archaeological sites, while keeping some 70 percent of the total area green.

▶ **Paquera** 39D1

This small town has lightened the heavy ferry traffic from Playa Naranjo, some 15 miles farther north, with a new service financed by the large Spanish-owned resort of Playa Tambor. Car and passenger ferries run four times a day and some have direct bus connections with Montezuma. The town itself lies a few miles inland. It is a useful place for stocking up on provisions, and offers some accommodations.

▶▶ **Parque Nacional Barra Honda** 38C3

Open: daily 8–4. Admission charge: expensive

Over 5,000 acres of hilly terrain punctuated by limestone peaks are riddled with 42 caves, the main interest of this national park. This area emerged from the sea 60 million years ago, and since then millennia of rain have eroded the calcareous rock and filtered below to create underground waterways, chambers, and vaulted ceilings. Spectacular stalactites and stalagmites are at their best in the caves of Terciopelo, Trampa and Santa Ana. The deepest, at 780 feet, is Santa Ana. Pozo Hediondo attracts hundreds of bats, and in Nicoa pre-Columbian human bones and artifacts have been found. Outside these caverns is a very hot, tropical dry forest, best appreciated from the look-out point above the caves. Wildlife is scarce but you may spot a raccoon or coati-mundi, coyotes, a flock of orange-fronted parakeets, or white-faced monkeys. Park headquarters are reached from Nacaome, 13 miles east of Nicoya, and two trails lead into the park. Guides are essential for visiting the caves.

▶▶ **Parque Nacional Guanacaste** 38B5

Open: daily 8–4. Admission charge: expensive

In 1989, 79,000 acres of land in northern Guanacaste were declared a national park. Starting on the plain at 650 feet above sea-level, this area rises a mile into the volcanic Guanacaste range and, together with the adjoining Santa Rosa park, provides essential migratory corridors for wildlife, as well as protecting some surviving stands of tropical dry forest. The evolving topography creates a variety of superb landscapes, but access is extremely difficult to the best viewpoints, on Cerro Cacao and Volcán Orosí, where biological research stations are located. Scientists are still identifying the great diversity of over 3,000 plant species, some 300 bird species, and 5,000 insects, not to mention monkeys, peccaries, tapirs, and even jaguars. Park infrastructure remains very limited, and information should be obtained from Santa Rosa's ranger stations. An alternative is to head for the atmospheric Hacienda Los Inocentes (tel: 256-5484), from where horse-back tours of the park are organized (see panel), or contact an agency in Liberia.

Los Inocentes

This beautifully preserved ranch on the northern boundary of Parque Nacional Guanacaste once belonged to the Viquez family. The two-story hacienda was built in 1890 of tropical hardwoods, and presided over an extensive ranch of some 8,000 cattle. Dairy farming continued under new owners until 1994, but since then the hacienda has been completely turned over to ecotourism, functioning as a hotel and organizing horseback tours of the surrounding pastures and volcanoes. Advance notice is required if you want to ride to the peak of the dormant Orosí volcano—a gruelling 14-hour trip.

47

Hacienda Los Inocentes: Brahma cattle once formed the livelihood of the region

■ **Costa Rica is becoming known as one of the world's top birdwatching countries, offering an astounding diversity that matches its varied topography. Waterbirds, seabirds, raptors, birds of the cloud forest or of the rain forest: all are present in astonishing numbers.** ■

Above, from left to right: rufous-tailed hummingbird, tricolored heron, blue-gray tanager, golden-collared manakin, green-crowned brilliant, turquoise-browed motmot

48

Right: limpkin

Below: Costa Rica's national bird, the clay-colored robin

National bird
With such an array of spectacular birds, it is surprising that Costa Rica has chosen as its national bird a rather understated and modest species called the clay-colored robin (*yigüirro*). As well as being visually uninspiring, it rarely even sings, except in April, during the breeding season. This coincides with the onset of the rains, an agricultural highpoint of the year and the reason for the robin's status.

Altogether, over 850 bird species have been identified in Costa Rica (as compared with 800 or so in the whole of North America), a quarter of which are migratory. Many ecotourism agencies cater almost exclusively for that obsessive and determined category of people, bird watchers, whose most precious items of luggage are their binoculars and life lists (their ongoing check-lists). For them, Costa Rica is definitely paradise.

Top ten Priority destinations are the rainforest area around La Selva, which claims over 400 species; Monteverde's cloud forest with 400; Chirripó and La Amistad parks with over 400 (although the full potential of the latter is still unexplored); Parque Nacional Corcovado, claiming over 360; Parque Nacional Braulio Carrillo with 350; the Wilson Botanical Gardens where ornithologists have recorded 330 species; Tortuguero's waterways, sustaining 309; Palo Verde, with an estimated 300; and the wildlife refuges of Caño Negro and Ostional, each of which has nearly 200 species, mainly waterbirds. Besides these major mainland destinations, several uninhabited Pacific islands are protected as seabird nesting sites. The Isla Bolaños off La Cruz (see panel on page 43) is home to the magnificent frigate bird, while the Gulf of Nicoya's Guayabo, Negritos and Pájaros islands conserve nesting grounds for brown pelicans. Laughing gulls, parrots, brown boobies, and white-tipped doves also circulate around here.

Waterbirds The lowland marshes and lagoons of Palo Verde, Caño Negro and Ostional attract countless wildfowl and waders, both migratory and resident, including huge flocks of black-bellied whistling-ducks, roseate spoonbills, blue-winged teals, wood storks, cattle egrets, white ibis, black-crowned night herons, neotropic cormorants, and, a Caño Negro specialty, permanent colonies of Nicaraguan grackle, a bird endemic to neighboring Lake Nicaragua. Another, lesser-known area for waterbirds is the delta of the Río Térraba, near Sierpe, where extensive mangrove swamps and tributaries harbor nearly 400 species of forest birds, seabirds, and wildfowl. In contrast, the waterways of Tortuguero are a well-trodden trail where some birds actually wait for snacks from the boatloads of tourists.

High visibility If you spot a male resplendent quetzal on a "joy flight" you will not forget it. Its long, silky green tail-feathers, scarlet belly, yellow bill and iridescent green crewcut are a stunning sight, matching the sonorous, deep-throated calls that fuse into a mellow flow. Also colorful and very audible are the parrot family, of which 16 species exist in Costa Rica. From tiny green parakeets to spectacular scarlet macaws measuring around 3 feet in length, they screech across the skies, flashing their brilliant plumage. However, this family is the most sought after for a caged, domestic existence, and once-common scarlet macaws may now number as few as 500 in the wild.

Chattering toucans are another typical, highly decorative inhabitant of lowland areas, and Costa Rica's six species are unmistakable, with huge curved bills and colorful, contrasting plumage. Flashy kingfishers and purple gallinules, blending turquoise and cobalt-blue plumage, exhibit their colors beside rivers and along the coastline.

Spinoffs If you see an airborne blur near a flower, it will be a hummingbird. More than 50 species of this extensive family live in Costa Rica, playing an important pollinating role as they feed from the nectar of red, orange, and yellow flowers. Some Ticos attract the birds to their gardens with flower-shaped feeders filled with sugared water. The extraordinary engineering that makes a hummingbird's wings flutter, rotate and hum at high speed allows it to hover, move backward and accomplish vertical takeoffs.

Also remarkable is the Montezuma oropendola, a weaver of intricate, pendulous nests that festoon tall trees. These nests are also a favorite feeding ground for the giant cowbird, and, when hung as decoration from the eaves of houses, are sometimes recycled as second-hand homes by the olive-backed euphonia (one of 45 species of tanager).

An early bird...
The best time for bird watching is from dawn until about 9AM, when activity slows, then again toward dusk as birds return to roost. Night prowlers may see and hear the bare-shanked screech-owl, the mottled owl, or crested owl.

49

Long-distance travelers
Over 200 species fly south to escape the cold North American winter. They include warblers, swallows, flycatchers, tanagers, finches, orioles, and raptors such as hawks, falcons, and eagles. Millions of these migrants cross Costa Rica to reach their wintering quarters in northern South America, and huge numbers of certain species remain within the country for the winter months.

Members of the parrot family range from tiny pygmy parrots to macaws over three feet in length

Arms to Santa Rosa

In the late 1970s Hacienda Murciélago, located in the newly designated northern section of the park, belonged to former Nicaraguan dictator Somoza, who found it convenient for zipping back and forth across the border. In 1978 the land was expropriated and added to Santa Rosa. In 1986 it was revealed that the remote Santa Elena peninsula sheltered a clandestine airstrip built by the CIA for sending arms to Nicaragua's Contras. Financing came via Irangate through a phantom Panamanian company founded by Lieut. Col. Oliver North. This completely violated Costa Rica's neutrality laws, and President Oscar Arias' subsequent annexation of the property is still generating friction between Costa Rica and the United States.

▶▶ **Parque Nacional Palo Verde**   *38C3*

Open: daily 8–4. Admission charge: expensive

Waterbirds are the incentive for exploring 40,000 acres of scenic, tranquil freshwater and saltwater marshes, lagoons, and channels formed by the basin of the Río Tempisque and Río Bebedero. These seasonally flooded areas change dramatically over the year and during the dry season there are vast concentrations of black-bellied whistling-ducks, blue-winged teals, wood storks, herons, and roseate spoonbills. Orioles, kites, egrets, and ibises are common, particularly in the mangrove forests.

Despite its astonishing ecological diversity (15 habitats), the park is named after the green-barked *palo verde* (horse bean), found in surviving tracts of tropical dry forest. Extensive biological research is being carried out at the OTS (Organization for Tropical Studies) station near the main park entrance south of Bagaces, but most visitors enter Palo Verde with a boat tour organized from Cañas, or from the fishing village of Puerto Humo, situated on the west bank of the Tempisque.

▶▶ **Parque Nacional Rincón de la Vieja**   *38C4*

Open: daily 8–4. Admission charge: expensive

The volcanic Cordillera de Guanacaste includes the dramatically beautiful park surrounding Rincón de la Vieja (6,217ft/1,895m), an intermittently active volcano that last erupted in 1991. Access to Sector Las Pailas is hard work along a rough, dusty road via Curubandé, signposted from the Interamerican Highway just north of Liberia. A toll is demanded for crossing private hacienda land, and it takes an hour to cover the 12 miles. From the park entrance, trails lead to cool waterfalls (many rivers flow through the park) or to steaming mud pots, geysers, sulfur hot springs, and other volcanic delights. The trail up to the crater of Von Seebach, with views over neighboring Rincón de la Vieja, is an arduous 5 miles, but it leads through remarkably diverse landscapes, home to some 257 bird species as well as ocelots, jaguars, sloths, and monkeys. The other entry point is at **Santa María**, 15 miles northeast of Liberia, on the equally bumpy road to Colonia Blanca. Both entry routes require four-wheel drive during the rainy season, but are just passable in high-clearance two-wheel-drive cars during the dry season.

One of many trails in and around Parque Nacional Rincón de la Vieja

▶▶▶ **Parque Nacional Santa Rosa**   *38B4*

Open: daily 8–4. Admission charge: expensive

This remarkably hot park preserves more than 120,000 acres of tropical dry forest and overgrazed pastures hugging the coastline of the Península de Santa Elena, where its purpose is to protect turtle nesting grounds. Easy of access and well structured, Santa Rosa was the site of three historic battles to preserve Costa Rica's independence. The first and most dramatic, in 1856, is well illustrated by the exhibits at the small museum of **La Casona**▶▶. This restored adobe and timber hacienda displays some wonderful old agricultural and domestic artifacts, 19th-century furniture, and old photographs and engravings. From here a short nature trail can be followed—it runs through tropical dry forest, where parrots, snakes, and iguanas hide among typical plant specimens, many of which are labeled. An uphill path leads to a lookout point dominated by the Monumento a Los Heros, a concrete arch dedicated to the victims of Santa Rosa's battles. The park headquarters, canteen, and campground lie just west of La Casona.

Dry Country Wildlife sightings are more likely during the dry season when animals emerge in search of water, but as the season progresses, Santa Rosa's aridity is accentuated by the hot dry winds sweeping in from the Pacific. Sightings of jaguars are not unknown and most visitors should see agoutis and tapirs. Birdlife is rich and varied and includes tinamous and great curassows. Insect life is also prolific and various (as anyone who has camped here will testify).

For a refreshing contrast, continue 7 miles south to the surfers' beach, Playa Naranjo, if you can—this road is not always passable even with four-wheel drive, so check before setting off. Alternatively, head north via the Interamerican and Cuajiniquil to the idyllic **Bahía Junquillal**, much favored during the rainy season by four of Costa Rica's turtle species, as well as by brown pelicans and magnificent frigate birds, whose aggressive aerobatics make a striking sight (see panel). The wide mile-long beach has two campgrounds.

Frigatebirds
Magnificent both in name and by nature, these huge seabirds can often be spotted in the Golfo de Santa Elena, around the Isla Bolaños and in the Bahía Junquillal. The combination of an immense wingspan and a light body makes it difficult for the bird to launch itself into the air from a normal standing or running position. For this reason it chooses only to land on high ledges or cliffs from where it can take off aided by wind currents in an ungainly leap. Frigatebirds in flight are, however, incredibly aerobatic as they chase and harass other seabirds into relinquishing their last meals. They never rest on the water, and spend the whole day on the wing.

A taste of the 19th century at La Casona

Flamingo fish
There are no pink flamingos in the Playa Flamingo area but the deep blue waters of the Pacific are teeming with vividly colored life. Sportfishing may involve wrestling with sailfish, blue and black marlin, amberjack, roosterfish, tuna, and some 25 other varieties. Divers may see white-tip reef sharks, grunts, yellow-tails, spotted eagle-rays, stingrays, eels, angelfish, octopus, starfish, seahorses, and, on a somewhat larger scale, whale sharks measuring up to 30 feet, spinner dolphins, pilot whales, and false killer whales.

▶▶ **Playa Conchal**   38B3

A short walk south across a rocky headland from the uninspiring, shadeless gray sands of Playa Brasilito (a focus for budget hotels and restaurants) brings you to this crescent-shaped beach of golden sand dominated by the crushed seashells of its name (*conchal* means "shell") and backed by lush vegetation. With no direct road access, Playa Conchal was for years a secluded getaway, but construction is underway of a low-rise hotel complex owned by the Spanish group Melia.

▶ **Playa del Coco**   38B4

This is the Tico family beach resort *par excellence* and offers a brash seaside atmosphere, complete with street vendors, fishing boats unloading their catches, loud open-air bars, garbage on the beach, uninspired food, and sandy streets. The sea itself is far from clean and any would-be swimmers should head for more pristine environments immediately south or north. Coco's popularity stems from its being only 21 miles west of Liberia along a paved road. That said, for those who want some good-natured nightlife and promenading with reasonably priced hotels and *cabinas*, this is where to go.

▶▶ **Playa Flamingo**   38B3

The status of Guanacaste's jet-set beach resort stems mainly from its 60-yacht marina, the first fuel dock for boats heading south down the Pacific coast after Acapulco in Mexico. It also boasts extensive diving and sportfishing facilities as well as the only nightclub and casino in the area, frequented by the likes of part-time residents Sylvester Stallone and Elizabeth Taylor. Despite this, Flamingo remains small in scale, with a cluster of badly designed hotels, condominiums and villas clambering around the headland of Punta Salinas. This offers lovely views over the adjacent Isla Plata and more distant volcanic-rock pinnacles of the Islas Santa Catalina, which attract divers.

Confusion sometimes arises as the name Playa Flamingo also refers to the blissful white sweep of Playa Blanca, which lies south of Punta Salinas and is joined to the north by **Playa Potrero**▶▶, **Playa La Penca**▶▶ and finally the remote **Playa Pan de Azúcar**▶▶▶, the latter monopolized by the relaxing upscale Hotel Sugar Beach. This string of fine, sheltered beaches is reached by a twisting unpaved road through pretty hills where you may see a troop of howler monkeys. Facilities are expanding but are still far from overdeveloped.

▶ **Playa Grande**   38B3

Immediately north of the popular Playa Tamarindo lies Playa Grande, favored for centuries by nesting leatherback turtles and now grandly labeled the Parque Nacional Marino Las Baulas de Guanacaste (from November to April access to the beach is restricted and payable. *Admission charge* expensive). It protects 1,100 acres of beach, forest and mangrove swamp full of blue-winged teals, black-bellied whistling-ducks, white ibis, cattle egrets, great blue herons, and muscovy ducks. Caymans, ctenophores, gray squirrels, howler monkeys, and white-faced monkeys are also present. The shadeless

Playa Flamingo's
sophisticated marina

sweep of the beach is popular with surfers but unsuitable for swimming. Canoeing, sailing, horse riding, and, in season, nocturnal turtle-watching tours are available through the Hotel Las Tortugas.

►► Playa Hermosa 38B4

This lovely crescent-shaped beach northeast of Playa del Coco is now seeing construction of a 320-room luxury hotel at its southern end. For the time being, a sprinkling of villas, hotels, *cabinas*, and restaurants front the beach, overlooked by a large villa complex. Activities include kayaking, windsurfing, canoeing, and snorkeling in crystalline waters. Beyond the northern point lies **Playa Panamá** ►►►, an equally beautiful, deserted beach with a campsite at the far end.

► Playa Junquillal 38B2

Halfway between Ostional and Playa Tamarindo, this wide, uncrowded beach is backed by dry forest and occupied almost exclusively by a handful of foreign-owned hotels. Swimming is dangerous here, but the hotels offer activities—or relaxation by a tranquil pool.

Out and about
The agency Ecotreks (tel: 654-4141) has an office in the Flamingo Marina Hotel, from where it organizes reasonably priced diving trips (including deep dives to 100 feet) to the Islas Santa Catallina, as well as kayaking and mountain-bike rental. Day-tours go as far as Arenal and, closer by, to the mangroves of Playa Grande. For sportfishing contact the Flamingo Marina (tel: 654-4203), which has a computerized database of over 100 boats.

Wide sands at Playa Sámara fill up on weekends during the dry season, but coconuts can drop at any time—beware!

▶ **Playa Naranjo** *39D2*

For years this ferry port opposite Puntarenas monopolized all public traffic across the Golfo de Nicoya. However, now that Paquera has a rival ferry service, local hotel owners have had to spruce up their image. A sprawling village without much of a beach (despite its name), Playa Naranjo now boasts a new complex by the ferry sideroad combining a hotel, pool, supermarket, car rental, and gas station. A short drive south through beautiful, wild hills brings you to Bahía Gigante▶▶, with its views of islands. A friendly, dynamic hotel here organizes water sports, horse riding, and island trips.

▶▶▶ **Playa Ocotal** *38B4*

This tiny (less than a half-mile long) and idyllic cove lies 2.5 miles south of Playa del Coco in a stunning setting, backed by hills of lush forest alive with parrots and monkeys. Tourist infrastructure is growing, but it remains a delightful spot and offers some excellent upscale accommodations. Great scuba diving is provided by Diving Safaris (tel: 670-0012), which operates on the beach, and by Guanacaste Tours, located at El Ocotal Beach Resort. Beyond the rocky headland to the south lies the small, black-sand beach of Bahía Pez Vela, where a lodge of the same name offers sportfishing. But above all don't miss a meal with a fabulous view from the hilltop hotel, El Ocotal.

▶ **Playa Sámara**   38B2

Seemingly endless off-white sands backed by coconut palms form this 3-mile beach, where outlying coral reefs keep the waves gentle. The consequently safe swimming combined with easy road access from Nicoya have made Sámara a popular Tico resort, and its airstrip flies in foreign and Tico owners of some large resort villas. Accommodations run the gamut of prices and the beachfront offers some breezy open-air restaurants.

Hotels pepper the road east before it swings around to **Playa Carrillo▶▶**, a beautiful crescent-shaped, palm-fringed beach ending in a forested headland dominated by a luxury Japanese-owned hotel, complete with a nearby airstrip and sportfishing boats. Otherwise this beach is superbly empty. The surrounding lush jungle continues along a rough but magnificent coastal track (viable only in the dry season with four-wheel drive) past Playa Camaronal to the extraordinary **Punta Islita▶▶**, where an innovatively designed, upscale hotel offers excellent accommodations, and the beach has safe bathing. An easier route, feasible with two-wheel drive, reaches Islita from the east passing through tiny villages and crossing undulating valleys on the way.

▶▶ **Playa Tamarindo**   38B3

The dirt road that leads downhill into the small resort of Tamarindo belies the upscale nature of the place. Long favored by wealthy Ticos as a spot for vacation homes, it is well endowed with stylish, inventively designed hotels, *cabinas*, expanding condominiums, and restaurants (which recently doubled in number in one year). The infrastructure has been slow to follow, forcing hotel-owners to band together to organize refuse collection and finance a paved access road.

The mile-long white-sand beach has rocky platforms that are exposed at low tide, and is edged by coconut palms and tamarind trees. Strong breezes make it good for windsurfing, and surfers can head around the southern point, which faces the tiny **Isla Capitan**. Papagayo Excursions (tel/fax: 654-4254) offers horse riding, deep-sea fishing, and estuary mangrove tours, plus turtle-watching at Playa Grande (see pages 52–53), while nocturnal social diversions are provided by beachfront open-air bars and restaurants. Despite the array of activities, the atmosphere at Playa Tamarindo is decidedly relaxed.

▶▶ **Playa Tambor**   39D1

Plum in the middle of the Península de Nicoya's southeast coastline lies **Bahía Ballena**, a magnificent horseshoe bay backed by deciduous forest whose beauty has been well exploited by the Spanish hotel group, Barcelo. Their sprawling, controversial, and heavily guarded resort occupies a central position (and is near to an airstrip), but as it is low-rise and surrounding vegetation still prolific, it barely alters the general aspect. A few miles south lies the lush village of Tambor, where a modest cluster of small beach hotels, shops, and restaurants caters for every budget. Ending the bay at its southern point is the Bahía Ballena Yacht Club & Watersports Association with a 30-boat marina, a lively Irish-run restaurant and scuba-diving, sailing, and sportfishing facilities.

Island-kayaking

The sea around the southeast corner of the Nicoya peninsula is generously sprinkled with uninhabited islands, the most famous being Islas Tortugas, whose pristine, jungle-backed beaches feature on countless travel posters. Boat tours run here from Puntarenas, Tambor, and even Montezuma, but the best way to explore these and some 15 other islands is by kayak. Bahía Gigante, between Paquera and Playa Naranjo, offers great paddling tours that include Isla Gitana, immediately offshore. This lush, private island is owned and operated by one of Costa Rica's great expatriate eccentrics, 80-year-old (plus) Carl, and offers rustic *cabinas*, a popular yachters' bar and friendly wildlife.

55

Beware the riptides

Costa Rica's Pacific beaches are not always what they seem. Riptides can carry even strong swimmers out to watery graves, and there are cases of drowning every year. No signs exist to warn visitors of the dangers, so it is your own responsibility to check on the safety of a beach and its waves. Never swim off a deserted beach without making enquiries locally. If caught in a riptide pulling you out to sea, don't struggle pointlessly against it. Instead, swim parallel to the shore to where you see breaking waves, which will help you back to the beach.

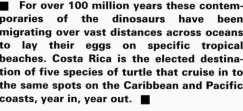

■ **For over 100 million years these contemporaries of the dinosaurs have been migrating over vast distances across oceans to lay their eggs on specific tropical beaches. Costa Rica is the elected destination of five species of turtle that cruise in to the same spots on the Caribbean and Pacific coasts, year in, year out.** ■

Threats to survival
Sea turtles are faced with innumerable threats that are far more destructive than the taking of eggs, meat and tortoiseshell. Beach-front constructions deprive turtles of safe nesting areas, and in contaminated waters turtles may die after ingesting plastic bags, or get trapped in floating debris that eventually strangles or drowns them. Above all they are menaced by fishing nets. More turtles die from accidental capture in nets than from all other life threats combined.

Leatherbacks, greens, hawksbills, loggerheads, and Pacific olive ridleys are the five species of sea turtle that for untold generations have nested on the beaches of Costa Rica. Their homing techniques still baffle scientists, but what is certain is that they commute long-distance between feeding grounds and nesting grounds, possibly following a specific smell or substance. Tagging by scientists has sketched the turtles' marine path, and a more precise picture is now emerging with the use of satellites. Since 1954, the world's longest ongoing turtle research station, the American-funded and -run Caribbean Conservation Corporation (CCC), at Tortuguero, has pioneered the protection of turtles, and today Costa Rica claims four major conservation sites. Visitors must follow strict regulations and are often accompanied by former turtle-hunters who have become guides.

Giant nomads In the Península de Nicoya, a new national park was created in 1991 at Playa Grande to protect nesting leatherbacks (*baulas*). This giant of the turtle world measures up to 8 feet and weighs around 1,500 pounds. Unlike other turtles, it does not have a hard shell but a thick, black, leathery skin, nor does it show strong fidelity to a particular nesting site. Solitary female leatherbacks come ashore on the Pacific coast between November and April to dig their huge nests, where they lay about 100 eggs in a laborious nocturnal operation, before covering them with sand and waddling back to sea. After 60–90 days the hatchlings emerge to make their way to the sea

Baby loggerheads (above) and freshwater turtles (below). Neither species is endangered yet

across the treacherous beach, easy prey for crabs, seabirds, and mammals. Only a tiny percentage survive. The eggs themselves have traditionally been plundered by villagers, although this habit is now changing.

Between February and July, leatherbacks also nest on the Caribbean coast, at Tortuguero and at the Gandoca-Manzanillo wildlife refuge. At the latter, regulations now limit the number of eggs that villagers collect, while the rest are hatched in incubators and the young turtles introduced to the sea.

Turtles

No room on the beach It takes luck to witness nesting leatherbacks, despite their tractor-like tracks, but quite the opposite is the case with Pacific olive ridleys, especially at Ostional. This much smaller species arrives in flotillas of hundreds, and sometimes there is so little room on the 3,000-foot beach that latecomers nest by the road. These amazing arrivals take place every month of the year but especially from July to December, and last 4–8 days. Again, villagers can collect eggs during the first 36 hours and even the research station is funded by the sale of eggs. Tagging of over 6,000 Pacific olive ridleys has charted their path north to the United States and south as far as Peru. Ostional is also visited, more rarely, by leatherbacks and greens, making it the second most important sea turtle hatchery in the world.

Vegetarians Research into green turtles is concentrated on the black-sand beaches of Tortuguero, which claims the largest hatchery in the western Caribbean, as well as less frequent visits from leatherbacks, hawksbills, and loggerheads. When Dr. Archie Carr started his research in the 1950s, greens were being heavily harvested by locals for their much-prized flesh. Unlike the jellyfish diet of leatherbacks or the sponges devoured by hawksbills—which make them toxic—the seagrass diet of greens makes them particularly tasty. Former turtle-hunters are now employed as guides or guards, and the CCC is working toward expanding the national park over the Nicaraguan border. Greens come to nest between June and November, when they lay 100–140 eggs each before continuing north to feed off Nicaragua's Miskito Coast, and then dispersing throughout the Caribbean.

Hawksbill turtles continue to be hunted illegally for their shells

Flapping in vain
"When the crashing wave breaks, they jump onto shore. They turtle along, dragging their shells in a rhythmic centuries-old minuet. They spawn deep in the sand, and when they attempt their return, they are flipped belly up and are left, flapping in vain, rocking back and forth stubbornly on their shells. Turtle in the soup, eggs in the gut of some turtle-bashing drunk. Sure, God made the animals first and then man. If the animals are dying, does the diviner divine who's next?" Abel Pacheco, *Deeper than Skin* (1972)

▶▶ **Refugio Nacional de
Fauna Silvestre Ostional** *38B2*

Open: daily
Located on the coast southwest of Nicoya, this 612-acre wildlife refuge protects the nesting grounds of the small Pacific olive ridley turtle. This species' homing instincts and the limited choice of potential nesting sites bring regular armadas to this spot, above all from July to December during the moon's last quarter, when you will see them arrive, looking like hundreds of floating boulders. Leatherbacks are occasionally seen between November and January, but hawksbill and green turtles are very rare here. A turtle research station (tel: 680-0467), located at the entrance to this black-sand beach refuge, provides information and basic dormitory accommodations, and there are a few *cabinas* in the village.

Airborne The coastal wetlands and forest are home to some 190 species of birds, including the brown pelican, magnificent frigate bird, royal tern, neotropic cormorant, and roseate spoonbill. Walks can be made along the seashore for some 11 miles north to Punta India or south along Playa Nosara to Garza and, at low tide, will reveal a wealth of sea urchins, anemones, crabs, and small fish trapped in the abundant rockpools. The entire beach has strong currents and would-be swimmers should note a memorial sign to a young American who drowned in 1992.

*Top: brown pelican
Above: the magnificent frigate bird*

▶▶ **Refugio Nacional de
Vida Silvestre Curú** *39D1*

This privately owned wildlife refuge, discreetly signposted from the road 4 miles south of Paquera, incorporates a mixture of pastureland, tropical hill forest, mangrove swamp, and idyllic beaches. It was established in 1933 by the Schutz family, who still run it, and named after the indigenous word for the magnificent Guanacaste tree. The hacienda's checkered history well reflects the environmental problems and solutions that Costa Rica is still finding. The initial decision to practice selective cutting of tropical trees, and to establish pasture and agricultural land, was followed in 1974 by an invasion of squatters, leading to the decision to protect both forest and mangroves and then, in 1983, the fragile marine habitat.

Ongoing activities Curú now has a small research center, used for educational programs. Current projects include reforestation, introduction of natural pest predators in order to eliminate pesticide use, preservation of turtle habitat, and the reintroduction of the spider monkey into the area. Eleven trails of varying difficulty wind through the refuge, and the fine, white-sand beach is ideal for swimming. Some 226 species of bird, 78 species of mammal, and 87 reptile species inhabit the refuge, including domesticated creatures that prowl around the house and research station. Visitors should book in advance, even for a day visit (tel: 661-2392. *Admission charge* moderate).

A short distance farther south at the village of **Valle Azul** is a newly established Butterfly Farm (*Open* Mon–Sat 8–4. *Admission charge* expensive), sheltered by a gigantic 150-year-old *Ceiba* tree. A short nature trail leads to the netted enclosure where you can watch nature's multicolored jewels flit from flowers to fruit.

▶ **Reserva Biológica Lomas Barbudal**   *38C3*
Open: daily 8–4. Admission charge: moderate
In 1986 it was decided to protect 5,430 acres of dry tropical forest and extensive grasslands in the middle of Guanacaste's hot, dry plains and hills. However, in 1994 disaster struck when flames destroyed much of the reserve, but regrowth is now underway. During the wet season Lomas Barbudal visually leaps out from the surrounding deforested savanna, but as the dry season advances it assumes a distinctly parched appearance.

Some mammals live here, but the reserve's biological importance lies above all in some 250 species of social and solitary bee (including the so-called Africanized "killer" bees), and in the numerous moth species. Local communities have been extensively involved in developing and manning the reserve, which is explained at a visitors' center in Bagaces, run by the Amigos de Lomas Barbudal. Access to the reserve is from Pijije on the Interamerican Highway, from where a gravel road leads to the park administration on the banks of the Río Cabuyo. A welcoming feature here is a freshwater pool.

59

During the dry season, thirsty trees become natural sculptures, and prone to forest fires

Gringo nose
The gumbo-limbo tree can be seen from Santa Rosa to Cabo Blanco. It attracts a variety of names, whether gumbo-limbo, *indio desnudo* ("naked Indian"), tourist's tree (in German) or, even more eloquent, gringo nose. These lyrical reactions are due to the way its ocher-colored bark peels to reveal a greenish under-bark. This photosynthetic process takes place during the dry season to feed the tree.

▶▶ **Reserva Natural Absoluta Cabo Blanco** *39D1*

Open: Wed–Sun 8–4. Admission charge: expensive
This is the longest-protected area in Costa Rica. The reserve was instigated in 1963 by a Swedish nature-lover, Olof Wessberg, who was far-sighted enough to recognize the importance of preserving and regenerating the last tracts of tropical rain forest on the peninsula. As a result, the numerous rivers running through the 2,900-acre reserve are always flowing, unlike those in the rest of this drought-ridden region, a clear environmental lesson. Visitors have been allowed in this "absolute" reserve only since the late 1980s, and recent overcrowding has led to two days of closure per week.

Forest trail One 3-mile trail leads from the park entrance over densely forested hills before descending to Playa Cabo Blanco, opposite Isla Cabo Blanco (topped by a light-house and a favorite nesting site for the brown booby). Typical trees are the lofty spiny cedar (some rise to 160 feet), gumbo-limbos, mayflowers, chicle trees, lemon-woods, and Panama woods, and wildlife here includes white-tailed deer, gray squirrels, tiger cats, howler, spider, and white-faced monkeys, and screeching para-keets. Watch out for rat-eating and grass snakes, boa constric-tors, vipers and coral snakes—the latter can be deadly.

Right: the deadly coral snake
Below: cattle grazing the parched grasslands of the Guanacaste region

▶ **Río Tempisque** *38C3*

This important 100 mile river has its headwaters high on the slopes of Volcán Orosí in the far north of Guanacaste, from where it flows southward through Lomas Barbudal and Palo Verde before emerging into the Golfo de Nicoya. Its once fertile valley attracted prehistoric settlers, and it has long been used for transport by boat, but sedimentation is now causing the water level to sink dramatically, making navigation hazardous. One of the problems is that local farmers build small dams along the Tempisque in order to redirect water for irrigation; another problem is deforestation along its banks, which leads to topsoil deposits. A new Chorotega-Indian-style hotel at Puerto Humo, Rancho Humo (tel: 225-2463), 16 miles northeast of Nicoya, offers boat tours along the Tempisque and into Palo Verde.

Ferry Visitors traveling north from the Central Valley to Guanacaste can cross the Tempisque on a car- and foot-passenger ferry. The turnoff from the Interamerican is 12 miles south of Cañas, from where it is another 15 miles to the embarkation point. Ferries run hourly and the crossing takes 20 minutes.

▶ **Santa Cruz** *38B3*

Santa Cruz is Guanacaste's burgeoning university and cultural center. It hosts numerous festivals but for visitors serves mainly as the gateway for Playas Tamarindo, Grande, and Junquillal. Along its handpaved streets, colorful old clapboard houses stand next to less appealing concrete low-rises, many of which have filled in a large section of the center that was devastated by fire in 1993. Most hotels are in or near the Plaza de Los Mangos, west of which lies the Parque Central, dominated by a weathered pink clock-tower, all that is left of a colonial church destroyed by an earthquake and now over-shadowed by a modern church. Three blocks farther west is the **Coope Tortilla**▶▶▶, an astonishing, barnlike building where a 12-woman cooperative dishes up some 500 meals a day to hungry locals and visitors seated at long wooden tables. One token man is employed to fuel the exterior tortilla ovens. The bustling atmosphere of black-ened pots bubbling on wood-fueled stoves is hard to beat, and you're unlikely to find a cheaper, more authentic meal anywhere.

Bulls
Not all those cattle you see scattered over the pastures of Guanacaste are destined for the dinner plate. Bull fighting is still a popular tradition throughout north-ern Costa Rica, and bullrings are a common, often precarious-looking, municipal fixture. However, in true pacific Tico fashion, bullfighters do not aim to kill the bulls. Quite the contrary, it is often the *montador* (climber) who gets hurt in his macho attempts to clamber onto the bucking bull's back and seize its horns.

▶ **Volcán Miravalles** *39D4*

The highest peak in the Cordillera de Guanacaste rises over 6,600 feet out of the hot savannah north of Bagaces. Although dormant, this volcano contains natural heat reserves that since 1994 have been exploited to produce geothermal energy, regarded as a more consistent source of energy than hydroelectric power (the latter formerly produced 85 percent of Costa Rica's energy needs). Instructive tours (contact Miratur, tel: 673-0260) of the plant and surroundings take in mountain trails, and extend to two-day expeditions to the summit, where encounters with wild cats are possible. Miravalles, like Rincón de la Vieja, has its own bubbling mudpots, Las Hornillas, reached from the village of Guayabo along a badly indicated road.

Drive Península de Nicoya

See map on pages 38–39.

Allow a long day for this circuit through the peninsula's heart, taking in the main towns and pottery centers, and ending at some stunning beaches. It can be covered in a sturdy two-wheel-drive vehicle. A detour to the Parque Nacional Barra Honda is possible.

Start at Playa Tamarindo and from there drive through Villareal to the junction at Huacas. Bear right and continue through wide open pastures with hills rising on both sides of the road and, in the dry season, splashes of brilliant yellow corteza trees. White Brahma cattle loiter in the rare shade provided by Guanacaste trees, or are herded by cowboys on horseback, as the road winds through tiny villages or past isolated farms. If the road is blocked by a *sabañero* and his herd, don't expect him to move it: the local habit is to weave your way slowly through the seemingly unconcerned cattle. About 12 miles farther, reach the crossroads at Belén. Turn right here toward Santa Cruz, entering a flatter rural landscape. **Stop at Santa Cruz▶** to sample an early but unusual Guanacaste lunch at the **Coope Tortilla▶▶▶** (see page 61).

Leave the town on the main road from the Plaza de Los Mangos and, shortly after crossing the Río San Juan, take a left turn towards Santa Bárbara. Grasslands, low hills in the background, clumps of green and flowering trees or royal palms contribute to the beauty of this route. After 6 miles (beyond Santa Bárbara), reach **Guaitíl▶▶** (see page 42). Visit the pottery workshops here, then continue to the hamlet of San Vicente to compare techniques and imagination. From here the bumpy gravel road winds through more villages, with the limestone hills of the **Parque Nacional Barra Honda▶▶** (see page 47) gradually coming into view. Tracts of forest may include quamwoods, wild cotton, and lemon woods. At Piave, along the turning to Nacaome, a detour may be made to the park, but the road needs a four-wheel-drive vehicle. Otherwise, to visit the park, continue 1.2 miles to the main road, turn left, and then drive 7 miles to a left turn where the park (another 3 miles) will be signposted. It is possible to continue by circling back to Nicoya, but time will be short and you may have to spend the night in Nicoya.

Stock up on fruit in Nicoya

Sorting the tomato crop

For those who have not made the detour to the park, the picturesque main route road finally leads into **Nicoya**►► (see page 45) where decorative fretwork buildings, often shrouded in bougainvillea, surround the town's historic church (it also functions as a museum). There is no shortage of *sodas* for refreshment, and the shady garden adjoining the church is a pleasant place to recover from the bone-shaking road. Leave Nicoya's main square by driving downhill from its southeast corner: this is the main road south that leads through Curimé and eventually reaches Playa Sámara, 21 miles south. Continue some 18 miles twisting through shorn hills dotted with palms, and past cattle and fields of melon and watermelon. After the neat village of Belén (another one!), the road climbs to overlook a magnificent wide valley edged with handsomely contoured hills. Mustachioed cowboys, traditional thatched buildings, and sprouting fences (see panel on page 81) are common sights in this area. Some 3 miles before Sámara turn right along a bumpy road to Barco Quebrada, which necessitates fording some shallow rivers.

Next stop is Garza, a pretty village straggling along a rocky cove that offers good swimming, bars, restaurants and some accommodations. The drive can end here, or continue a few more bone-rattling miles to the beaches and hills of **Nosara**►►► (see page 46).

THE NORTH

Previous pages: horseback is the only means of transportation in the rugged mountains on Laguna de Arenal's southern banks

The North Unfolding northward from the natural mountainous barrier of the Cordillera Central and the Cordillera de Tilarán is a patchwork of landscapes encapsulating Costa Rica's incredible natural riches as much as its environmental woes. Volcanoes, waterfalls, mineral springs, rushing rivers, marshes, cloud forest, rain forest, and rolling cattle pastures combine to create this concentrated topographical diversity. Towns remain small in scale and points of interest are well scattered over a network of rough roads, so this is certainly a region where a car is advisable. Watch out in the rainy season when many roads become impassable, and make sure your clothing is adaptable to rapid changes in temperature. The northern region is also home to a handful of Costa Rica's pioneering eco-lodges, whose isolated

Map labels:

NIC

Punta Castilla

Isla Machura

Barra del Colorado

Isla Calero

Isla Brava

San Juan

Trinidad

Colorado

Chirripó

Refugio Nacional de Fauna Silvestre Barra del Colorado

119m Cerro Tortuguero

Zona Protectora Tortuguero

Llanura de Tortuguero

Encina

Canta Gallo

Suerte

Parque Nacional Tortuguero

n Carlos

Toro

Sardinal

Sarapiquí

Pangola

Boca Río Sucio

Muelle

HEREDIA

Chilamate

Puerto Viejo de Sarapiquí

La Selva

Tigre

La Virgen

Sucio

San Pedro

Tortuguero

LIMÓN

Griega

Cariari

Esperanza

Zancudo

Zona Protectora La Selva

Las Horquetas

Teresa

Jiménez

Rara Avis

Río Frío

Rita

Roxana

Villafranca

Llanura de Santa Clara

Río Jiménez

Parque Nacional Braulio Carrillo

Santa Clara

Guápiles

Guácimo

Jiménez

rablanca 2906m

Volcán Barva

Rainforest Aerial Tram

Jardín Botánico Las Cusingas

Pocora

Parismina

Germania

Sacramento 2047m

Cerro Honduras

San José de la Montaña

Zona Protectora Acuíferos Guácimo y Pococí

Cairo

Florida

nta Bárbara

Barva

San Isidro

Yurquí

Parque Nacional Volcán Irazú 3432m

Volcán Turrialba 3328m

Heredia

Santo Domingo

San Isidro

Volcán Irazú

Monumento Nacional Guayabo

Peralta

Reventazón

Zona Protectora Río Pacuare

Lajas

Pacuare

SAN JOSÉ

Guadalupe

Llano Grande

Santa Cruz

San Pedro

Escazú

Pacayas

See drive page 84

See drive page 84

Enforced myopia
"Go up and down mountains. Touch clouds and shiver with cold. Sometimes waterfalls thunder, at other times wide rivers flow with clear and resonant waters, occasionally currents so deep that you can barely see the bottom from the top of a narrow bridge studded with crosses in memory of accidents. Coming down, you always arrive at a meeting of bridge and river; going up, you always run into mist for miles of enforced myopia." Carmen Naranjo, *Believe it or not* (1991)

67

locations make unusual demands on even the most well-seasoned travelers. Try the tractor ride to Rara Avis for good measure or, more serenely, a boat downriver from Puerto Viejo de Sarapiquí to reach Oro Verde.

Hot spots An increasingly popular center for visitors is along the shores of Laguna de Arenal, where water-sports, fishing and horse riding vie with the attractions of the rumbling Volcán Arenal, most sybaritically observed while indulging in a natural water massage at the hot springs of Tabacón. Budget travelers home in on Fortuna de San Carlos, a useful tour center, while serious bird-watchers head for the lush rain forest of La Selva or the wetlands of Caño Negro. Boat-trips from Puerto Viejo de Sarapiquí chug northeast along the Nicaraguan border and

THE NORTH

Resplendent quetzal
Both sacred (for the Maya) and elusive, the resplendent quetzal (illustrated on page 173) lives all year round in the high-altitude cloud forests of Central America, from southern Mexico to Panama. Today its numbers are decreasing alarmingly due to the destruction of its natural habitat. The nesting season—March to May—offers the best chance of sightings, when male and female can be seen swapping shifts for incubating the eggs. Nests are built in the hollows of dead trees. The brilliantly colored male's long green tail feathers are spectacular, especially in flight, and are at their best in the spring.

eventually into the Amazonian-style waterways of Barra del Colorado and Tortuguero (see pages 133 and 142–143), another birdwatchers' paradise. These tours are best organized through agencies in San José. One of the world's largest volcanic craters, Poás, is another crowd-puller, easily accessible from San José. However, the favorite destination on the northern trail is the cool hill country of Monteverde and Santa Elena, where well-organized cloud forest reserves offer brilliant flashes of the resplendent quetzal, as well as endless hiking possibilities. Now well established on tour itineraries, with a wide range of accommodations, Monteverde is suffering from overpopularity and a notable influx of gringos—not quite the idyllic Quaker retreat it once was.

Eco-enlightenment This is the area where you can learn how the rain forest functions as the planet's lungs, a complex and sophisticated interactive system. There is no shortage of information or experts, and private environmental initiatives are mushrooming, particularly within the vicinity of the Limón highway as it cuts through the Parque Nacional Braulio Carrillo on its way to the Carribbean. Farther north, as the road descends to humid lowlands, pockets of rain forest give way to desolate logged landscapes where plantations, sawmills, and skinny white cattle have taken over, all of them bugbears of environmentalists. But *campesinos* (farmers) on horseback, farms hidden in lush valleys, and tiny villages with their inevitable *sodas*, *pulperías* and central squares give an equally true picture of Costa Rica's rural reality.

Self-sufficient homesteads are a Tico tradition in the lush hills north of Monteverde

► Bosque Eterno de los Niños
(Children's Eternal Forest)
66B2

This remarkable project has, since 1988, succeeded in acquiring and protecting over 42,000 acres of cloud forest, an area that now practically encircles the Monteverde Cloud Forest Reserve (Reserva Biológica del Bosque Nuboso de Monteverde).

Children from 30 countries, from Australia to Saudi Arabia, finance the activities of the Bosque Eterno de los Niños, namely conservation, international environmental education, reforestation, and the establishment of biological research stations. Local communities are closely involved through school projects or by adopting farming methods compatible with conservation. Problems such as fires, poaching, logging, and squatters remain, and the number of forest guards is insufficient to patrol such an area, but the organization and communication skills of the managing group inspire confidence for the future.

A small section of the forest, **Bajo del Tigre►** (see page 77), lies in Monteverde itself, but more interesting are the trails surrounding **San Gerardo►►**, an isolated research station situated 2.5 miles from Santa Elena. The scenic landscapes at over 4,000 feet include views over Arenal and reveal just how fantastic is the region's biodiversity. Horses are available for trekking. Contact the Monteverde Conservation League in Monteverde (tel: 645-5003/5305, fax: 645-5104) for information about access and dormitory accommodations.

► Ciudad Quesada
(San Carlos)
66C2

A humid gateway to the north, often known by its former name of San Carlos, Cuidad Quesada lies at the foot of the Cordillera Centra. It is an important agricultural center for sugarcane, citrus fruits and cattle, and its lively cattle fair in early April is one of Costa Rica's largest.

The town is of limited interest but the main square is home to a crafts cooperative, a colorful vegetable market, and even a casino, in the Hotel La Central, while local *talabarterias* (saddlemakers) are known for their finely crafted leather saddles. Carnivores can indulge in a prolific selection of steaks at local restaurants before heading on. A small tourist office (*Open*: weekdays 8:30–11:30, 12:30–5) is located on the main road at the southern entrance.

Infant initiative
At the origin of the Bosque Eterno de los Niños was a group of Swedish children who, concerned by the demise of the rain forest, raised money which they sent to the Monteverde Conservation League. From that point the project mushroomed, and schoolchildren from Britain, USA, Germany, and Japan were soon actively working to raise funds. Its educational work continues in informative newsletters juxtaposing serious articles with pages designed for young children.

Much pride is taken in a cowboy's accessories, the best being from Ciudad Quesada

Heliconias

Although the name heliconia derives from Mt. Helicon, the Greek mythological home of the Muses, these decorative flowers are native to Latin America and some islands of the Pacific. They develop in secondary forest in humid lowland tropics or higher up in the cloud forest, and are pollinated by hummingbirds. Flat, two-dimensional leaves grow vertically on long stalks, and the plants are easily mistaken for their close cousin, the banana palm. From the stalk the colorful flower branch emerges, usually bright red, yellow, or pink. Some 50 flowers blossom on each inflorescence, lasting anything from a few days to months, before they die and rot away.

After a strenuous climb and a slippery descent, the trail ends at Fortuna's waterfall

▶ **Fortuna de San Carlos (La Fortuna)** *66B2*

A strange phenomenon: the numerous hotels and restaurants of this nondescript town somehow manage *not* to have views of Arenal looming to the west. Yet backpackers flock here, and the town buzzes with guides and tour agents offering trips on horseback, by jeep or boat to the nearby sights of Volcán Arenal (by day or by night), the Venado caves, Caño Negro, or Río Frío. Commercial sharks abound and prices vary, but a reliable multilingual guide service is provided by Gabino at the Vegetarian Restaurant (tel/fax: 479-9178) on the south side of the church. Pura Vida, based at the Hotel La Central (tel/fax: 479-9004), also offers reasonable rates. Hikers can explore the lower slopes rising towards Arenal, or head 3 miles southwest of town to the **Catarata Río Fortuna**▶▶, a magnificent waterfall thundering down to a jungle pool. The access trail winds uphill past isolated farms and agricultural land before penetrating forest where jaguars are said to roam.

▶ **Guácimo and Guápiles** *67E1*

The interest of these two towns, 7 miles distant from each other, lies in their surroundings. Banana companies have transformed much of the character of the region but it is attracting an increasing number of conservation-inspired projects, all on or just off the Limón highway. Number one is **EARTH (Escuela de Agricultura de la Región Tropical Humedo)**▶▶ (tel: 255-2000, fax: 255-2726), which lies at Pocora, immediately southeast of Guácimo. Since 1990, students from all over Latin America have come here to follow university courses in sustainable tropical agriculture, and trails through a private rain forest reserve are also open to tour groups and independent visitors. Situated opposite, the **Hotel Las Palmas**▶ (tel: 716-5289) has developed a 2½ hour trail through its own reserve, with river, waterfall and heliconia garden.

Gardens Closer to Guápiles, accessible by a 3-mile gravel road from a turnoff at the Soda Buenos Aires, is the **Jardín Botánico Las Cusingas**▶▶ (tel: 710-0114 for messages. *Admission charge* moderate). Run by a dedicated US/Tico family, this project preserves a tract of secondary rain forest (with a two-hour trail) beside an experimental garden for medicinal plants, and is developing an educational center for adults and children. More commercial in spirit is **Costa Flores**▶ (tel/fax: 717-5457. *Open* weekdays. *Admission* expensive guided tour), Costa Rica's largest heliconia farm, 9 miles east of Guápiles. Part of the garden has been landscaped beside a restaurant, and the entire area attracts hummingbirds and butterflies.

Rain forest The private 420-acre reserve of **Bosque Lluvioso**▶ (tel: 224-0819.

Open daily. *Admission charge* expensive) makes an easy introduction to the primary rain forest. Trails (from half an hour to four hours) have been designed for visitors such as families who might want easy routes, and facilities include a riverside restaurant. Guided tours are available, or you can follow the trails using a guidebook. Access is by a 2-mile dirt road running south between Río Costa Rica and Río Blanco. Very close by, reached from a short track leading north from the Río Corinto, is the **Centro Ecológico Morpho**► (tel: 221-9132), another rain forest reserve that organizes environment-related workshops with tent accommodations and trails for visitors to follow. Future plans extend to a natural history museum and a rainforest research laboratory.

Crowning this region's offerings is the **Rainforest Aerial Tram**►►► (tel: 257-5961. *Open* daily 6–3:30. *Admission charge* very expensive), an extraordinary enterprise that opened in 1994. The open cable cars float visitors above the jungle canopy along a 2-mile route, taking about 1½ hours. Observation stops can be made on request to the accompanying guide, but this is not a zoo, so do not expect to see wildlife swinging along beside you. Bird watchers should aim for the very early morning; otherwise afternoons are less crowded but booking is always advisable. Access by tractor down from the highway is followed by a short trail that leads to the unobtrusive information center and restaurant.

The Rainforest Aerial Tram

Dr. Perry
The inventor of the jungle cable car is Dr. Donald Perry, an imaginative Californian professor of tropical biology who, since 1974, has been developing various methods of exploring the fascinating world of Costa Rica's forests. Adopting mountain-climbing techniques, he started with a rope web system strung over the jungle canopy, continued at Rara Avis with an automated web, which included observation platforms, and in 1992 started the ambitious aerial tram project. Installation logistics were mind-boggling, but in October 1994 the aerial tram finally opened.

Rain forest palms

One of the most characteristic plants found in the subcanopy (30–80ft) of primary rain forest is the palm, and at La Selva 32 species have so far been identified. The most common is the *Welfia georgii*, distinguishable by its brilliant orange young leaves and its long, serpentine growths that spread over the forest floor. The seeds of this palm are much appreciated by monkeys, agoutis, and other mammals, which, in their turn, attract the hungry bushmaster viper. Another common rain forest palm is the *Socratea exorrhiza*, recognizable by its triangular web of spiny roots.

La Selva's bridge gives access to some 2,000 plant species

▶▶ **Laguna de Arenal**   66A2

This mirrorlike expanse, reflecting Volcán Arenal (see page 83) at its eastern end and skimmed by windsurfers at its western end, is Central America's largest man-made lake. In 1973 an existing lake was enlarged by flooding the original town of Arenal, and this is now a confirmed center for water sports (windsurfing above all), fishing (rainbow bass), and horse riding around its shores. A severely rutted road runs from the volcano, along the northern banks, to curve eventually round the windier, western end, where it cuts south to Tilarán (see page 81). Accommodations are scattered up slopes beside the road, and nearly all offers fabulous vistas across the water to the Cordillera de Tilarán, but telephones are still scarce so communications are difficult. The wild southern banks are most easily accessible on horseback.

Mineral soak The Tabacón Resort▶ (tel: 222-1072. *Open* daily 10–10. *Admission charge* expensive) lies 7 miles west of La Fortuna and is a spa built to take advantage of Arenal's thermal springs. Five pools, a restaurant, jacuzzis, massages, and landscaped gardens are part of the package, but for less formal surroundings and budget prices follow a sideroad opposite that leads down to a creek where there are changing rooms and sandy bottomed mineral pools. A few miles southeast of Nuevo Arenal (a useful budget stop) along a killer stretch of road is the **Arenal Botanical Garden (Jardín Botánico Arenal)**▶▶▶ (tel: 694-4273. *Open* daily 9–5. *Admission charge* inexpensive). This small, beautifully landscaped garden offers a fantastic array of over 1,000 varieties of native and exotic plants, all labeled, and is alive with butterflies and hummingbirds. Opposite the entrance is a trail leading down to a lakeside picnic and swimming area.

From Nuevo Arenal westwards, the lake loses its luxuriant slopes and is set in bleaker, drier cattle pastures. This end of the lake is where windsurfers can indulge in winds of over 30 knots during the dry season. Numerous lakeside hotels offer water sports and fishing facilities.

▶▶▶ **La Selva**   67D2

This OTS (Organization for Tropical Studies) station reigns over 4,000 acres of protected rain forest adjoining Parque Nacional Braulio Carrillo. An average annual rainfall of over 150 inches combines with 62 percent primary rain forest to make it one of the top four places in the world for rain forest research.

American and Costa Rican scientists flock here to study the remarkable biodiversity, which includes more than half (over 400) of Costa Rica's bird species. Tapirs, jaguars, sloths, coatis, and howler monkeys are among the 113 mammal species that lurk in the shadows of this spectacular reserve, while butterflies, amphibians and reptiles add to the abundance. The 30 miles of well-marked trails cross the humid forest, and are best followed with an informative guide, but as this is primarily a scientific and educational establishment, access to nonspecialist visitors is severely restricted. Reservations, even for a day visit, must be made well in advance through the OTS office in San José (tel: 240-6696, fax: 240-6783. *Admission charge* expensive). Access is from the main road just south of Puerto Viejo along an unmarked turning west from a bus stop.

▶ **Los Chiles** 66B4

A straight, flat road slices through northern Costa Rica to reach the Nicaraguan border at Los Chiles, a dilapidated town that serves as a base for touring the wetlands of Caño Negro (see page 80). This sparsely populated area is characterized by vast orange groves, sugarcane plantations, and sawmills piled high with gigantic logs. Los Chiles itself has some atmospheric old clapboard houses but very limited accommodations. Most visitors head directly for the banks of the Río Frío, just west of the main square, where boats can be rented to take you into Caño Negro. Alternatively, contact El Parque restaurant (tel: 471-1090, fax: 471-1032) on the main square for a reasonably priced boat tour.

It's the cicadas
"There is a voiceless murmur at first, brilliant, then vibrant, that grows, stuck to the earth. There are thousands of voices. Myriads of screeches. It isn't the sound of the trees or the rivers, it isn't human voices. It's the cicadas. Their voices grow under the green, in the dust, in the gardens. They move the leaves, stir the river, build forever and ever, as if they were never going to end, maddening, in waves surging from the ground, fanning down from the houses, forever and ever and ever..." Yolanda Oreamuno, *The Spirit of My Land*

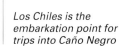

73

Los Chiles is the embarkation point for trips into Caño Negro

Herbal medicine

■ **The medicinal secrets of tropical plants have still to be extensively explored by scientists, but for centuries indigenous people, Afro-Caribbeans, and descendants of the Spaniards alike have relied on them. Every Costa Rican market has stalls devoted to folk remedies, and herbal medicines are now gaining a hold on visitors seeking an alternative to antibiotics.** ■

Go to no doctor

In the words of Mr. Selvyn Bryant of Old Harbour, transcribed by Paula Palmer in her folk-history of Talamanca's Afro-Caribbeans, *What Happen*, "One time machete cut these three finger, all three right to the bone. Go to no doctor. Just get the cocoa and scrape it on there, tie it up. Machete chop off this finger too, when I was a boy, and I wave it till this end piece practically come off, and my mother take it and just clamp it on back and get cocoa and bandage it up. Go to no doctor."

Ongoing tradition

Herbal medicine is by no means dying out in Costa Rica. In 1981 an international congress on medicinal plants took place in San José, and delegates were taken to Bribrí and Puerto Viejo to investigate traditional cures used by *curanderos* (healers). More recently, concern about diminishing knowledge among indigenous communities led to a series of workshops among the Talamanca and Guaymi populations, so that they could share and renew confidence in natural medicine.

Ironically, in a country that boasts a highly developed public health service, with over 85 percent of homes covered by health centers and a life expectancy of 75 years (just behind North America's 76 years and well ahead of all other Central American states), folk remedies still play a major role in daily life. Talamanca Indians, Afro-Caribbeans, and the Ticos of the capital are all well acquainted with the medicinal uses of plants and fruits. Stinging nettles, cocoa pods, coconuts, manioc, knot-grass, mango leaves, passion fruit, aloe, ginger, custard apples, pineapples, leaves of the breadfruit tree, sap of the tallow tree—all of these, and hundreds of others, may be brewed into teas, made into solutions, or applied directly to wounds.

Mystical application Plant cures are traditionally used by Costa Rica's Indian population in mystical rituals performed by a shaman (*awapa orjawa*), a crucial spiritual role inherited through the male line. Armed with an *ulu*, a balsawood stick painted with images of the god Sibu, mythological plants and animals, and wearing a pouch around his neck containing magic stones to detect illness or pain, he launches into ritual chants before administering the appropriate remedy. Ceremonies only take place at night. Every Talamanca Indian acquires an intimate knowledge of the use of plants for everyday problems: ulcers are cured with a preparation of leaves from the *frailecillo* (cassava marble), colic with an infusion of white mustard leaves, arthritis and hair loss with a preparation of leaves from the guarumo and quina trees. An extract of the cycad plant treats snake bites, as does the juice of no fewer than 18 lemons, drunk over six intervals of 10 minutes.

Tie it up The Afro-Caribbean population of Limón is particularly resilient (with a genetic resistance to the tropical killer, malaria) and shares medicinal knowledge with neighboring Indians. General good health means that medicinal care is most commonly needed only for childbirth, snake bites, or accidents such as machete cuts. Midwives and snake doctors were once the most respected members of a Talamanca Afro-Caribbean community, the latter working in a semi-mystical fashion similar to that of the Indian shaman. For machete cuts the common remedy was simply to apply a peeled green cacao pod. The sticky inner cacao flesh was bandaged to the wound and left there until it healed.

Brew it up Tico market stalls bristle with bunches of leaves, vines, roots, or cactus leaves, all labeled for their respective treatments. For facial inflammations, try a tea made from the fragrant river valley shrub, queen-of-the-night (whose genus *Datura* is a source of antidotes for certain pesticide poisonings). For allergies apply the squeezed sap of papaya leaves, for intestinal worms take a morning draft of coconut and pineapple juice, for diarrhea choose from manioc, the boiled young leaves of the guava tree or passion fruit, for arthritis boil the root and top of the sulfur plant or use a preparation of ripe plantains, for coughs and bronchitis make an infusion of oregano, for insect bites apply a solution made from the leaves of the natural blue... the treatments and ingredients are endless.

Certain plants have multiple uses. An infusion of the aloe vera cactus relieves bronchitis, diabetes, or colitis, and the gelatinous leaves are used externally for burns, rashes, and dry skin—something the cosmetics industry appreciates too. The geranium, brewed into a tea, is said to help sore throats, hysteria, and menstrual disorders. And for a really fortifying energy kick, try drinking an infusion of *culantro de coyote* (spirit weed).

Leaf of life
The seemingly miraculous *hoja de aire* (the leaf of life, air plant or miracle plant) not only has leaves with the ability to grow after being separated from the plant, but is also said to cure coughs and colds.

Gnarled roots and bundles of leaves hardly seem inspiring, but curanderos (healers) know their hidden properties

Butterflies
Blue morphos are only one of the 545 butterfly species identified in the Monteverde region, while the whole of Costa Rica claims over 1,000 species. After metamorphosing from caterpillars to chrysalids, most butterflies live for only a month, though exceptions such as the longwings species live as long as 9 months, helped by their pollen diet. Otherwise, nutrition is obtained from flowers, rotting fruit, and even dead insects and bird droppings. Butterflies cannot maintain their body temperatures and need sunlight to heat their muscles for flight, which is why, in cool, cloudy conditions, they can be seen roosting under leaves.

Monteverde's cloud forest supports over 500 butterfly species

▶▶▶ Monteverde   66A2

Monteverde is famous for two things: firstly its cloud-forest reserve, and secondly a farming community founded by American Quakers in the 1950s. The combination makes it one of Costa Rica's top tourist destinations, despite the awful roads that lead there.

Pastoral straggle The village straggles several miles along a ridge between Santa Elena and the reserve, so you have to hike between points of interest, but the cool climate, fragrant pine trees, and lovely views make walking very pleasant. Numerous conservation projects and ecologically minded hotels, and a constant influx of students and volunteers contribute to the earnest and "alternative" atmosphere. From January to mid-February, the mood changes somewhat, with a festival of classical, jazz, and Latin music.

Forest Priority destination is the **Monteverde Cloud Forest Reserve (Reserva Biológica Del Bosque Nuboso de Monteverde)▶▶** (tel: 645-5122. *Open* daily 7–4, entrance possible earlier. *Admission charge* moderate), a 25,000-acre private reserve owned by the Tropical Science Center of San José. It has well-marked trails, and a fantastic array of wildlife, including jaguars, ocelots, bellbirds, and the resplendent quetzal, as well as (possibly) the golden toad, once found only here and now feared extinct.

Nevertheless, some visitors go home disappointed (if they get in at all—numbers are restricted and reservations are essential in the high season), and it takes forethought to ensure that your visit lives up to expectations. A good time to go is between February and April, when birdwatching and weather are at their best. From the visitor center, with its hummingbird feeders, follow one of the many trails that enable you to spend the entire day alone, if your legs are up to it. Howler monkeys and quetzals are comparatively easy to see overhead. Other forest-dwellers are more secretive, but just try standing still—violet saber-wing hummingbirds may come and investigate you, and antbirds and trogons will emerge from the undergrowth. It is best to start early in the morning: by early afternoon, cloud and mist have often descended. For a really spectacular sight, follow the main trail up to the Continental Divide and watch the clouds build up and flow eerily over the ridge itself.

Other places to visit There is plenty of wildlife, even around some of the hotels and boarding houses. In the grounds of Pensión Flor Mar, run by Quaker bird-enthusiasts, you may see emerald toucanets, brown jays, and masked tityras—even, perhaps, a two-toed sloth. A short distance downhill from the main reserve, **Reserva Sendero Tranquilo** (tel: 645-5010. *Open* daily. *Admission charge* expensive), is a small private reserve and farm offering personalized cloud-forest tours. At the junction with the main road stands a Monteverde landmark that has nothing to do with the wildlife— **La Lechería**, the cheese factory (*Open* tours weekdays 1:30. *Admission charge* inexpensive), which is a model of high-technology but environmentally respon-sible production (though plastic-wrapped, sliced Monteverde cheese tastes as bland as any mass-produced product). Toward the center of Monteverde village, next to the central grocery cooperative, is **CASEM**, a women's cooperative selling souvenirs and craft items (not all are made locally). Just opposite are **Meg's Stables** (tel: 645-5052), offering horse riding tours to local lookout points and, next door, a popular bakery and coffee shop selling American cakes.

Education From here, Monteverde's rural road winds past a river to reach another clus-ter of activity, incuding the offices of the **Monteverde Conservation League►►** (tel: 645-5003/5305, fax: 645-5104). The league publishes information on environ-mental issues, especially its main project, the Bosque Eterno de los Niños (see page 69), and the **Bajo del Tigre►** trail through secondary and tertiary forest (downhill from the cheese factory and good for birdwatching). Signposted from the main road near here is **Monteverde Butterfly Garden►►►** (*Open* daily 9:30–4. *Admission charge* inexpensive guided tour), with over 40 species of local butterflies. At the Santa Elena end of the village, the **Parque de Aves** is a small private reserve of secondary forest (*Open* daily from 7. *Admission charge* inexpensive).

77

On the rough and rutted road to Monteverde

Boat trips from Puerto Viejo give views of monkeys, caymans, and countless birds

▶▶ **Parque Nacional Braulio Carrillo** 67D1

Open: daily 8–4. Admission charge: expensive

Less than 30 minutes' drive from San José, the main highway to Limón cuts through this magnificent park, too often admired only from the comfort of a vehicle. Rugged mountain peaks, primary forest, dormant volcanoes, thundering waterfalls, deep canyons, and semi-permanent cloud and/or rain combine to create a unique environment of 10,900 acres. There are three entrances with facilities, information points, and trails: two on the highway, and a third on the slopes of Volcán Barva along a rough road from Sacramento, only passable during the dry season. A five-hour trek here (with potential sightings of quetzals along the way) brings you through volcanic landscapes to the crater lake of Danta.

Wild variety Braulio Carrillo has extraordinary diversity. Where it abuts the reserve of La Selva (see pages 72–3), the low altitude of 650 feet nurtures hot and humid rain forest, in contrast to the cool, cloudy southern section (around the highway), which rises from 5,000 to 6,600 feet, culminating at 9,534 feet on the summit of Volcán Barva. These more accessible highland areas are clad in oaks, mountain cypresses, cedars, magnolias, mosses, and the distinctive gunnera, or "poor man's umbrella." Birdlife is correspondingly rich, including the three-wattled bellbird, king vulture, solitary eagle, and resplendent quetzal, while mammals include coyotes, agoutis, and various wild cats. A short walk along one of the trails should provide views of owls, butterflies, squirrels, cuckoos, and flycatchers. Watch the ground itself for huge red-legged tarantulas, and be well prepared for rain and cool temperatures (see also page 71 for the nearby Rain Forest Aerial Tram).

Stopping the rot
The Sarapiquí region has long been a target for timber companies, much to the ire of conservation organizations. Absurdities exist, such as precious mahogany being felled in order to make 2 million palettes annually for banana transportation, and there are other environmental problems too. Pesticide-spraying is widespread and is having serious effects on humans, with an estimated 4,000 banana-plantation workers reported sterile and a recent increase in the number of babies born with deformities.

▶▶ Parque Nacional Volcán Poás   66C1

Open: daily 8–3:30. Admission charge: expensive

The spectacular crater of Poás slips elusively from view as clouds drift across this stark, powerful landscape. Park authorities have even felt obliged to signpost warnings that visitors may not see the crater at all, but the 1,600-acre park always offers easy trails through cloud and dwarf forest, and some 79 bird species. This is the most visited national park, and includes a museum, cafeteria, auditorium and gift shop, from which a short path leads to the crowded lookout point. Here, if you are lucky, you will gaze out over the 2-mile crater, its lake and steaming fumaroles backed by a cone of slag. Visualize the *azufreros* (sulfur-collectors) who, as recently as the 1950s, transported the yellow mineral on foot to sell to medicine-makers. Poás' second crater lake, Laguna Botos, is located along a short trail to the south. The self-guided La Escalonia trail leads through the cloud forest, rich in bromeliads, lichen and mosses. Birds that you might encounter include the mountain robin, brown jay, and scintillant hummingbird. Measuring a mere 2.5 inches from bill to tail, this may be the second smallest bird in the world. Plenty of insects here are considerably larger.

▶ Puerto Viejo de Sarapiquí   67D2

This nondescript riverside town is the starting point for river trips down the jungle-edged **Río Sarapiquí▶▶** to the Río San Juan, that forms the Nicaraguan border. From here boats can continue east through the swamps of Barra del Colorado to enter the waterways of Tortuguero. Organized tours from San José are the cheapest, but boats can be hired from the dock at hourly rates. *La muelle* (dock) is located at the eastern end of a dirt-road straggle of budget hotels and restaurants. Vast banana and pineapple plantations have eaten up much of the virgin rain forest of this humid region, leaving only a few pockets, notably at La Selva (see pages 72–73), Rara Avis (see page 80) and downriver around **Oro Verde**, an ecotourism center in a huge area of rain forest.

Boom!

Poás was active in the 19th century, and erupted in 1889, but it was in 1910 that this volcano really left its mark. A major eruption resulted in a cloud mushrooming some 2 miles above, and left a gigantic hole measuring over 5 miles across. One hour later an estimated 640,000 tones of volcanic debris started showering the Central Valley. Constant rumbling and violent emissions of burning rock culminated in the next major eruption in 1953, which ten years later led to the formation of the lake. Occasional geyser eruptions continue, and in 1989–1991 gas emissions led to acid rain damaging surrounding coffee and strawberry plantations, as well as aggravating asthmatic conditions.

A rare cloudless and steamless view of the Poás volcano, thought now to be coming out of an active phase

Arrow-poison frogs

Of the 160 or so amphibian species that lurk in Costa Rica's more watery environments, the arrow-poison frogs (*Dendrobates spp*) are the most toxic. These tiny, gaudy frogs, ranging in palette from bright red with black dots to fluorescent green with black markings, have long been caught by the Indians for their poisonous skin secretions, which were used for soaking arrow-tips prior to hunting. When the toxin penetrates the bloodstream by arrow or through an open wound, it causes neuromuscular contractions that can lead to paralysis and death. Researchers have identified nearly 300 alkaloid compounds secreted by arrow-poison frogs, including analgesics 200 times more powerful than morphine.

Innocuous-looking, perhaps, but the arrow-poison frog's toxin can be fatal

▶▶ **Rara Avis**   67D2

One of Costa Rica's most remote ecotourism projects was founded in 1983 by a biologist and former manager of La Selva, Amos Bien, to explore economic alternatives to logging the rain forest. The 3,200-acre private reserve bordering Braulio Carrillo and La Selva provides a clear demonstration of the benefits of conservation, with related projects such as research into the harvesting of ornamental and medicinal plants, a butterfly research farm and a rain forest nursery garden.

Access to this pioneering project is, come rain or shine, by a gruelling four- or five-hour tractor ride from Las Horquetas, a village situated 11 miles south of Puerto Viejo. The demanding journey offers an explicit picture of the transition from desolate, logged cattle ranches into dense, rich virgin rain forest. This, too, is where Donald Perry first developed his AWCE (Automated Web for Canopy Exploration) in 1987, a precursor to the more sophisticated aerial tram (see panel on page 71). A variety of accommodations is available, and reservations are essential (tel/fax: 253-0844).

▶▶ **Refugio Nacional de Vida Silvestre Caño Negro**   66A3

This little-visited wildlife refuge in the far north of Costa Rica encompasses 25,000 acres of lowland swamp crossed by the Río Frío before it drains into the Lago Caño Negro. During the dry season the area is reduced to small lagoons and channels, but nothing deters the cattle egrets, roseate spoonbills, white ibis, wood storks, black-bellied whistling-ducks, and neotropic cormorants (it shelters Costa Rica's largest colony of the cormorants) that inhabit these wetlands. The surrounding grasslands, marsh and forest are home to several monkey species, sloths, otters and a few wild cats, while caymans and 30 species of freshwater fish profit from the rivers. The best way to visit is by organized tour from La Fortuna (see page 70) or from Los Chiles (see page 73).

▶▶ **Santa Elena**   66A2

A few miles northwest of Monteverde, Santa Elena offers a budget alternative and is reached by equally rough and dusty roads. Number one attraction here is the **Reserva Santa Elena**▶▶▶ (tel/fax: 645-5238. *Open* daily 7–5. *Admission charge* inexpensive), a locally managed conservation project opened in 1992, which offers 5 miles of trails through 765 acres of cloud forest. This land is 83 percent exuberant primary forest, rich in dripping epiphytes, vines and mosses; pumas, howler monkeys, and quetzals also inhabit the reserve. Less visited than Monteverde's cloud-forest reserve, yet offering the same flora and fauna and equally well organized (with rubber boots, rain-ponchos, and guides for hire), Santa Elena's reserve is an attractive alternative. It lies about 3 miles northeast of town along a bumpy track.

Whisked away The center of Santa Elena town is the main crossroads, around which are the bus terminal, some reasonable accommodations, restaurants, a bookstore, a bank, and tourist information at the Albergue Santa Elena. Horse riding tours around this beautiful region are offered by Caballeriza La Estrella (tel: 645-5067) on the San José road. The more adventurous Canopy Tours (tel/fax: 645-5243) winch visitors in harnesses 130 feet up through the trees to observation platforms. The system is expanding and relocating to the Cloud Forest Lodge, where the organizers plan to install a network of seven platforms connected by rope. Also in Santa Elena is the **Serpentario▶** (tel: 645-5238. *Open:* Mon–Sat 9–4. *Admission charge* inexpensive), a small snake farm.

▶   **Tilarán**   *66A2*

There is little scenic or other interest in this small, windy town just south of Laguna de Arenal. It nevertheless makes a useful stopover for bus travelers and provides reasonably priced hotels and restaurants, mostly situated around the Parque Central. People are friendly and arrangements can be made here for fishing trips, water-sports, or tours to Volcán Arenal. A useful source of information is the American-run budget Hotel Yasmine (tel: 695-5043). South from here is a stunningly beautiful, though rough drive along a road that winds through rolling pastures and tiny dairy-farming communities to reach Santa Elena and Monteverde—allow at least two hours to cover the 20 miles.

Living fences
The pastures of Costa Rica are often bordered by living fences. These sprouting wooden pickets are actually living branches planted in the soil. Once the posts have been planted they grow for decades, occasionally requiring pruning, and providing a pleasantly leafy barrier. Only a handful of tree species are suitable; most farmers use a dense, local wood, and swear by specific, well-timed methods to ensure growth. Branches should only be cut during the waning phase of the moon in March, and are then "cured" for three or so days by placing them on an incline, before the final planting.

81

A hole in your shoe? On-the-spot repairs at Tilaran

■ **Constant cloud is the easily definable characteristic of Costa Rica's extensive cloud forest, which starts at elevations of around 5,000 feet. This is where rain forest becomes a seemingly paradoxical world of abundant tropical plants flourishing in cloud, rain, and cool temperatures.** ■

Tapirs
Of the 100 or so mammal species found in cloud forests, Baird's tapir was once numerous. This particular species can be found from southern Mexico to northern South America, where it hides in thickets and swamps during the day, emerging only at night. They are much sought after by hunters for their meat, and this, combined with their intolerance of man's presence and sensitivity to habitat disturbance, is leading to their gradual disappearance.

Hot lips (top) flourishes in the mist and drizzle of the Parque Nacional Braulio Carrillo

The low cloud of Costa Rican cloud forest is produced by moisture-laden trade winds blowing in across the Atlantic and over the Continental Divide, where they cloak the forested mountains in a veil of mist, drizzle, and rain. As a result, these dripping forests and their numerous waterfalls and streams are an essential watershed for drier areas at lower elevations. The Monteverde area is the most renowned of Costa Rica's cloud forests, but this same ecosystem continues down the spine of the country and can be explored near San Ramón (Los Angeles Cloud Forest), in valleys around Cerro La Muerte and at the national parks of Braulio Carrillo, Tapantí, Chirripó, and La Amistad.

Flora and fauna The sheltered tracts of evergreen forest are thick with lush ferns, palms, epiphytes, mosses, and lichen, while at higher elevations oaks with gnarled roots and buttress trunks take over, before vegetation finally dwindles into wind-sculpted dwarf forest on exposed ridges (making in total about 2,500 species of plants). Insect life is astonishingly varied, and resplendent quetzals, three-wattled bellbirds (practicing their loud, unmistakable "bong" call high in the canopy), clay-colored robins (Costa Rica's national bird), wrens, hummingbirds, flycatchers, woodpeckers, trogons, owls, and hawks all figure among the 400 or so species of birds.

Hot lips Among the begonias, heliconias, monsteras, and philodendrons of the understorey are "hot lips" (*Cephaelis elata*), named after their large red leaves. The roots contain chemicals used in pharmaceutical products, while the flowers, blooming most of the year, are firm favorites with hummingbirds and butterflies. Butterflies are another of the cloud forest's colorful inhabitants: about 500 species hover and flit through the undergrowth in search of their host plants, and often play a crucial pollinating role.

▶▶▶ Volcán Arenal   66B2

This near-perfect 5,358-foot volcanic cone rises majestically out of the lush pastures and forest at the eastern end of Laguna de Arenal. Intermittent rumbling, explosions, and nocturnal fire-spitting are the mesmerizing features that draw visitors to its base by day and night. Cloud often obscures the summit, but when lava flows cascade, incandescent rocks fly and Arenal roars, few forget it. Its flanks have been declared a national park (*Open* daily 8AM–10PM. *Admission charge* expensive) but the nocturnal light show can be witnessed equally well from outside the boundary. Continually active and evolving in form since 1968, Arenal is extremely dangerous and nobody should venture onto its slopes. Any appearance of a lull in activity is deceptive: this is an erupting volcano, and in recent years three imprudent hikers have died of gas emissions or burns.

Blanket of fire Lively but ancient, Arenal is 2–3 million years old. No records exist of eruptions during the Spanish colonial period, but mineral samples suggest that it was booming between 1200 and 1500. Records of crater activity started in 1937. Then, 31 years later, Arenal moved into its current phase, which kicked off with tremors followed by an eruption on July 29, 1968, that killed 87 people. The town of Pueblo Nuevo was eradicated, large tracts of farmland and forest were destroyed, and 1,500 acres were blanketed in molten lava before the colossus entered a quiet phase of hot gas and ash emissions. Fumaroles soon appeared in the newly formed craters, and a lava flow started advancing toward the Tabacón river valley at the rate of 30–100 feet a day. Today, vegetation has reappeared among the boulders and solidified lava, but vulcanologists consider the Tabacón area particularly vulnerable to hot avalanches.

Night views Night tours are arranged from Fortuna and even from San José, but visitors with their own transport can drive to a good viewpoint on Arenal's western side, which offers the best sight of the inferno-like activity. Drive to the park entrance then branch right along a rough track which leads to several hotels and the Arenal Volcano Observatory, a residential observation center open to vulcanologists and visitors.

Arenal, a natural light show

Seismic mysteries
Major zones of seismic activity follow the boundaries of the tectonic plates making up the earth's rigid surface layer. Costa Rica's volcanoes are at the fragile meeting of the Cocos Plate in the Pacific, and the Caribbean Plate. This string of volcanoes continues south through the Andes and north through Mexico, making for a particularly volatile area.

Drive Cloud forest, rain forest, and plain

See map on pages 66–67.

This loop takes you through an extraordinary variety of landscapes and climates. It is possible to cover the route in a strenuous day (five or six hours' driving) but, better still, spend a night on the way in order to stop and explore.

Before setting off, make sure that your clothing is designed for rapidly changing climatic extremes.

If starting from San José, head out on the highway to Limón, which for over 40 miles presents an unusually well-maintained surface. Enjoy it while it lasts. While winding through the semi-permanent drizzle of **Parque Nacional Braulio Carrillo►►**, stop at one of the pull-offs, the better to admire dramatic vistas over the cloud forest. Clouds permitting, you may see parrots flying over the tree canopy below or birds of prey soaring over the ridge. Just before a tunnel beneath the 6,715-foot peak of Cerro Hondura is a toll booth (inexpensive) and soon after it the road crosses a bridge over the Río Sucio. It is possible to pull in after the bridge and walk down a path to the river for a close view of the strange meeting of a clear water current with a yellow, sulfurous stream straight from Volcán Irazú. Soon after, you pass the entrance to the **Rain Forest Aerial Tram►►►** (see page 71) on the right, though the actual structure is invisible from the highway. This entire mountainous area presents fantastic views over dense virgin rain forest, while the roadside is thick with "poor man's umbrella" (gunnera) and palms.

Left: cattle-ranch in the Póas region

Between here and Guápiles are numerous private ecological projects (see pages 70–71): watch closely for signs if you decide to visit any of them. About 15 miles beyond the Zurquí tunnel, at Santa Clara, take a turn to the left that cuts straight through an extensive, flat and much hotter plain of palm-heart and pineapple plantations and cattle ranches. All of it was once clad in dense rain forest, well exemplified farther north by the lush research grounds of **La Selva►►►** (see pages 72–73; you must make an advance booking to visit). After 26 miles from the Santa Clara turn, the straight road arrives at **Puerto Viejo de Sarapiquí►** (see page 79), worth a stop to take a leisurely boat trip along the **Río Sarapiquí►►** in search of crocodiles, howler monkeys, and exotic birds. Police road-checks are common around here, as many Nicaraguan immigrants use the river to enter Costa Rica illegally.

From Puerto Viejo, continue west, stopping for wholesome Tico sustenance at Restaurant Jacaré, about 3 miles from Puerto Viejo on the left, or at Chilamate to look at the botanic garden, birds and butterfly enclosure of Selva Verde Lodge. Near here you will see a roadside pottery vendor: the pots in traditional Guanacastecan style will have been brought from Guaitíl and prices are reasonable. At La Virgen, an alternative food and/or kayaking stop is possible at Rancho Leona on the banks of the Sarapiquí river. From here the road starts twisting wildly as it climbs through the villages of San Miguel, Ujarrás and Cariblanco, all of which offer picturesque rural scenes against a backdrop of increasingly spectacular mountainous scenery. Soon after

Cinchona, the Catarata La Paz comes into view on one of the many hairpin bends: this thundering waterfall is fed by a river that cascades straight down from **Volcán Poás►►** (see page 79), situated 6 miles west of the junction after Varablanca. A short trail leads behind the waterfall, offering a close view of the impressive curtain of water. To the east of the road looms the even higher volcano of Barva, within the boundaries of the Parque Nacional Braulio Carrillo.

If not making a detour to see Poás, continue south through pine forests and rolling hills of strawberry and coffee plantations, stopping to sample fruits and *cajeta* sold by numerous roadside vendors. A clear fork in the road eventually offers the choice of returning to San José via Alajuela or Heredia.

Wildlife comes in all guises

THE CENTER

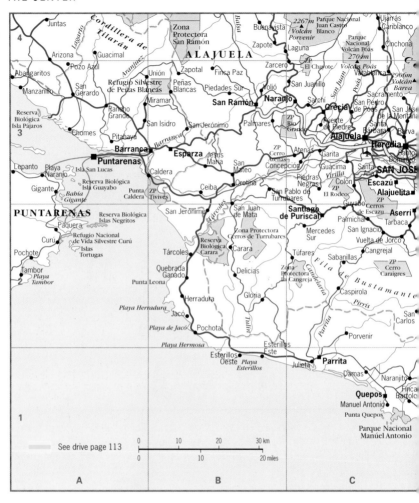

See drive page 113

The Center This section covers an area spilling over from the Central Valley, north to the mountain towns of Sarchí and Zarcero, south to the magnificent Cerro La Muerte, east to Turrialba and west to the corresponding shores of the Pacific. All places mentioned can be reached on daytrips from San José if necessary. The Central Valley (or, more correctly, plateau) is the heart of Costa Rica's economic life, where some 60 percent of the population is concentrated, attracted by the extreme fertility of the volcanic soil and an easy springlike climate. Twisting roads are common currency as they negotiate sharp changes in altitude, and landscapes take on epic proportions. Coffee plantations are still the most common sight on the cultivated slopes, with sugarcane, corn and dairy farms following closely behind.

Previous pages: all roads lead to San José, the forward-looking capital of Costa Rica

On the road to San José At the heart of the valley lies the capital, San José, which, whatever your itinerary, you will see more than once. All roads and flights lead there and it long ago outstripped its urban rivals, Cartago,

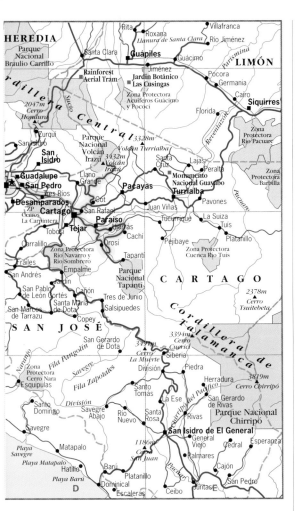

Carara crocs
American crocodiles have hardly changed in the past 200 million years. They reach lengths of up to 10–20 feet and may live 60–100 years. Their eggs are buried in the sandy banks of a river, where the porous shell absorbs moisture to help the embryo develop. Survival of these embryonic crocodiles generally averages only 2 percent, but at the Reserva Biológica Carara (see page 109) it has been estimated that barely 0.5 percent actually develop. Local sharpshooters and egg-trampling cattle are partly to blame, but river pollution and fertilizers also create havoc.

Eye to beady eye with an iguana— before it hits the pot

Alajuela, and Heredia. Although not the most visually inspiring of cities, it nevertheless makes a friendly, lively place to spend a few days between trips, and its museums provide an important cultural introduction to the country. The only rival town in terms of infrastructure and interest is Heredia, a mere 20 minutes from the capital by car, and recently improved by two comfortable new hotels, a sure sign that it is waking up to its potential. For those wary of San José's errant muggers, traffic, and pollution, it makes a pleasant enough base with a distinctive character due to the presence of a large university. All towns of this region have suffered from earthquakes and volcanic eruptions, and evidence of colonial history is thus conspicuous by its absence. Amends are made by the relaxed, rural atmosphere of the region's small communities, such as Barva, Atenas, Santa Ana, Zarcero, and even the burgeoning international community of Escazú, another viable alternative to staying in San José as it is well supplied with bed-and-breakfasts and some more upscale hotels.

Luminous frogs croaking
"In the wide valley below, the lights of the city sparkled, a myriad of tiny luminous frogs croaking in the pool of darkness. Here and there in the distance, patches of light could be seen, some weaker, others stronger. They all indicated the positions of towns on the *meseta*, as if clusters of stars had fallen from the constellations above. More than forty years ago there'd been fewer luminous frogs. San José wasn't as spread out then, and most people in the villages were without electricity..." Fabian Dobles, *El Targua* (1984)

Under the giant mango trees
"...It was easy to see that nobody felt like working on such a hot afternoon. In the Parque Central, without a doubt, under the giant mango trees, policemen, the druggist, shoeshine boys, a few students, and numerous beggars fanning the flies away with their open, bony hands would be resting like animals in a zoo. Meanwhile the cantinas would be deserted, because the drunks preferred to doze on the lawn of the Parque Juan Santamaría..." Fernando Duran Ayanegui, *Monday* (1988)

Seductive wilds Head out into the wilds and it is a different story. Thrill-seekers can choose between whitewater rafting on the Río Reventazón, bungee-jumping near Atenas, mountain-biking in Tapantí, horseriding, or any number of water sports on the coast. But much of the enjoyment can be more passive. You can peer vertiginously into the crater of Volcán Irazú, whose desolate landscape has been said by visiting astronaut Neil Armstrong to resemble the surface of the moon—when this still-active volcano is not showering its spectacular slopes with ash, as it does sporadically. You can explore the national archaeological site of Guayabo, concealed in a rich rain forest setting. Compare the magical Orosí Valley, unfolding in seductive splendor, with the brooding valleys of cloud forest around Cerro La Muerte, where the resplendent quetzal resides. Take the beautiful route through Orotina to the Carara reserve and watch scarlet macaws roosting at dusk, or hike through dense rain forest nearby to see a thundering waterfall. If you have four-wheel drive, explore the backroads off the *costanera* (coast road) where tiny villages rise into the foothills of the central mountains and offer stunning ocean views.

Star turn You may encounter a brasher atmosphere in the coastal towns of Puntarenas, Quepos (both of which have embraced tourism as a new source of prosperity following the demise of their ports) or the tackiest of Costa Rican resorts, Jacó, best avoided unless you have booked in at the design-conscious Villa Caletas hotel, perched high above the coastline to the north. Between these main towns are some reasonable beaches, most offering some form of accommodations and alternating in suitability for surfing or swimming. This coastal stretch was also chosen as the location for sequences of *1492*, the film relating Christopher Columbus's early Caribbean incursions. Ultimately, however, nothing can beat Costa Rica's most popular national park and beaches, at Manuel Antonio. Conservationists are anxiously monitoring developments here, as this tiny reserve and its stunning surroundings are becoming engulfed by tourist facilities and crowds, with the environment suffering as a result. Manuel Antonio's future development will serve as a measure of Costa Rica's real dedication to the environmentally responsible tourism it espouses.

Getaway For those really wanting to escape the crowds, this central region is not the most recommended, as the proximity of major points of interest to San José makes them easy targets for tour groups and domestic tourism. Compared with other parts of the country, roads, public transportation, and communications are quite manageable, though road signs are still rare. Isolated and less-visited exceptions do exist, however, and there are some outstanding lodges hidden away in mountain retreats or on the coast. Environmental projects are not absent and are generally wildlife-oriented, whether concerned with butterflies, crocodiles, iguanas or scarlet macaws. Of particular significance is Turrialba's CATIE, one of the world's leading centers in agronomical research.

► **Alajuela** *88C3*

This provincial capital was founded in 1782 with the name of Villa Hermosa, but its distance of only 12 miles from San José has always left it on the sidelines, and life here is decidedly unhurried. Today, the population of 50,000 enjoys a peaceful existence in and around the verdant Parque Central, where the dense mango trees are said to house a sloth or two. Alajuela's warmer climate (it is 660 feet lower than the capital) attracts city-dwellers for a stroll, while the proximity of the airport, barely 2 miles southeast, brings a few tourists to its limited hotels. Every April the town springs to life for Costa Rica's most ambitious cultural festival, and in July a craft fair is held under the name of the Fiesta de Los Mangos.

The only permanent point of interest is the **Museo Juan Santamaría►** (Avenida 3/Calle 2, tel: 441-4775. *Open* Tue–Sun 10–6. *Admission free*). This focuses on the 1856 battle when an Alajuelan-born drummer-boy, Juan Santamaría, torched the hideout of William Walker's filibusters (see pages 32–33) . The exhibits give a haphazard background. A statue of the hero stands in the Parque Juan Santamaría, two blocks south of the Parque Central.

Out of town Alajuela's environs hold interest, notably Zoo-Ave► (tel: 433-8989. *Open* daily 9–5. *Admission charge* moderate), at Garita about 7 miles west. This 5-acre bird zoo features 116 Costa Rican species alongside some rare imported birds, making a good introduction to the country's colorful birdlife. You can further sharpen your natural history knowledge at the **Butterfly Farm►►** at Guácima, near San Antonio de Belén (tel: 438-0115. *Open* daily 9–3. *Admission charge* expensive), the world's second-largest exporter of butterfly pupae. Bees and botanical wonders are also to be seen. This farm offers a choice of two-hour guided tours and can also arrange hotel pick-ups from San José.

An owl butterfly exhibits its silken finery at the Butterfly Farm near Alajuela

Alajuela's popularity has waned in the face of San José's socio-cultural life (below)

La Negrita

Miracles have accompanied this statue ever since it was discovered in 1635 in the forest that once grew on this site. The legend goes that, after the statue was found by a young girl, it was installed by a priest in the local parish church. Twice over it disappeared to return to the forest, and only stayed put once a basilica had been built on the spot. Even the spring water from behind the church is thought to have curative powers, another good reason to attract thousands of pilgrims, some of whom end their journey crawling on their knees, every August 2.

Las Ruinas, Cartago

▶ **Atenas**   88C3

High in the hills west of San José lies what residents and the *National Geographic* claim to be the town with one of the best climates in the world. Atenas dominates a sunny region of rolling coffee plantations, and can be taken in by a short detour if you are driving to the Pacific via Orotina. There are few tourist-oriented facilities and this adds to its rural charm, though a minor hiccup has occurred recently with a marked increase in the number of resident snakes—particularly the deadly fer-de-lance.

▶ **Cartago**   89D2

Costa Rica's former capital of Cartago dates from 1563 but was officially replaced at independence by San José in 1823. Sadly, most of its colonial past has disappeared in the rubble of major earthquakes, thanks to Volcán Irazú, which looms near by. In testimony to Cartago's former glory are the roofless arches of **Las Ruinas**▶▶▶, which rise sculpturally beside the Parque Central. The original church was erected in 1575, but the destructive 1841 earthquake enforced massive reconstruction, which was blighted by another quake in 1910, leaving only these walls. They now enclose a pretty graveyard splashed with crimson bougainvillea. The old bell is suspended over the central arch. Flanking the southern side of the square are some decorative old clapboard houses displaying fretwork eaves and interior archways.

Six blocks east of here rise the massive walls and white cupolas of the **Basilica de Nuestra Señora de los Angeles**▶▶, a stylistic hotchpotch though vaguely neo-Byzantine. Demure winged angels enhance the façade, while the interior features heavily decorated pillars, tiles and stained glass. The basilica was built in 1926 to replace an earlier structure destroyed in the earthquake, but its national importance lies in one statue, that of Costa Rica's black patron saint—La Negrita. Don't miss her shrine, which is packed with offerings, abandoned crutches and other items testifying to her miraculous healing powers. Other churches dot the town but these spiritual concerns have not prevented the growth of a surprisingly un-Costa Rican shanty town on the eastern outskirts.

Right: Cartago's Basilica, ornate home of La Negrita

Escazú combines rural pursuits with services for wealthy Tico and foreign residents

▶▶▶ Cerro La Muerte (Death Hill)   89E2

This 11,480-foot pass is where the Interamerican Highway reaches its highest point in Costa Rica. Temperatures plunge, the air thins, and the road often disappears behind thick banks of fog or rain. The name was earned when farmers used to trudge across on foot, and today the road to the pass is dotted with white crosses that mark fatal accidents. The paramo-type vegetation that cloaks the highest points of Cerro La Muerte makes for fascinating, if eerie, exploration. Even at this altitude, hummingbirds can still be found, as can rufous-collared sparrows and jays. The vegetation itself is stunning, the subtle shades of gray-green and strikingly architectural foliage being worthy of any garden designer.

Quetzal valley If you are approaching the pass on the beautiful stretch from Cartago, a scenic detour can be made by turning off just after Empalme to Jardín and **Santa María de Dota▶▶**, then returning to the Interamerican Highway via Copey, known for its trout restaurant. About 6 miles south of here, at marker 80, lies the blissful 'quetzal valley' of **San Gerardo de Dota▶▶▶**, reached by a twisting road descending to the west. This cool, tranquil valley, crossed by the trout-rich Río Savegre, offers exceptional hiking through cloud forest as well as a chance of spotting a resplendent quetzal (March–May is the best time). Two hotels cater to bird-watching and trout-consuming visitors. At marker 89 on the Interamerican Highway is a restaurant, Las Torres, opposite which a dirt road leads up to a cluster of radio masts. This peak offers breathtaking views across mountains and valleys, west to the Pacific beaches and, on exceptionally clear days, east to the Caribbean.

Before the Interamerican
It was only in the 1920s that a cart trail was first laid over the Talamanca mountains. Before that, farmers from the fertile southern valleys had to accomplish excruciating journeys on foot, herding pigs and loaded down with 110-pound packs of blackberries, rice, or corn, to trade at San José's market. Often barefoot and wearing little more than a thin shirt and trousers, they negotiated the Cerro La Muerte pass in bitterly cold and permanently wet conditions.

►► Escazú 88C3

Escazú is virtually joined to San José by a sprawl of chic western suburbs. Witches were once said to proliferate here, but craftspeople and an international community seem to have replaced them. Easy access (15 minutes' drive and frequent buses), cooler temperatures, colorful, luxuriant vegetation and wide views make it a favored haven for wealthier Josefinos and expatriates. Escazú is also a good place to relax after a long-haul flight and still get a flavor of Costa Rica's birdlife. Clay-colored robins (the national bird) are common in gardens here, as are rufous-tailed hummingbirds, great kiskadees (a bird that calls its name) and Montezuma oropendolas.

Escazú's main square is dominated by a church flanked by some old adobe houses. Elsewhere there are new shopping centers, hotels, and modern houses, in bizarre contrast with the rural scenes of cows and ox-carts along the main road winding up to San Antonio de Escazú. From San Antonio there is a steep 2,300-foot climb to the mirador of Pico Blanco. Bed and breakfasts abound in this area, and there are plenty of reasonable eating-places. A car is essential, as buses go no further than the main square and the climb from there is a long and steep one.

► Esterillos 88B1

The seemingly endless palm-fringed beach of Esterillos lies in a flat, featureless region of plantations to the southeast of Jacó and is reached by three main turnings from the coastal road. Esterillos Oeste (West) leads to a breezy section of the beach. The currents are dangerous but it offers budget accommodations. Esterillos Este (East) is a similarly unspectacular beach but has the advantage of a slow descent to the sea and safe swimming. The small community has a handful of mid-range hotels. Hikes can be made to nearby rain forest waterfalls. A third, unnamed turning farther east leads to a campsite and the popular old Hotel El Delfin.

►► Grecia 88C3

Halfway between Alajuela and the crafts town of Sarchí lies Grecia, a well-maintained hill town that is dependent on the surrounding coffee, sugarcane, and pineapple plantations. Its verdant main square is dominated by the bulky church of Las Mercedes, an unusual construction of bolted metal plates that dates from 1958. Its vaulted interior is dedicated to the cult of La Virgen de las Mercedes.

95

The powerful spires of Las Mercedes in Grecia

Entomological aesthetics
Just south of Santo Domingo de Heredia, on the San José road, lies an extraordinary private museum, the Joyas del Tropico Humedo (Jewels of the Rain Forest). This was set up by a couple from Oregon to display, using a more aesthetic approach than usual, hundreds of butterflies and over 50,000 insect species collected from the world's rain forests. Arranged into mandala-like paintings, mosaics or in trails creeping over the ceiling, the iridescent and often brilliantly colored insect world assumes other dimensions, but the display also has an educational role. The museum is open daily 9–5 and located 300 yards west of the Río Virilla bridge. Entrance fees are inexpensive.

New windows in Heredia's old Basilica

▶ ▶ ▶ **Heredia**   88C3

Of all Costa Rica's provincial towns, Heredia is perhaps the one with most character and interest although this aspect is, as yet, little exploited and you certainly would not believe it from the outskirts. Founded in 1706, Heredia predates both San José and Alajuela, and today much of its population of 55,000 is connected with Costa Rica's second-largest university, whose campus lies east of the center, injecting the town with youthful dynamism. Spanish-style tiled roofs, adobe houses, and stately stone buildings are plentiful, while the higher, northern slopes of the town command sweeping views across San José, the valley and distant mountains.

Faith and fun At the center of the grid of streets stands the impressive Basilica de la Immaculada Concepción (1797), whose leprous façade belies a completely renovated interior with pristine stained-glass windows and church bells from Peru. An unusually squat, solid design (sometimes classed as "seismic baroque") has helped the church withstand the earthquakes that have toppled most of its contemporaries. A domed side-chapel with a separate entrance from the adjoining garden is the site for constant prayer. Equally intense promenading takes place on Sundays under the huge centennial trees outside, around the focus of live bands playing in the white kiosk.

Military imagination Opposite the church and its garden, on the north side of the Parque Central, stands an elaborate stone post office, dating from 1915, next to the colonial-style Palacio Municipal. However, the jewel in Heredia's architectural curiosities is a military fort, El Fortín, built by the eccentric President Alfredo Gonzalez Flores early this century. His curious approach to military strategy produced a beehive of a tower with slits that enlarged outwards, so letting bullets in easily. Three blocks south of the Parque is a lively central market where leather goods and wickerware are sold beside the usual abundant display of edible produce. Like San José's Mercado Central, the market is also a good place for cheap meals. Take time to wander around Heredia's pretty central streets and, towards sunset, do not miss the outrageous natural light show painting the valley skies, best watched from the top floor bar of the Hotel Valladolid, designed with precisely that idea in mind.

Beyond the town Between Heredia and Barva lies the **Café Britt** ▶ ▶ plantation and coffee-mill (tel: 260-2748 for reservations. *Open:* tours at 9, 11, and 3, transportation from San José. *Admission charge* expensive), a must on tour group itineraries as its presentation includes costumed actors. Caffeine addicts can indulge in tasting

The odd beehive fortress is a striking landmark on the main square

Buses to Heredia
Bus connections between Heredia and San José are frequent and easy: from Avenida 7 & 9 Calle 1 in San José buses leave every 5–10 minutes daily between 5AM and 10PM and from Avenida 2 Calle 12 every 20 minutes. In Heredia the San José buses leave from Avenida 4 Calle Central, one block south of the Parque Central.

the various roasts and buy stocks at factory prices. On a lower key and certainly less visited is the **Museo de Cultura Popular▶▶** (tel: 260-1619. *Open* weekends 9–6. *Admission charge* inexpensive), located in a northeastern suburb of Heredia and well signposted from the main road. At the back of a garden, an attractive mid-19th century adobe farmhouse displays an eclectic collection, including an ancient gramophone (the caretaker will crank it up for you to play pre-World War II hits).

Barva and upward A pleasant stop can be made south of Heredia at Santo Domingo de Heredia, but more atmospheric is **Barva de Heredia▶▶**, a few miles north. This entire village is protected as a national monument, because of its harmonious and well-preserved central square, flanked by traditional adobe houses with a brilliantly white church set among palm trees. The peaceful atmosphere and easy access to the capital have attracted a growing colony of artists and craftspeople. North of Barva the road forks. To the right it winds up through cool, pine-clad hills to **San José de la Montaña▶▶**, where several mountain lodges offer outdoor activities and bird-watching or onward trips to Volcán Barva (see page 78). The left fork leads to Volcán Poás (see page 79) and/or northwards through the Cordillera Central to Puerto Viejo de Sarapiquí (see page 79 and Drive, pages 84–5).

■ **Earthquakes and volcanic eruptions have wrought havoc on much of Costa Rica's architectural heritage, but some remnants exist, hidden in urban pockets or engulfed by San José's low-rise concrete jungle. Each surviving style reflects a momentous stage in the nation's history.** ■

To every house a story
One of Los Yoses' strangest mansions is Casa Matute, an elaborate 1920s construction purchased in 1935 by a Venezuelan, Matute Gomez, who was fleeing political persecution following the fall of his dictator brother. He moved in with his daughters and, it is said, a minor fortune in gold coins fresh from the Venezuelan treasury. Flamboyant parties and eccentric behavior were the rule until 1951, when Matute mysteriously disappeared to Panama, where he died in obscurity. The sole remaining resident was his daughter Isola, who lived alone in the enormous house until her death in 1990. Her heirs were her housekeeper and chauffeur, and the house has now become a buzzing nightspot.

Casa Verde, one of San José's many century-old houses to be converted into a hotel

Costa Rica was transformed in the mid-19th century as a result of the expanding coffee trade. New horizons, money and status brought a blossoming of architectural styles, above all in San José. In many cases they were inspired by European designs, in others they appropriated the more climatically suitable Caribbean colonial style. For several decades the capital enjoyed this new-found prosperity and cultural refinement, becoming the third city in the world to have public lighting and later boasting art deco cinemas. Pressure came during the 1950s when Costa Rica's population boomed to a million, double that of the 1930s. Then followed a catastrophic period of aping North American norms. Up went the cheap concrete blocks and down came the elegant façades of the immediate past. Today the majority of Costa Rican towns are indistinguishable from one another, although each has notable exceptions to the mediocre rule.

From *ranchos* to adobe In the Península de Nicoya and southern Costa Rica, *ranchos* are common sights. These originated in the indigenous culture, but are built today not only for touristic interest but often also as well-ventilated sitting-spaces attached to stuffier modern homes. Traditional *rancho* floors were of beaten earth or pounded logs, from which split bamboo walls rose to a palm-leaf roof, so allowing air to circulate freely while keeping rain at bay.

The main architectural innovation of the Spanish Conquest was adobe-building. Walls were built of mud inserted into a wooden or bamboo framework then limewashed in bright colors. Sloping tiled roofs often extended to shelter shady verandas that ran the full length of the (usually L-shaped) house. There are plenty of picturesque surviving examples in the Central Valley (Escazú, Heredia, and, above all, Barva de Heredia) as well as in the Guanacastecan towns of Liberia and Nicoya, where the *puertas del sol* were developed (see panel on page 44).

Clapboard Although concrete and corrugated iron have made inroads into urban Costa Rica, they have not eradicated the widespread use of clapboard in rural areas for simple one-story farms or generously propor-

Spanish-colonial in San José contrasts with the 1990s

tioned two-story mansions, embellished with intricate, fretwork eaves and sometimes raised on piles. This "Caribbean Victorian" architectural form reached heights of fantasy at the turn of the century under the proprietorial eye of wealthy coffee barons and hacienda-owners, and was extended in the New Orleans-style frame houses of the United Fruit Company, still visible in Golfito. San José's aristocratic Barrio Amón has preserved some wonderful early examples, many of which have been transformed into exclusive hotels. Casa Verde (c1910) belonged to the wealthy owner of a cattle ranch near Limón, and the 100 percent mahogany Hotel Santo Tomás (1910) was the domain of a coffee planter's family. L'Ambiance combines a Moorish layout (internal patio with fountain) with European detailing, while two neighboring residences followed the turn-of-the-century fashion for Moorish style to the last arch and stained-glass panel. In the 1920s, wealthy residences spread to an inner suburban ring from Los Yoses to Paseo Colón, and are preserved today as numerous hotels.

Solid appeal Commercial architecture of the period looked straight to Europe, adopting neoclassical style with a vengeance. Pillars, porches, pediments, and balustrades bristled over façades, while decorative stonework became the rule for banks, colleges, hospitals, churches, and government buildings. San José's Correo (post office), built by an English company in 1914, typically blends neoclassicism with ornate flourishes. Interesting exceptions include the Escuela Metálica, a prefabricated import of cast-iron plates from Belgium, and San José's crown jewel, the Teatro Nacional, a combination of a neoclassical exterior with a sumptuous neobaroque interior modeled on the Paris Opera House. However, since World War II, innovative architecture has been abandoned in the public domain.

Caribbean genesis
Early Afro-Caribbean settlers of the Talamanca coast were turtle fishermen, whose temporary huts, built for shelter during their fishing season, were the precursors of typical homes in the region today. They were made of planks cut from the rawa palm, raised on piles and thatched with a common swamp palm. The palm would only be cut after the new moon when it was insect-free. Thatch has since been replaced by zinc roofs, a great error as zinc is hot and ugly while thatch, if properly made, provides good insulation for years as well as looking better.

Jacó is easy to reach by car for a budget escape from the capital

▶   **Jacó**   *88B2*

This hot seaside resort offers a cheerful resort atmosphere within easy reach of the capital (110km away), so it makes a popular Tico destination. Cheap *cabinas* first sprang up to cater for surfers who came for the almost constant waves, but Jacó has since developed facilities for a lazier crowd, with shops, restaurants, and hotels all located along an uninspiring low-rise strip backing the long curve of the bay. Water sports, sportfishing, and river-rafting activities are extensive, but swimmers should be careful as the currents here can be fatal and the beach is quite badly polluted. A useful tour and travel agency is Fantasy Tours (tel/fax: 643-3365), which is located above the Jacó pharmacy.

For more inviting beach surroundings with calmer waters, head 3 miles north to **Playa Herradura**▶▶▶, where fishing-boats anchor in the bay, trees give welcome shade, and *cabinas* and a campsite provide budget accommodation. High above the coast here is one of Costa Rica's most inspiring luxury hotels, Villa Caletas, definitely worth the precipitous 2-mile ascent for a drink or gourmet lunch with a spellbinding view. Farther north still, at Punta Leona, a string of exquisite beaches backed by rain forest have unfortunately been overrun by a very questionable mass development. This spot, together with Playa Herradura, was chosen in 1992 for the filming of *1492*, Ridley Scott's film about Christopher Columbus.

▶▶▶   **Monumento Nacional Guayabo**   *89E3*

Open: daily 8–3.30. Admission charge: expensive
Part of Costa Rica's largest archaeological site has been sensitively excavated at the heart of pristine natural surroundings, and combines easy nature trails through primary and secondary forest with a unique close-up view of the country's indigenous past. Although the site itself is in no way comparable to Inca or Mesoamerican monuments, its circular mounds, stone causeways, walls, aqueducts, water tank, tombs, and petroglyphs (see panel) offer a clear picture of a sophisticated pre-Columbian structure. It is thought to have been occupied from 1000 BC until AD 1400.

Mysteries Since 1968 an estimated 10 percent (5 acres) of the total area has been excavated by the University of Costa Rica. Although it is known that Guayabo's apogee was AD 300–700, a question mark remains over why it was abandoned before the Spanish Conquest: disease and war are two hypotheses. Construction techniques reflect both South American and Mesoamerican influences, and interpretation of many of the uncovered petroglyphs remains incomplete. What is certain is that Guayabo was ruled by a *cacique* (chief) who exercized both political and religious power over a large region, and that the inhabitants were specialists in a variety of trades.

Trails The 1,300-yard self-guided Los Montículos trail winds through luxuriant rain forest where turquoise morpho butterflies, toucans, loriots, and oropendolas may cross your path as you climb to a lookout point over the archaeological site. From here the path continues down through the site before circling back to the entrance. A

Petroglyphs
So far 53 petroglyphs (carved stone slabs) have been unearthed on the causeways and around the mounds of Guayabo, and most are displayed in San José's museums. One petroglyph exhibited in the undergrowth of Guayabo's main trail shows a crude bas-relief carving of a jaguar and a crocodile, both of which lived in the area until relatively recently. For the Talamanca Indians, the crocodile/alligator symbolized Sibu, their god, and the jaguar (an animal considered to have supernatural attributes), a shaman.

second trail, Los Cantarillos, leads from the amphitheater at the entrance, down through rain forest to the Río Lajitas. There is a small visitors' center opposite the entrance, and Spanish-speaking volunteer guides are available.

▶   **Orosí**   *89D2*

Cradled in the heart of the beautiful coffee-growing **Orosí Valley▶▶** lies this small, much rebuilt town, whose main interest is a simple church dating from 1743. It is lined with paintings and has two ornate shrines flanking the wooden altar, one with a polychrome statue of San Francisco. An adjoining monastery now houses the **Museo Franciscano▶▶** (*Open* daily 9–5. *Admission charge* inexpensive), which displays an odd assortment of religious statuary, colonial paintings from Mexico, silver, vestments, and even an ancient typewriter. On the southern edge of town are two *balnearios* (thermal pools) whose recreational grounds cater mainly to families. Opposite Los Patios *balneario* and restaurant is a small regional tourist office (tel: 533-3333). For sublime views over the valley, stop at the Mirador de Orosí, on the road to Paraíso.

Coffee plantations punctuated by flame trees clad the slopes of the Orosí Valley

Valley flames
A recurring sight in the Orosí Valley is the fiery orange glow of the flamboyant or flame tree (*Delonix regia*), creating a luminous contrast with the undulating slopes of dark green coffee-bushes. One of the world's most strikingly beautiful trees, this native of Madagascar resembles a delicate flame-colored umbrella, and its dense clusters of flowers bloom from early spring until late summer. The fern-like foliage later gives way to long brown seed pods—hence the Greek name *Delonix*, meaning "long claw". The common Costa Rican name for this tree is *malinche*.

The charming Franciscan church of Orosí is Costa Rica's oldest still in use

Lankester Gardens: floral surprises

Beneath the surface
The turquoise waters of Manuel Antonio, are particularly transparent during the dry season. Anybody with a snorkel and mask will be mesmerized by the life around the coral reefs that line the coast and islands between the park and Quepos. Green turtles also discovered these beaches long ago, and pre-Columbian inhabitants developed a sophisticated system of wooden traps in rocky inlets, where, at low tide, the turtles would be left high and dry. These are still visible at either end of Playa Blanca

 ▶ Paraíso   89D2

"Paradise" is a surprising name for this nondescript little town 5.5 miles southeast of Cartago, but it was allegedly coined by exhausted Spaniards after they had struggled up from the Caribbean coast to reach cooler climates. Today Paraíso only serves as a stopover for visitors before or after a trip to the **Jardín Botánico Carlos H Lankester▶▶▶**, signposted from the main road northwest of town. These botanic gardens (*Open* daily 8:30–3:30, visits on the hour. *Admission charge* inexpensive) were founded in the 1950s by Charles Lankester, an aspiring English coffee-planter, and are now managed by the University of Costa Rica. Often referred to as orchid gardens, the 26-acre area in fact harbors a wealth of tropical plants, from bamboo to bromeliads, ornamental plants, aloe, palms and amaryllis, as well as a wilder part of regenerated rain forest at the back. February to May is the best time to see the 800 species of orchids in bloom.

▶▶▶ Parque Nacional Manuel Antonio   88C1

Open: Tue–Sun 8–4. Admission charge: expensive
Manuel Antonio's modest 1,687 acres combine white-sand beaches backed by lush tropical forest, with snack-seeking white-faced monkeys, sloths, grunting howler monkeys, iguanas, and the poisonous manzanilla tree. Above all it is the spectacularly jagged coastline and exquisite sheltered waters that have made its reputation. These attractions are also the park's downfall, as human overload has caused considerable damage. Quotas limit visitor numbers, but the lack of buffer zones around the park inspires little confidence. Some of the park land is still privately owned, and has been exploited by clandestine tree-cutting. Worse still, the surfeit of hotels nearby brings pollution. Note that the river that you must wade through to enter the park is labeled "contaminated".

True paradise On a brighter note, the beautiful coastline starts with the blissful sweep of Playa Espadilla Sur and continues beyond the densely forested headland of Punta Catedral to the magnificent **Playa Blanca▶▶▶**, also known as Playa Manuel Antonio or Playa Tres. Picnic tables, showers, and troops of tame (to the point of being irritating) white-faced monkeys add to this beach's popularity. From here, trails lead uphill past Playas Gemelas and the "sloth trail" to end steeply at another sheltered but rockier cove, Puerto Escondido. Those lucky enough to visit the park by boat will see the curiously eroded cliff, Punta Serrucho, which divides this bay from the final beach, Playa Playita.

Rare specimens Visitors who have come for the wildlife should not be put off by the beach-party atmosphere around the bars and hotels. Waterbirds, including tricolored herons, willets and Amazon kingfishers, feed beside the tidal pools and mangrove creeks, and the tiny offshore islands are refuges for common terns, magnificent frigate birds and brown pelicans. Tracts of primary forest shelter bully trees, cow trees, Santa Marías, silk cottons, and the increasingly rare black locust tree. Monkeys are numerous (including the endemic but endangered squirrel monkey), as are agoutis and iguanas, and three-toed sloths are usually easy to see. Park rangers may be able to help you find them (as elsewhere in Costa Rica, it helps if you can ask in Spanish)—or look for the handlike leaves of cecropia trees, which sloths love to eat. As you wander the trails, look for coatis crossing and listen for orange-collared manakins in the undergrowth—the males snap their wings as they gather to display.

▶ **Parque Nacional Tapantí**   89D2

Open: daily 8–4. Admission charge: expensive
Promoted from being a wildlife refuge to the status of national park in 1992, Tapantí offers the dubious attraction of having the greatest amount of rain and cloud cover in the country (315 inches annual rainfall). The well-maintained dirt tracks of this 14,800-acre park straddling the northern Talamanca mountains are especially popular with mountain bikers, and there are swimming areas in the cool rivers, whose torrents are also exploited for hydroelectric energy. With altitudes rising from 4,000 to 8,000 feet, bird and plant life is varied, but cloud forest dominates and butterflies are abundant. The entrance is along a poor road 5 miles southeast of Orosí.

Tombolo
The wedge-shaped headland of Punta Catedral, connected by a thin neck to Playa Espadilla Sur, was once an island. Sand gradually built up in the intervening channel over a period of hundreds of thousands of years, until finally a tombolo, or sand bridge, was formed. Grass, shrubs, and eventually trees took root to form the present luxuriant picture.

Manuel Antonio offers sublime scenery both under- and over water

▶▶▶ Parque Nacional Volcán Irazú   89D3

Open: daily 8–3:30. Admission charge: expensive

The stark gray lunar landscape of Irazú, studded with a lime-green crater lake, offers a spectacular contrast to the access route that twists up through fertile volcanic-soil valleys. This is perhaps Costa Rica's easiest park to visit, as the main crater lies only a few minutes' walk from the parking lot, but go early to avoid both crowds and cloud.

Thunder The name of this 11,257-foot subconical volcano derives from an indigenous word meaning "thunder and earthquake mountain," and ash-showers continue to worry residents of nearby Cartago. Documented since 1563, Irazú's activity means that access to some of its craters may be restricted, but the principal lake, an almost perfect circle with steeply inclined walls, and the smaller Diego de La Haya crater are usually accessible. If the trail is open to the western side, you may have rare views of both oceans and, with a telescope, of Lake Nicaragua. Care should be taken walking over the loose lava shingle, and pay attention to warning signs—Irazú's fumaroles are capricious. Concern was rekindled in December 1993 when Irazú reawoke, and many vulcanologists feel another major eruption is imminent.

Flora and fauna Surrounding vegetation is premontane and montane wet forest, partly lichen-draped, interspersed with open grass- and scrublands. Birds are scarce due to deforestation and volcanic activity, but include clay-colored robins, mountain robins, owls, hummingbirds, and volcano juncos. Rabbits, gray foxes, armadillos, porcupines, coyotes, and tiger cats can also be spotted. If using your own car, take the opportunity to stop on a bend of the access road at another of Irazú's unique features, the Restaurant Linda Vista, where walls and the bar have accumulated layers of paper money and visiting cards from thousands of visitors over the years.

▶▶ Puntarenas   88A3

Long reviled as a brash and badly maintained port, Puntarenas now presents a spruced-up image. Its position on a narrow spit of land jutting into the Golfo de Nicoya makes it a strategic point for ferries between the Nicoya peninsula, islands and the mainland, as well as for Josefinos from the capital, only 1½ hours away. Hotels proliferate, and open-air bars and restaurants dominate the breezy, tree-lined Paseo de Las Turistas, sharing the shore with fishermen bent over their nets. Stylish hotels and a yacht club are located at the entrance to the spit, where a single access road gradually fans out into five main avenues, terminating at the lighthouse at the western end. The beach lining the Pacific side is now clean enough to swim from, but avoid the dirty, silted waters of the lagoon, where ferries also dock.

A new fast road from San José has encouraged Puntarenas to polish up its attractions

Faded glory The port was founded in the 18th century, and in the latter half of the 19th century all Costa Rica's coffee exports were channeled through it. Puntarenas lost much of its coffee business when the Atlantic railway to Puerto Limón was opened, and although it remained for some time the most important Pacific port, that role was also lost in 1981, when a new port opened to the south at Caldera. Much of its charm lies in the legacy of the cosmopolitan old days—a large Chinese population, countless colorful clapboard houses, a water village toppling into the lagoon on the northern side, some rough-looking *cantinas* (bars) and a sprawling, old-fashioned market. You can trace Puntarenas' evolution at a new **marine museum**, behind the crenellated walls of a former prison (*Open* Mon–Sat 9–noon, 1–5. *Admission charge* inexpensive) on Avenida Central, just east of the town's sturdy stone church.

Cruising Puntarenas is the starting point for numerous yacht or cruiser tours of the islands in the Golfo de Nicoya, although in all cases transport can be arranged from San José. The pioneering Calypso Tours (tel: 233-3617) fishes and snorkels its way around Islas Tortugas and the wildlife refuge of the Islas Negritos, and offers a luxury "royal cruise" to Punta Coral. Bay Island Cruises (tel: 296-5551) takes passengers to Islas Tortugas and neighboring islands.

Tuna fishing in the Pacific off Puntarenas, still a busy fishing port

Chinese imports
In the early 1900s Puntarenas had a population of some 2,000 Chinese, who flocked there to work in the docks. Although many have moved away to the capital, the port still has an active Associación China, founded in 1909 by the main families. Their superb old meeting-house, its ornate interior worthy of a Chinese Buddhist temple, sadly disappeared in the 1940s, though a photo remains on display at the museum. The new building on Avenida 1 dates from 1949 and offers a strangely anachronistic atmosphere, with flags and banners dedicated to Taiwan's Nationalist Party.

■ **One of the pleasures of this country is its fabulous range of exotic fruit, piled high in the markets, sliced open at street stands, liquified into a *refresco* or dangling from a tree. Some will be immediately familiar, but the appeal of others may need explanation.** ■

Pejibaye (top) is grown extensively by indigenous peoples

The coconut
Quintessential fruit of tropical beaches, the coconut is exceptionally multifunctional. The fresh white meat and milk is often used as a blending ingredient, particularly on the Caribbean coast, and young coconuts (*pipa*) are sold on stands in all coastal regions as refreshing drinks. The green casing is hacked off to open the nut, at the same time creating a convenient "spoon" to scoop out the flesh. Both the milk (which resembles water when fresh) and the flesh are highly nutritious. Coconut oil, made by heating the white meat, is traditionally used as a sunscreen and skin softener.

Breadfruit *(fruta de pan)* The large, seedless fruit of the breadfruit tree was introduced to the Caribbean by Captain Bligh, who brought it to Jamaica from Tahiti. It is found above all on the Caribbean coast, where it is eaten fried, roasted or boiled, and is an excellent source of vitamins A, B, and C.

Cashew apple *(marañon)* Yes, the kidney-shaped nut also has a fruit from which it grows. This bright scarlet, pear-shaped fruit has delectable, soft, sharply flavored flesh whose strong perfume is a favorite for jams and drinks. Watch out for the nut that grows from the fruit: this is only edible once roasted, otherwise it is poisonous.

Guava *(guayaba)* The guava is cultivated throughout the tropics for its thin-skinned, lemonlike fruits, whose aromatic pink pulp is rich in vitamins A and C, iron, and calcium. It can be consumed raw, cooked into jams and jellies, or served as a juice. Guava leaves are also used to make tea as a treatment for amebic dysentery.

Mango *(mango/manga)* Seen in the city square of Alajuela, arid Guanacaste and throughout the tropics, the "king of fruits" is ubiquitous. Maturing fruit dangle prolifically from the tree from March to October—but be careful, some people are allergic to the sap and skin. The male mango (*mango*) is greener, smaller, and harder than the more generous, yellow female (*manga*), which contains a fibrous orange pulp. Green *mangos* are used for chutneys, preserves, and pies, and Ticos also eat this male variety sprinkled with lemon and salt.

Mombin *(jocote)* When Spaniards first set eyes on this, they called it a plum. In fact this dark-green- to red-skinned juicy fruit has a spicy flavor, and is consumed in large quantities from August to October. A wild, yellow-skinned cousin called the hogplum is a favorite with tapirs.

Mountain apple *(manzana de agua)* Like the breadfruit, the mountain or Malay apple was introduced from Tahiti to the Caribbean by Captain Bligh in 1793. The crisp white flesh of this small, oval, pinkish fruit tastes very similar to that of apples, and is eaten raw or stewed into jams. A distant, equally delicious

de tropico

PALMITO EN TROZOS

PESO NETO: 410 g
PESO ESCURRIDO: 220 g

Sin azúcar ni preservantes

Todo Natural
PESO NETO: 200g

Piña
DESHIDRATADA

Ingredientes: Piña deshidratada • Producto Centroamericano procesado en Costa Rica por TODO NATURAL S.A. Tel. 25-1104, La M.S. 2583

cousin, the **rose-apple** *(manzana rosa)*, has the bonus of being rose-perfumed.

Palm-fruit *(pejibaye)* This is the Tico fruit *par excellence* and is considered sacred by the Guaymi Indians. Like small coconuts, *pejibayes* grow in clusters amongst the fronds of the *pejibaye* palm-tree. *Palmito*, or palm-heart, is extracted from the base of the same tree. The glossy, orange fruit is only eaten cooked, and is often blended with mayonnaise to soften its dry texture, whose flavor is a cross between chestnut and pumpkin.

Papaya/pawpaw *(papaya)* Forty-five varieties grow all over the tropics, but the papaya is indigenous to Central America. Yellow-, green- or orange-skinned, the elongated fruits grow in clusters at the top of a hollow trunk beneath a spray of leaves. The flavor of the slightly bland, though wonderfully smooth, orange flesh is heightened by a sqeeze of lime or lemon juice.

Soursop *(guanábana)* The hardly inspiring English name of this prickly, kidney-shaped fruit bears no relation to its subtly flavored white pulp, from which a sweet-sour juice is extracted to make *refrescos* or ice cream. It is a relative of the custard-apple, also found in Costa Rica.

Starfruit *(carambola)* The starfruit's shiny, pale yellow skin conceals a very juicy white flesh.

Chiverre
The notoriously sweet Tico tooth meets its match when Easter arrives, and mounds of large green and white striped fruits appear on roadsides and in markets. This is the *chiverre*, a member of the pumpkin family that somewhat resembles a squash. For centuries Ticos have transformed the *chiverre* into a sweet jam by mixing its dried pulp with a block of brown sugar, *tapa dulce*. The resulting stringy texture and sugary taste is an essential ingredient in pies made for the Easter feast.

Papayas, mangoes, bananas, plantains and cashew apples (at back of cart)

Stilt-houses lining the estuary date from Quepos' less sophisticated past

▶▶▶ Quepos

Quepos' origins as a major banana-exporting port are apparent in the neat little plantation villages lining the access road. These are now surrounded by more lucrative oil-palms, whose advent ended the port's importance. However, Quepos has a new *raison d'être*, namely as a base for visitors to the park of Manuel Antonio (see pages 102–103). From the picturesque town center, a road winds 4 miles along the cliff to reach Playa Espadilla Norte and the park entrance. This stretch (known as Manuel Antonio) is the focus for burgeoning hotel and restaurant developments, many with fabulous ocean views, some with private beaches and nearly all very upscale. Budget travelers should either stick to downtown Quepos or take a bus directly to the *cabinas* that are clustered near the park entrance.

The choice Apart from some funky bars, discos, a handful of souvenir shops, restaurants, and even a small casino, the attractions of downtown Quepos lie in its sleepy, tropical port atmosphere, enlivened by a dynamic foreign population. Useful information on hotels and tours is given at the Quepos Activities Center (tel: 777-1526), located opposite the bus station. Sportfishing is big business here (try Jim Geary, tel: 777-1839), as are other water activities. High Tide Ocean Kayak Tours (tel/fax: 777-0403) organizes nature tours, snorkeling, and kayaking, while Tarzan's Mother (tel: 777-1257/0191) offers two daily cruises along Manuel Antonio's idyllic coastline. Scuba-diving is available through the Hotel Byblos (tel: 777-0411). Taximar (tel: 777-1170) offers day trips to the Isla del Caño or Bahía Drake, with snorkeling and fishing en route; whitewater rafting is offered by Ríos Locos (tel: 777-1170). Swimmers should be wary of dangerous riptides at Playa Espadilla Norte.

Conscience The rampant, thoughtless, and often destructive development of the Manuel Antonio area is provoking a few reactions. One rare set-up that seems out of place in this hedonistic resort is the wildlife breeding center of **Jardín Gaia▶▶▶**, 1½ miles from Quepos on the coast road (*Open* daily except Wed 9–noon, 1–5. *Admission charge* moderate). Here, animal enclosures with details of the plight of certain species stir visitors' consciences. The Italian owners are also extremely active in raising local environmental consciousness and lobbying for buffer zones around the park.

▶▶ Reserva Biológica Carara 88B2

Open: daily 8–4. Admission charge: expensive

This 11,600-acre reserve is one of Costa Rica's last habitats for scarlet macaws, and a nesting ground for over 100 pairs, best seen at dusk as they return to roost in the mangrove swamps at the mouth of the Río Grande de Tárcoles. Carara offers rich biodiversity due to its transitional position between the dry northern forests and the humid tropical forests of the south. Its rivers and lagoon are home to crocodiles, roseate spoonbills, boat-billed herons, blue-winged teals, howler, and white-faced monkeys, deer, and peccaries. Two trails lead through the reserve: a short half-mile trail starts at the main entrance, about 2 miles south of the Río Tárcoles bridge, and a longer 2.5-mile trail starts about 500 yards past the bridge. Black-hooded antshrikes, long-tailed hermit hummingbirds, and armadillos are quite often encountered, and you may see nesting pairs of the macaws, in hollows up large trees.

Alternatives Anyone interested in crocodiles should indulge in a 2½-hour Jungle Crocodile Safari (daily according to tide) along the river: contact Hotel La Guaria (tel: 661-0455) in the village of Tárcoles. Another, more strenuous diversion in this area is to the **Manantial de Agua Viva▶▶**, a spectacular 660-foot waterfall reached by a 2.5-mile trail through dense forest adjoining Carara. The *catarata* (waterfall) is signposted on the main coastal road, and the entrance to this private reserve (tel: 236-4140. *Open* Dec–mid-Apr 8–3. *Admission charge* moderate) is a few miles uphill from the Villa Lapas hotel.

Scarlet macaws
The brilliant blue, yellow, and red plumage of this tropical bird has been its downfall. Christopher Columbus was the first to smuggle a scarlet macaw to Europe, and baby macaws now fetch up to $1,500 on the black market. Poaching and destruction of their habitat has made them an endangered species, but scarlet macaws can be seen on Costa Rica's Pacific coast, in Carara and at the Parque Nacional Corcovado.

109

Scarlet macaws fetch high prices—an attractive incentive for poachers

Saturday is market day all over Costa Rica, not least in San Ramón

▶▶▶ **San José**   89D3
See page 116

▶　　　**San Ramón**   88B3

A visit to the agricultural community of San Ramón is best made on Saturday mornings, when you can see the farmers' market in full swing. Fruit, vegetables, and truckloads of cattle are brought into town to be haggled over by local *campesinos* (farmers). On a weekday, the small museum (*Open* Tue–Fri 1–7. *Admission charge* inexpensive), in the old municipal palace on the main square displays a reproduction *campesino* home from the turn of the century, while photographs and panels recount local history. During the coffee-harvesting season (November to January), visit the local processing plant, the Cooperativa de Café.

The surrounding mountainous region is particularly beautiful and, 11 miles to the north, offers a private reserve, the **Los Angeles Cloud Forest**▶▶ (tel: 228-4603. *Open* daily. *Admission charge* moderate), owned by former president Rodrigo Carazo and his wife. The 2,000 acres of cloud forest are crossed by an easy one-mile trail (guides are available). Next to the reserve is the charming Villa Blanca hotel, under the same ownership, which organizes horse-trekking.

▶　　　**Santa Ana**   88C3

The location of this once-dusty rural town, on the highway 9 miles due west of San José, has given it a new identity as a satellite of the capital, much favored by expatriates wanting to settle beyond Escazú. Yet the old rural spirit prevails and roadside stalls announce the town's specialty—plaited onions. They even hang from the eaves of houses in town and onions are served in roasted form by local restaurants. Wander in the center, which still harbors some picturesque old buildings in adobe and clapboard, wreathed in brilliant crimson bougainvillea.

Hibiscus
The large pink, orange, or blood-red flowers that grace the hedges and gardens of the Central Valley are those of *Hibiscus rosa-sinensis* or, as it is locally known, the *amapola*. Athough a very common sight in Costa Rica, it originated from tropical Asia, which has a similar climate. Horticulturalists have developed over 5,000 varieties of this flower.

► **Sarchí**   88C3

Once a sleepy little village where inhabitants whiled away the day painting oxcarts, Sarchí is now an overwhelmingly commercial center for buying crafts. It is invaded daily by tour buses, and customers are even plied with free buffets at the workshops. A new Mercado de Artesanía combines restaurants, bars and craft shops and there is also a cooperative, but the commercial leader of Sarchí remains the Fabrica Joaquín Chaveri. Small workshops surround the garden at the back, where oxcarts are laboriously painted, and the front shop displays an enormous range of hardwood furniture, bowls, platters, boxes and, parrot-headed walking-canes in tropical woods. This is the place to buy your folding cowhide rocking chair, a traditional feature of many hotel verandas throughout the country. Sarchí's main square has an attractive twin-towered 1949 church, set in a garden where even the benches, like the local bus shelters and trash cans, are painted in Sarchí floral style.

► **Turrialba**   89E3

This small town was once devoted entirely to agriculture, but a prosperous new era has opened up with the development of kayaking and whitewater rafting on the nearby Río Reventazón, considered to be one of Costa Rica's top destinations. There are reasonable accommodations in the town, and more upscale establishments in the very scenic surroundings. For easy wildlife-spotting, look closely at the trees in the central square, where sloths laze the day away.

Back in 1942 Turrialba saw the founding of CATIE, a pioneering center specialising in agronomical research, that continues to experiment with tropical crops over an area of nearly 2,500 acres. The extensive laboratories, library (recognized as one of the world's best information sources on tropical agriculture), experimental plots and greenhouses can be visited on a five-hour guided tour (tel: 556-1149. *Admission charge* expensive), which needs advance booking as numbers are restricted.

Oxcart genesis
Sarchí's painted souvenir oxcarts, resplendent with floral motifs, are not an old tradition. Although wooden oxcarts were introduced from Nicaragua in the mid-1800s to haul coffee beans, it was not until 1903 that an inspired *campesina* decided to decorate the wheels. Soon after, metal axles and sectioned wheels led to even more elaborate designs while preserving the original star-shaped motif. Around 1915, painting spread to the body of the cart and colors evolved from grays and greens to today's standard orange. When motorized transport took over in the 1960s, Sarchí's oxcart painters turned to the tourist trade, though some carts are still in use in San Antonio de Escazú.

Oxcart, Sarchí: a breakaway design abandons the floral tradition

THE CENTER

Opposite: the ruined church, Ujarrás

Mystical history
The church of Ujarrás was pre-dated by a venerated shrine dedicated to the Virgin del Rescate de Ujarrás. In 1565, according to legend, she appeared from inside a tree trunk to an Indian fishing in the Río Reventazón. Goaded into action, the Indian carried the trunk back to Ujarrás but, as he proceeded, it became heavier and heavier until finally, on his arrival, it could not even be lifted by a gang of helpers. Local Franciscan fathers interpreted this as a sign to build a shrine. When the incident of the pirates took place a century later, it was assumed that the Virgin had saved the day, as they advanced no further than Turrialba.

▶▶ **Ujarrás**   88C4

The abandoned village of Ujarrás nestles in the Orosí Valley at the base of steep cultivated slopes running down to the Cachí reservoir. In 1883 a flood wiped out the village, and today there is little here except a swimming pool and a few restaurants. However, in the middle of chayote plantations stands the star of Ujarrás, the atmospheric ruins of the church of **Nuestra Señora de La Limpia Concepción**, built in 1681–1693 to commemorate the retreat of the pirates Morgan and Mansfield, who threatened to sack Costa Rica. A century later the church was destroyed by an earthquake and today the old stone walls stand in a carefully tended garden of flowering shrubs.

About 2 miles northeast is the Cachí dam and adjacent Charrara recreation area (closed Monday), with pools, a restaurant, trails, and rowboats. A few miles further towards Orosi stands the unique **Casa del Soñador (Dreamer's House)**, a whimsical one-man work by the aging folk-sculptor Macedonio Quesada. Woodcarvings are still made by one of his four sons, who will show you round the simple house, faced with bas-reliefs and sprouting carved figures at every corner.

▶▶ **Zarcero**   88C3

This mountain village of ruddy-cheeked inhabitants harbors the work of another of Costa Rica's idiosyncratic sculptors (see Ujarrás, above). This artist uses topiary as his medium. The astonishing garden fronts a pastel-colored church, dating from 1895, whose horseshoe steps seem designed to lead the eye to the creations of Evangelisto Blanco, the park gardener. For some 30 years he has trimmed and pruned these cypress bushes, rejecting lucrative offers to apply his talents elsewhere, and as a result Zarcero's Parque Central offers a vegetal gallery of animals and human forms—from faces peeping out of niches to elephants, huge standing figures, a cat riding a motorbike, and even a populated bullring.

Visit the impeccably maintained and highly decorated church, and do not forget to sample Zarcero's gastronomic offerings while you are there: fudge (*cajeta*), candied orange, honey, cheese, and wonderfully thick cream.

Delicately painted designs embellish the wood-paneling of Zarcero's church

Drive Valley and volcano

See map on pages 88–89.

Make an early start to complete this very full one-day circuit, which takes in Cartago and Volcán Irazú before meandering through the enchanting Orosí Valley. Cultural stops are included and, if time allows, a therapeutic soak in a mineral pool.

From San José drive out through San Pedro on the highway to **Cartago►** (see page 92). Negotiate the confusing streets of this town, stopping to look at **Las Ruinas►►►**, before heading out northeast toward Cot. At a major fork, branch left to Potrero Cerrado, then wind up through beautiful agricultural valleys and pineforests to reach eventually the national park of **Volcán Irazú►►►** (see page 104). On the way back down stop at the Restaurant Linda Vista for a snack in an intriguing setting.

Backtrack to Cartago then drive east out to Paraíso, stopping just before at the **Jardín Lankester►►►** (see page 102). In Paraíso itself, drive through the main square and follow signs to Cachí. This part of the Orosí Valley is blanketed with rich fields of cane, coffee and macadamia, and the road twisting down to the Cachí reservoir offers plenty of views as well as the gushing Los Novios waterfall. A right turn from the main road leads shortly to **Ujarrás►►** (see opposite) and its melancholic ruins (above). If hunger strikes, indulge at a modest little open-air restaurant at the junction. From here return to the main road and continue around the lake, passing the hydroelectric dam channeling water into a spillway, before winding uphill to the carved Casa del Soñador.

The road continues through stunning, undulating landscapes of coffee plantations, with the foothills of the Cordillera de Talamanca looming up towards the south. At **Orosí►** (see page 101) stop to look at the venerable church and/or relax in the thermal pools. Do not miss the panoramas from the mirador outside town, before heading back through more bucolic landscapes to Paraíso, then Cartago and San José.

■ **Costa Rica's handicrafts may not compare with the range available in Guatemala or Mexico, yet the country continues to play a strategic role as a marketplace for artisans from north and south. Indigenous peoples have rediscovered old craft skills, and tropical woods inspire skilled North American carvers.** ■

Craft sources
Near San José, San Vicente de Moravia (usually called Moravia) is a good crafts center with a wide choice of shops and an *artesanía* market. Also nearby, at Bello Horizonte, uphill from Escazú, are the showroom and workshop of Biesanz Woodworks (tel: 228-1811); its products are sold in hotels and craft shops throughout the country. Jay Morrison's furniture is displayed in San José at Magia (Calle 5/Avenida 1 & 3) and at his Tierra Extraña showroom in Piedades de Santa Ana (tel: 282-6697). Further afield, the CASEM crafts cooperative in Monteverde sells clothes and knickknacks inspired by local nature. See also San José (pages 120–121) and Sarchí (page 111).

Folding rocking chairs are easily exported

Since pre-Columbian days when Costa Rica's indigenous peoples extensively traded their stunning pottery, gold ornaments and stone carvings, handicrafts have taken a downward turn. Gone are the intricately carved metates and the inspired zoomorphic jade and gold pieces. Today you are more likely to see primitive gourds, baskets and weavings. However, the growth of the tourist market has given the necessary impetus not only to the development of new directions but also to a revival of old traditions. Add to this an influx of North American craftspeople, usually inspired by Costa Rica's wide range of tropical woods, and the crossroads position of Costa Rica on the Latin American map, and the result is a steadily growing crafts industry.

Indigenous traditions Of all Costa Rican traditional handicrafts, it is the pottery of Guaitíl (see page 42) that carries off the prizes. In pre-Columbian days, the pottery of the Chorotegas of the Nicoya peninsula was acclaimed and commissioned by Zapotecs and Aztecs, and traded to southern Costa Rica and Panama. Today the kilns of Guaitíl are firing again in an impressive revival that spurns modern technology. Similarly, with the help of an enlightened Tico artist, the Boruca Indians have now rejected synthetic dyes and threads and revived traditional techniques with backstrap looms, usually installed in a family kitchen. Like the Talamanca Indians, they continue to make carved gourds and incorporate symbolic designs into fine string baskets (*chácaras*) of natural fibers. Crudely carved balsawood masks are made by the Borucas for their Diablitos celebration, while iguana-skin drums are produced by more remote indigenous groups.

Bring on the ox Ubiquitous to the point of overexposure, the painted oxcart is a distant reflection of old *campesino* traditions transformed into easily packable miniature versions, the ultimate Tico souvenir. These decorative objects are hand-painted at Sarchí (see page 111) where visitors can watch craftsmen at work at the pioneering Chaveri workshop, which dates from 1903 and developed for the nascent tourist market in the 1960s. Sarchí has since become *the* crafts town of the country and this is where visitors can stock up on every imaginable transformation of tropical wood. Bowls, platters, teapots, trays, boxes, jewelry, parrots... there is no shortage and the quality is generally high. Although materials come straight from the tropical forest, the high profit margin on these comparatively small objects makes

Crafts

Animals assume mystical status in Guaitíl's centuries-old forms and designs

them ecologically acceptable compared with large-scale commercial logging. Another typical Tico souvenir is the collapsible leather and wood rocking chair, a Spanish inheritance that is easily transportable.

Foreign input Perhaps the most beautifully crafted wooden items come from the workshop of Barry Biesanz. Rosewoods, lacewood, ironwood, purpleheart, tigerwood, balsam of Peru, satinwood, and many others of Costa Rica's 1,500 tree species are transformed into combs, bowls, and boxes, often combining two or three woods in one perfectly joined piece. In harmony with a strictly conservationist attitude, his expanding Escazú workshop, Biesanz Woodworks, maintains a seedbank, a rare-wood nursery and, whenever possible, uses fallen or dead trees. A similar approach is expounded by Jay Morrison and his company, Tierra Extraña, through their reforestation program. Morrison produces extraordinarily crafted furniture made from native Costa Rica woods, and, like Biesanz, allows their textures, grains, and colors to influence his designs.

New directions Whether adapting indigenous beeswax whistles (*ocarinas*) into clay and adding an animal head or two, or importing Mexican silver from Taxco, clothes and textiles from Guatemala, ceramic-bead necklaces from Colombia, embroidered panels from Panama or llama-wool jackets from Ecuador, Costa Rica is reestablishing itself as Latin America's handicrafts crossroads. Parallel to this, a renewed interest in and intelligent promotion of indigenous crafts, plus the dynamism of talented expatriates, may take future Costa Rican crafts beyond banana-paper, the latest novelty.

What's in a gourd?
If you spot a short-trunked tree with long spreading branches and green, volleyball-sized spheres hanging from them, you are looking at a calabash tree. Gourds and maracas are made by hollowing out calabash fruits, then letting them dry for several days. The hard shells can be incised or beautifully polished, and odd shapes can be created by binding the fruits as they dry. Their usual function is as a container for food or water, a custom of the Afro-Caribbeans as well as the indigenous people of Talamanca.

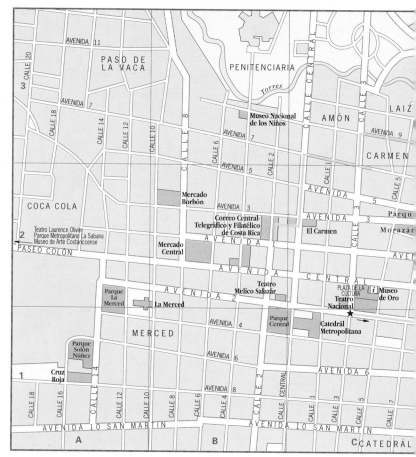

San José

Nestling at 3,770 feet in the Meseta Central (Central Plateau), the capital of Costa Rica is a crossroads between the country's natural sights. As well as being the hub of the nation's political, economic, and cultural life, San José also maintains a well-oiled tourist infrastructure, offering just enough to keep visitors busy for a few days before they head out to more distant forests, volcanoes and beaches. The small scale of the downtown (287,000 inhabitants), easy grid layout, mild spring-like climate, and lively cultural life create a pleasant introduction to the country, although belching buses, heavy traffic, and crowded sidewalks leave little desire to stay long. It is relatively safe compared to other Latin American capitals but pickpockets and muggers are on the increase even here. Whatever its drawbacks, San José retains a distinctly provincial, small-town flavor—where else does a president drive his own car and flag down passing motorists when he runs out of gas?

New look Although founded in 1737, San José only replaced Cartago as Costa Rica's capital in 1823, following a short civil war. Its socioeconomic zenith was

SAN JOSÉ

Left: central San José

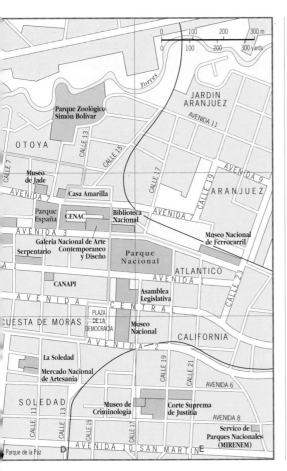

Safety
The days of San José being a safe city are over, and although the level of danger is far below that of neighboring countries, tourists are considered easy game. Beware of certain areas—the Coca Cola bus station being number one, closely followed by central streets south of Avenida 2 and around Parque Central. Conmen and conwomen (often masquerading as prostitutes to trap unsuspecting male visitors) abound, so be wary of any nocturnal street contact, however harmless it may seem. Also watch out for the *chapulines*, teenage gangs who organize distractions, all the better to rob their chosen victims.

Below: San José sprawls some 4 sq mi across the central plateau
Left: lottery-ticket seller

reached toward the end of the last century, when the coffee trade was booming: most of the capital's more impressive public buildings date from this period, as do the surviving pockets of plantation owners' homes. Earthquakes, property developers, and a population explosion have taken their toll, leading to the replacement of numerous old architectural gems with characterless concrete edifices. Government buildings range from the elegant old Legislative Assembly, immediately north of the Museo Nacional, to aberrations such as the tower-block headquarters of the ICT (tourist institute) or the uninspiring law-courts complex southeast of the center. As a welcome contrast, the center is dotted with verdant squares, and the old airport at La Sabana has been transformed into a large park where the silhouettes of surrounding hills are easily visible. This, too, is part of San José's small-town appeal, which suits the scale of so diminutive a country.

Central zone Most points of interest are located within a dozen or so blocks bordered to the north by Barrio Amón (Avenida 7–9), to the south by Avenida 6, to the west by Calle 16 (with its infamous Coca Cola bus station) and to the east by Calle 19. Avenida Central bisects the city east–west with odd-numbered avenues running parallel to the north and even-numbered avenues to the south. For several central blocks it becomes a pedestrian street. West of La Merced church it is renamed Paseo Colón, an upscale business neighborhood whose quiet side-streets harbor some elegant small hotels. Beyond here lie La Sabana and the embassies of Rohrmoser. A few blocks east of the Museo Nacional, Avenida Central skirts the prosperous residential area of Los Yoses before entering San Pedro, another elegant suburb and also site of San José's university.

Churches There are no outstanding churches left in San José but a few neoclassical examples have recently had facelifts following the 1991 earthquake. The Catedral Metropolitana (Avenida 2/Calle Central), and adjoining archbishop's palace date from the founding of San José in the early 18th century, but were virtually destroyed by the 1821 earthquake and not rebuilt until 1871. Looking equally pristine is La Soledad (Avenida 4/Calle 11), an eclectic 1909 construction

San José street life is lively, and food and drinks are easily available

La Merced, fronted by one of the mystery spheres from southern Costa Rica

with two symmetrical towers flanking a central atrium. The small plaza in front once hosted seasonal fairs but has now been supplanted by the adjoining square in front of the overbearing ICT tower block. La Merced, unmistakable in its strategic location where one-way traffic careers round to Avenida 2 from Paseo Colón, is in a neo-Gothic style mixed with the neoclassical.

Culture Tickets to cultural events are astonishingly inexpensive thanks to government sponsorship—so make use of them. San José boasts some 15 theaters, and, if your Spanish is up to it, an outing to a show (the majority are comedies) should be on your agenda. Otherwise, English-language plays are regularly staged at the Teatro Laurence Olivier. Music is similarly a high priority for Josefinos, who are justly proud of their National Symphony Orchestra: you may catch it in full melodic swing at the Teatro Nacional or on tour in a provincial capital. Plentiful cinemas offer the full gamut of Hollywood productions, often screened in San José before they reach Europe, while independent foreign films can be seen at the University Cinemateca in San Pedro or the Sala Garbo off Paseo Colón. And don't miss the dance and theater performances staged at the CENAC complex (see Galería Nacional de Arte Contemporaneo y Diseno, page 120).

Tourist information
The ICT (Instituto Costarricense de Turismo) has a public office next to the Museo de Oro on the Plaza de La Cultura/Calle 5 (tel: 222-1090. *Open:* weekdays 9–5, Sat 9–1). This is not to be confused with the ICT administrative block on Avenida 2/4. There are plenty of brochures about Costa Rica's natural sights as well as photo files supplied by various hotels around the country to lure you to them. English-speaking officials will also advise. For information, bookings, and discounted tickets to the national parks, go to their central office, the Servicio de Parques Nacionales, part of the ministry concerned with natural resources (MIRENEM, Calle 25/Avenida 8 & 10, tel: 257-0922. *Open:* weekdays 8–4). Extensive listings of cultural events can be found in the weekly *Tico Times* or *Costa Rica Today.*

THE CENTER

Jade

Costa Rican jade is actually jadeite, as opposed to the denser nephrite jade used in Asia. Jade has been unearthed only in graves in Guanacaste and on the Atlantic side, some carved according to Olmec or Maya traditions but the majority made in a distinctive Costa Rican style. From about 300 BC to AD 500 jade was considered the most valuable material for ritual objects used by priests and shamans, as it attracted and absorbed energy as well as being associated with agricultural fertility. Carving techniques varied from elaborate string-sawing and carving in the round on the Atlantic side to Guanacaste's tradition of carving into the curved surface of a polished jade piece.

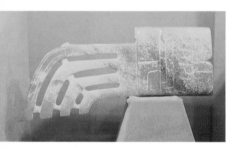

A finely carved and etched jade piece, c300 BC, from the Península de Nicoya, on display at the Museo de Jade

▶ **Galería Nacional de Arte Contemporaneo y Diseño (National Gallery of Contemporary Art)** *117D2*

Avenida 3/Calle 15, tel: 223-4919.
Open: Tue–Sun 10–4. Admission charge: donation
In 1994 an old liquor distillery was successfully renovated to create a dynamic cultural complex (CENAC), sprawling between the Parque España and the Parque Nacional. In its southeastern corner stands this impressive museum of contemporary art and design, which displays a permanent collection of Latin American art and temporary exhibitions of international artists and designers. Check the performing arts program, and explore the whole complex, which dates from the late 19th century.

▶ **Mercado Central (Central Market)** *116B2*
Avenida Central/Calle 6
This is the place for a close encounter with Josefinos (the people of San José)—a far cry from the muted calm of the hotel circuit. Colors, odors and bustle are typically Latin American, and the goods range from live chickens to medicinal herbs—the latter all labeled for their respective uses, and sold at an overwhelming number of stalls. A few vendors target the tourist trade with leather goods, hammocks, or pottery, and the surrounding streets are teeming with impromptu salesmen. The covered market area is also the best place in San José to sample traditional Tico food at rockbottom prices. One drawback is the concentration of pickpockets, who take advantage of the market crowds.

▶▶▶ **Museo de Jade (Jade Museum)** *117D2*
Instituto Nacional de Seguros,
Avenida 7/Calle 9, tel: 223-5800 ext 2581
Open: Mon–Sat 8–5. Admission: free
The odd location of this museum, hidden away on the 11th floor of the social security building, belies its immense interest. Jade is not the only exhibit here: the entire display gives a fascinating account of Costa Rica's pre-Columbian civilizations and their links with Mesoamerica and South America. Besides the extensive collection of superbly crafted jade pieces, there are exquisite gold pieces, mainly produced by the Diquis, numerous well-preserved or restored examples of anthropomorphic and zoomorphic pottery, and a fabulous array of *metates*. These elaborately carved three- or four-legged andesite stool-like objects are unique to Costa Rica, and held great sculptural and symbolic significance. Some date from as early as 500 BC. The last room holds fertility symbols, from phallic sculptures to terracotta models of copulating couples or pregnant women.

▶▶▶ **Museo Nacional (National Museum)** *117D1*
Avenida 2/Calle 17, tel: 257-1433
Open: Tue–Sun 8:30–4:30. Admission charge: inexpensive
Housed in the imposing Bellavista fortress (1887), whose corner tower is still pockmarked with bullet holes from the 1948 civil war, this museum offers a sweeping overview of Costa Rica's history. It incorporates a lovely breezy garden

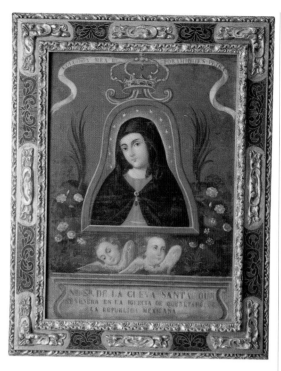

Armchair history
Weary of museums? Then try going to a Tuesday night performance at the decorative little Teatro Melico Salazar (Avenida 2/Calle Central, tel: 222-2653). This government-sponsored show features the National Dance Company interpreting Costa Rican history, myth, and legend in sumptuous costumes, with a background narration in Spanish.

Nuestra Señora de la Cueva (left) and San Roque (below), both at the Museo Nacional

courtyard with fine views over San José and the mountains of Escazú. Follow the collection in a counter-clockwise direction, starting on the south side of the courtyard and ending at the front entrance overlooking the Plaza de la Democrácia. Pre-Columbian exhibits include petroglyphs from Orosí and Guanacaste, imaginative **metates** including flying-panel versions, staff heads, gold ornaments, carved funerary stones and several stone spheres from the Palmar region (see pages 156–157). Colonial furniture of the 17th century is followed by the Sala Historica, where panels and captions in Spanish and English, often highly critical, outline the socioeconomic effects of colonialism. Photos and documents end with the Nobel prize certificate presented to President Oscar Arias in 1987.

▶ **Museo Nacional de Ferrocarril**
   (National Railroad Museum)   *117E2*
Avenida 3/Calle 19, tel: 221-0777
Open: Tue–Sun 2–9. Admission charge: inexpensive
Housed in the original Atlantic railroad terminal (1908), this small museum is devoted to a railroad that transformed the nation's economy but closed in 1990 due to endless landslide damage (see page 132). Old photos, a model railroad and some real rolling stock chart the colorful history of the Jungle Train. Every day at noon five passenger coaches would rattle away from San José, rolling past farms and coffee plantations, cutting high above the Río Reventazón and across precarious-looking bridges before descending through jungle to the humid tropics around Siqueres, and eventually Puerto Limón.

Gold pendant of a harpy eagle, Museo de Oro

▶ **Museo Nacional de los Niños (National Children's Museum)**   *116B3*

Avenida 9/Calle 4, tel: 233-2734
Open: Wed–Sun 10–12, 2–5. Admission charge: moderate
This new addition to San José's museum circuit, opened in 1994, is aimed solely at children, with didactic and interactive displays covering children's rights, the universe, living creatures, health, communications, city life, and Costa Rican history, and numerous scientific exhibits. The striking, fortresslike setting on the north side of town is actually a former prison.

▶▶▶ **Museo de Oro (Gold Museum)**   *116C2*

Beneath the Plaza de La Cultura, entrance on Calle 5, tel: 223-0528
Open: Tue–Sun 10–5. Admission charge: moderate
This spectacular display is one of the highlights of Costa Rica, and certainly of San José. Pre-Columbian gold, nothing more, nothing less, is the subject, whether hammered breastplates with fine repoussé work, *tumbaga* (an alloy of copper and gold) or intricately sculpted ornaments cast with the lost-wax method. The latter technique was probably introduced to Costa Rica from Venezuela and Colombia around AD 400 and obviously fired the imagination of the craftsmen, who created miniature versions of armadillos, alligators, frogs, parrots (symbol of intelligence), or butterflies (the Bribrí symbol of femininity). Explanatory panels in Spanish and English give background information about alloys, craft methods and the function and significance of decorative designs, and the entire collection is dramatically spotlit in its shadowy setting. An ironic climax comes in the form of some glass-bead necklaces astutely exchanged by the Spaniards in 1502 for local gold ornaments. The same underground complex, an innovative 1975 design belonging to the Banco Nacional, houses temporary art exhibitions and the Museo Numismatica. The city tourist information office is located at the entrance.

▶ **Parque Metropolitano La Sabana**   *116A2*

San José's largest city park offers a temporary bucolic escape from the frenzy of downtown traffic and crowds. Josefino joggers, aspiring soccer stars and local families share the shady lawns and lake, all of which were landscaped from the former airport. The imposing terminal building at the eastern end now houses the **Museo de Arte Costariccense**▶ (*Open* Tue–Sun 10–5. *Admission charge* moderate). Permanent and temporary exhibits here are firmly national in scope and of variable quality, but the Salón Dorado occasionally presents free chamber music concerts. Don't miss the lofty ground-floor café with views through the trees. At the western end of the park is the national stadium, also used for international rock concerts, beyond which lies the spacious suburb of Rohrmoser, a favorite with embassies and diplomats. A gymnasium, free tennis courts, and an Olympic swimming pool (not always open) occupy the southeastern corner of the park.

▶ **Parque Morazán**   116C2

Avenida 3/Calle 6–9

These flourishing gardens covering four city blocks include two oddities—the domed and colonnaded Templo de la Musica (Music Temple), which has a distinct French 18th-century style, and the Escuela Metálica, made of bolted metal plates, which was shipped in pieces from Belgium in 1890 before being assembled to house 1,000 students.

Escuela Metálica: not only the style but also the entire building came from Europe

▶ **Parque Zoológico Simón Bolívar**   117D3

Avenida 11/Calle 7 & 9, Barrio Amón, tel: 233-6701
Open: weekdays 8–3:30, weekends 9-5. Admission charge: inexpensive

After gazing at gold versions of Costa Rica's fauna at the Museo de Oro, you can come here to see live specimens that you may not have had the luck to see in the wild. The zoo offers a good round-up of wild cats, coatimundis, reptiles, tapirs, monkeys, sloths, reptiles, and birds.

THE CENTER

Let there be opera
The construction of the Teatro Nacional was paid for by a special coffee tax that the 19th-century coffee barons imposed on themselves. The incentive had come when the Italian opera-singer Adelina Patti was touring Guatemala but was unable to extend her visit to Costa Rica because it had no appropriate concert hall. Not wanting to be left out of the *fin de siècle* swing, the plantation owners decided to tax every bag of coffee exported from Costa Rica. Within a short time they were able to call upon European architects, muralists, and decorators to fashion this remarkable construction.

A lyrical Muse at the Teatro Nacional

▶ **Plaza de La Cultura** *116C2*

This busy central square just behind the Teatro Nacional is home to the Museo de Oro and the tourist information office, both beneath the Banco Central. Recent restructuring of the plaza was financed by McDonald's, of hamburger fame, which presides in all its garish glory over the northern flank. Peruvian musicians haunt the precinct, and vendors do a fast trade in T-shirts, cheap Guatemalan clothes, jewelry and animal-shaped clay flutes. The streets immediately to the northeast are what is known as San José's red-light district, a decidedly low-key affair.

▶ **Serpentario** *117D2*
Radamida building, Avenida 1/Calle 9 & 11, tel: 255-4210
Open: daily 9–6. Admission charge: inexpensive
If you are considering trekking through Costa Rica's rainforests, this small exhibition will alert you to potential reptilean dangers. Live snakes and a few frogs are displayed, and a bilingual biologist is on hand to explain the niceties of species, such as the venomous fer-de-lance, that you may encounter.

▶▶▶ **Teatro Nacional** *116C2*
Avenida 2/Calle 3 & 5, tel: 221-5341
Open: weekdays 10–noon, 2–6. Admission charge: inexpensive

This ornately decorated 1890s building reflects the heyday of San José when coffee-barons and bankers flocked to see operas and concerts in a gilded interior worthy of, and modeled after, the Opéra de Paris. The neoclassical exterior is less impressive than the interior, nor is it helped by an uninspired revamping of the square outside. Much of the dazzling decoration within was badly damaged by the 1991 earthquake, and a million-dollar restoration has only just been completed. But still gloriously intact are the Carrara marble statues and grand staircase, gold-leaf moldings, and the original ceiling mural, *Alegoría*, depicting coffee-harvesters reaping the profitable crop that paid for the building (see panel on this page). Try to go to a free Sunday morning concert (11AM) to soak up the old-world atmosphere. A peaceful coffee shop to the left of the foyer holds art exhibitions and makes a useful escape from the crowds of tourists on the café-terrace of the Gran Hotel de Costa Rica outside.

Walk **Old San José**

See map on pages 116–117.

This walk takes you past several downtown sights and circles around some oustanding old buildings in Barrio Amón before returning to the center. Allow two hours for a leisurely stroll.

From the **Teatro Nacional**►►► walk east down Avenida 2 to the **Plaza de La Democrácia**, home to a crafts market, with the Museo Nacional towering above. Walk around the square and across Avenida Central on to Calle 15, dominated by the **Legislative Assembly (Asamblea Legislativa)** building. Keep going north on Calle 15 to reach the **Parque Nacional**, a lovely square whose centennial trees encompass the **Monumento Nacional**, a bronze homage to the Central American nations' spirited rejection of William Walker. A short detour can be made east along Avenida 3 to see the old **Atlantic railroad terminus** and its **museum (Museo Nacional de Ferrocarril)**►. On the northern side of the Parque Nacional stands the **Biblioteca Nacional** and, on the northwestern corner is the entrance to the **Galería Nacional de Arte Contemporaneo y Diseño**►►.

Marimba players get the action going in downtown San José

Continue along Calle 15 to Avenida 7 where you turn left (downhill), passing the very elegant Mexican Embassy on your right, to reach the **Parque España**. The **Museo de Jade**►►► lies on the upper floors of the modern block in front of you. Turn right up Calle 13, circling past the wide stairways of the neo-baroque **Casa Amarilla** (yellow house), now the Ministry of Foreign Affairs, before reaching Avenida 9. Turn left and enjoy a downhill stretch that passes several decorative clapboard residences, some now converted into hotels, notably the mintgreen **Casa Verde** on the corner of Calle 7. Two blocks farther is a Moorish folly, the **Casa Morisca**, where you should turn left up to Avenida 7. A few yards' detour to the left here brings you to the Caribbeanstyle **Alliance Française**, from where you backtrack, passing on your left the **Hotel Santo Tomás**, converted from a 1900s coffee baron's residence. Walk straight on and turn left at Calle Central, which, after two blocks, reaches the **Iglesia del Carmen**. Cross the square on your right to Calle 2 and end at the **Correo Central**—a remarkable building dating from 1914.

Practical details

Beat the bill
Hotels make heavy surcharges on phone calls, so for prolonged long-distance calls or faxes the Telecom office may prove useful. A bonus is that payment can be made by credit card. It is located on Avenida 2/Calle 1 & 3 (*Open:* Mon–Thu 7AM–10PM, Fri–Sun 7AM–midnight). Avoid evenings, when lines are long.

Getting around Despite the easy central grid system, street numbers soon disappear as you enter the outer districts. Instead, addresses are given with reference to a nearby landmark—which could be the American Embassy or Pizza Hut. Each block is counted as 100m, so '125 metres al oeste y 200 metros al norte de la Cruz Roja' means roughly one-and-a-quarter blocks west and two blocks north of the Red Cross.

The center can easily be covered on foot, and buses run from suburbs such as Los Yoses or San Francisco, which are quieter places to stay. Destinations are marked on the front and fares are paid to the driver. Taxis are inexpensive, but make sure *la maria* (meter) is functioning. If not, negotiate a reasonable fare.

Buses to outlying towns leave from designated stops— contact the tourist office for details

Shopping San José has a wide range of shopping, although Sarchí (see page 111) is acknowledged to be the country's main crafts center. A reasonable, though repetitive choice of leather, bamboo, wicker, and ceramic goods, as well as locally made and Guatemalan clothes, is sold at stalls inside **La Casona** (Avenida Central & 1/Calle Central), or head out to the handicraft market of **Las Garzas** in the outlying suburb/village of Moravia (100m south and 50m east from the Red Cross). A rather disappointing government crafts cooperative, CANAPI, is located on Avenida 1/Calle 11, and at the **Mercado Nacional de Artesanía** on Calle 11 behind La Soledad church. **Anda** (Avenida Central/Calle 5 & 7) sells reasonably priced indigenous baskets, weaving, gourds, and masks. For high-quality goods including jewelry, try **Galería Suráska** (Avenida 3/Calle 5). **Atmosfera** (Avenida 1 & 3/Calle 5) displays paintings, hangings, and some indigenous work.

Books in English and Spanish as well as overpriced crafts are stocked by **The Bookshop** (Avenida 1/Calle 1 & 3), and foreign magazines and newspapers at Lehmann's, a few steps away. Coffee gourmets should head for **La Esquina del Café** (Avenida 9/Calle 3) where every possible Costa Rican coffee bean and roast can be sampled and bought. Department stores such as **La Gloria** (Avenida Central/Calle 4 & 6) can be useful, but if you are looking for high fashion, investigate the upscale shopping centers on the road to Escazú (Multiplaza being Costa Rica's largest) or in San Pedro.

Nightlife Cautious first-timers to San José could check out **El Pueblo** in Barrio Tournón, a tourist-oriented complex that offers a Spanish pueblo-style maze of bars, restaurants, and nightclubs, aimed at a mature clientèle. A newish Josefino hot-spot is **Casa Matute** (Avenida 10/Calle 21), a stylishly converted old mansion housing bars, a restaurant and a disco with live music, all spilling into the garden until 4AM. Not far away is **Akelare** (Avenida 4 & 6/Calle 21), a sprawling old house open for drinking and dining, with live bands at weekends. More sober and elegant in style is **L'Habanera** (Avenida 9/Calle 11 & 13), a smooth cocktail bar with resident pianist, again located in a beautifully restored mansion.

Long-standing and still popular is **El Cuartel de la Boca del Monte** (Avenida 1/Calle 21 & 23), a relaxed bar/restaurant with background rock (the decibels rise at weekends), live music on Mondays, good *bocas* and great cocktails. Small and intimate with occasional live music, **The Shakespeare** (100m south of Pizza Hut, Paseo Colón) is plastered with old movie posters, and is favored by the intelligentsia after a show at the adjacent Laurence Olivier theater or a film at Sala Garbo. Live blues, jazz, and calypso throbs at **Soda Blues** (Avenida 10 & 12/Calle 11) while mariachi bands haunt **La Esmeralda** (Avenida 2/Calle 5 & 7) between serenading appointments round town. For Latin rhythms, try **Salsa 54** (Avenida 1 & 3/Calle 3), which incorporates a special stage for star-turns, or **Las Tunas Discoteque** in La Sabana Norte.

Time for a snack before the bus leaves

Top of the bill
Costa Rica boasts plenty of homegrown bands specializing in anything from reggae to rock and roll, salsa, merengue, Latin folk, or traditional and experimental jazz. Cantoamerica and Oveja Negra are two popular local dance bands that blend Latin and salsa influences with reggae and calypso from Costa Rica's Caribbean coast. Good old rock is pounded out by Café con Leche, Liverpool, and Grupo Cuartel at different nightspots round town, while Marfil, La Banda, Los Brillanticos and Grupo K-lor cover a wide range of contemporary Western hits and tropical classics.

Crafts are sold daily on Plaza de la Cultura and Plaza de la Democrácia

THE CARIBBEAN

Punta Castilla

Isla Machura

NIC

5

Isla Calero
Barra del Colorado

San Juan

Isla Brava

Trinidad

Colorado

Chirripó

Refugio Nacional de Fauna Silvestre Barra del Colorado

119m Cerro Tortuguero
Zona Protectora Tortuguero
Tortuguero

Sarapiquí

Sardinal
Boca Río Sucio

Llanura de Tortuguero

Suerte

Canta Gallo

4

HEREDIA

Muelle
Puerto Viejo de Sarapiquí
La Selva
Tigre
Zona Protectora La Selva

Encina

Parque Nacional Tortuguero

Sucio

San Pedro

Tortuguero

Cariari

Esperanza

Sierpe

Rara Avis

Griega
Teresa

Las Horquetas

Zancudo

Río Frío

Jiménez

Parismina

Rita
Roxana

Villafranca

Parque Nacional Braulio Carrillo

Santa Clara
Guápiles

Llanura de Santa Clara

Río Jiménez

LIMÓN

3

Jiménez

Guácimo

Parismina

Canal de Tortuguero

Pocora
Germania

Manila

Cordillera Central

2047m Cerro Honduras

Rainforest Aerial Tram

Jardín Botánico Las Cusingas
Zona Protectora Acuíferos Guácimo y Pococí

Cairo

Siquirres

Batán

Cuatro Millas

Sucio

Zurquí

Parque Nacional Volcán Irazú

3328m Volcán Turrialba

Florida

Matina

Estrada

Larga Distancia

Barbilla

Porte
Moí

San Isidro

3432m Volcán Irazú

Santa Cruz

Reventazón

Zona Protectora Río Pacuare

Bristol
Stratford

Liverpool

Llano Grande
Tres Ríos

Lajas
Peralta

Zona Protectora Barbilla

Río Blanco

Pacayas

Cot

Monumento Nacional Guayabo
Turrialba

Pacuare

1617m Cerro Tigre

Banan

2 ZP Cerro
La Carpintera
Cartago

San Rafael

Juan Viñas

Pavones

Asunción

Tejar
Paraíso

Cervantes

Tucurrique

La Suiza
Tuís

Zona Protectora Río Banao

Tobosi

Cachí

Chirripó de Atlántico

2251m Cerro Matama

Fila de Matama

Orosí

Pejibaye

Platanillo

Zona Protectora Río Navarro y Río Sombrero
Empalme

Tapantí

Zona Protectora Cuenca Río Tuís

Chirripó Abajo

Estrella Vall

Jardín

Parque Nacional Tapantí

CARTAGO

2378m Cerro Tsuitebeta

Reserv
Hito

San Marcos
Tarrazú
Cañón

Tres de Junio

Valle d

Santa María de Dota
Copey

Salsipuedes

Cordillera de Talamanca

3394m Cerro Cuericí

Parque Nacional Chirripó

Teliré

San Jos
Cabéca

SAN JOSÉ

1

Fila Pangolín

San Gerardo de Dota

3491m Cerro La Muerte

Siberia

2435m Cerro Punibeta

Zona Protectora Cerro Nara

Savegre

Fila Zapotales

División

Santo Tomás

Piedra

3819m Cerro Chirripó

Parque

Internacional

Fila Dúrika

Savegre Abajo

Río Nuevo

Herradura
San Gerardo de Rivas
La Ese
Rivas

Chirripó del Pacífico

La Amistad

A

B

The Caribbean For centuries the province of Limón was geographically and culturally isolated, its Afro-Caribbean population even banned from traveling into the Central Valley until after the 1948 civil war. Communications with the rest of the country greatly improved with the completion of the Limón highway in 1987, but even today telephones are rare outside the provincial capital. Climatic conditions are extreme, with almost constant high humidity and rain interspersed with brilliant sun and clear light. Go to Limón and you will enter a completely different atmosphere and culture, far closer in spirit to the islands of the Caribbean than to Costa Rica's Tico regions.

Hit the hammock Tourism is increasingly important in this region. Although much of the low-lying terrain is blanketed with monotonous plantations, Limón is also a naturalist's fantasyland. High on tourist itineraries is Tortuguero, an area crisscrossed by canals and rivers, including the whitewater rapids of the Río Pacuare. It attracts hundreds of bird species and its beaches are nesting grounds for turtles. More marshes and lagoons are found around Barra del Colorado, Río Estrella, and Manzanillo, the latter another turtle favorite.

Rising to the west is the daunting Cordillera de Talamanca, whose foothills harbor the Reserva Biológica Hitoy Cerere and indigenous reserves. However, the region's greatest attraction lies along its shores, in a string of seductive white beaches edged with coral reefs in true Caribbean tradition. Fling yourself into a hammock at Puerto Viejo or Cahuita, sip a fresh coconut and let a sybaritic vacation mood take over.

The facts
Limón is, after Guanacaste, Costa Rica's least densely populated province, with only 8 percent of the country's total population. Average temperatures are the highest in the country, oscillating between 91°F during the day and 68°F at night; rainfall is also very high and seems to fall by the bucketload in Tortuguero. The best months are March and October, when hot, sunny days produce luminous seas and skies.

Hammocks
Hammocks are sometimes thought to have been introduced from the tropical islands of the Caribbean, but they are native to Costa Rica too. Cabécar Indians high in the remote sierra use hammocks made from the coarse fiber of the sago palm. Every traditional hut has at least two that are used for resting, for visitors or for children during the day.

131

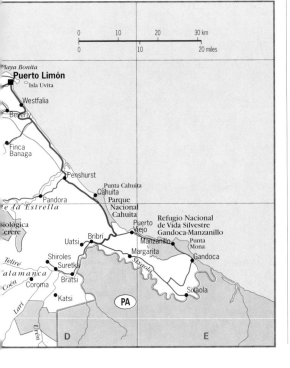

Pages 128–129: temperatures on the Caribbean coast can top 90°F, making Cahuita's waves a welcome relief

The Atlantic railroad

■ Costa Rica's jungle train ground to a halt in 1990 due to continuous landslides and lack of funds for repairs. Gone are the days of the seven-hour run from San José to Puerto Limón, but the railroad's effect on the country's development can still be felt. ■

Working for the Company "There was plenty of work in Andromeda. The Company needed to open a great swath through the mountains, breaking rocks on the riverbanks, filling and leveling and building bridges to carry a train through the marshy virgin forest, good for the cultivation of bananas, and in the process revive some of the plantations abandoned years earlier when the river had carried away the old railroad." Carlos Luis Fallas, *In the Shadow of the Banana Tree* (1941)

Construction took 20 years and was to tranform Costa Rica's economy, demography, and society. Before the railroad was completed, in 1890, the nation's burgeoning coffee exports were transported by a long and costly route from the port of Puntarenas, right round Cape Horn and from there to Europe. It soon became obvious that if Costa Rica was to prosper, a port had to be developed on the Atlantic coast, with easy access from the Central Valley's coffee plantations.

Hacking In 1870, the daunting contract went to Minor Cooper Keith, a young, worldly wise American who, within a few decades, rose from being a Texan pig farmer to one of Costa Rica's richest men and husband to the president's daughter. His first major task was to hack the 120-mile route from Cartago to Limón through rugged mountains, precipitous gorges, and dense jungle, in extreme climatic conditions. The laborers brought in from Italy and China for the job were devastated by diseases such as yellow fever and malaria, and also dysentery. About 4,000 died on the first 20-mile stretch alone, so Keith turned to the West Indies for sturdier workers who were better accustomed to the hot, humid climate.

Below: locomotive imported from Philadelphia in 1939

Debts and profits Meanwhile, Keith was juggling with the vast $8 million debt that had been contracted with British banks to finance the operation. His astute negotiations brought gratitude from the Costa Rican government in the form of huge tracts of land and the railroad concession itself. This propelled Keith and Costa Rica to the next economic catalyst: bananas. Conveniently situated alongside the railroad track, his new plantations flourished, and when the railroad was finally operational, bananas were in the freight alongside coffee. Keith was responsible for forming the notorious United Fruit Company.

132

► **Barra del Colorado** *130B5*

Located in the far northeast, this small town is internationally famous for sportfishing off the coast and in the adjoining wildlife refuge. It can only be reached by small plane or by boat, the latter from the north via the Río San Juan, from Puerto Lindo in the west or from Moín and Tortuguero to the south. The refuge covers 227,000 acres of channels, lagoons, islands, marshes, and hills crossed by three rushing rivers. Annual rainfall approaches 240 inches, flooding much of the low-lying land, leading rivers to change course, and nurturing a large mosquito population. Temperatures and humidity are permanently high, with rain only letting up significantly in March. Those willing to confront these extremes will enjoy great birdwatching and sportfishing, catered for by several lodges.

► **Bribrí** *131D1*

The tiny town of Bribrí forms the entrance to an Indian reserve that spreads along the Panamanian border southwest of Puerto Viejo. A handful of restaurants, shops, a bank, and an incongruous new courthouse make up the facilities. A right turn at the junction in front of the school takes you 1 mile to Uatsi (also called Volio), a scattered community known for its crafts. Follow the sign across a suspension bridge for one outlet, a cluster of thatched stilt-houses displaying gourds and baskets.

Back at the school junction, the left turn leads through beautiful, mountainous landscapes opening up to the southeast across the Río Sixaola. This is Panama, easily accessible by boat for local inhabitants who go there to shop. After entering the confines of the Bribrí reserve the gravel road reaches Shiroles, 11 miles from Bribrí. There is a good family restaurant, Se Yamida, here that also rents rooms. **En route** are hamlets and rural scenes of farmers leading cattle, and women washing or carrying baskets of vegetables on their heads. At Suretka is the innovative Centro Cultural Namsöl, run by the non-governmental organization CODEBRIWAK to defend indigenous rights (see panel).

Bribrí's central restaurant and bus stop is the social focal point for local indigenous communities

Indigenous awakening
The impressively equipped CODEBRIWAK is the sign of an increasing indigenous consciousness. Initially an informal committee, it is now a recognized association of the two main Talamancan Indian groups, the Bribrí and the Cabécar, who number some 7,000 altogether. Their health needs are catered for by only one clinic in Bribrí, and until recently there was no sociocultural education to keep their traditions alive. The activities of this center, built in traditional style, will at least supply the latter.

▶ **Cahuita**   *131D2*

Funky, laid-back, hip, and sometimes dangerous, Cahuita is the main beach center on the Caribbean coast. Lush vegetation, white sandy beaches fringed with classic, swaying coconut palms, and a lively tourist infrastructure have long made it a favorite with backpackers. It lies 27 miles southeast of Puerto Limón on a curved bay ending at Punta Cahuita (Cahuita Point), where you can still see flourishing examples of the sangregao trees, or *cawi*, from which the area probably derived its name (see panel). In June the trees' generous boughs burst into a mass of yellow flowers. This promontory forms the **Parque Nacional Cahuita▶▶▶**, a 2,637-acre park designed to protect over 54,000 acres of marine habitat, including extensive coral reefs.

Bearings There are three turn-offs to Cahuita from the coastal road, but all join up with the village's main street, which runs parallel to the beach. At the northern end, edging the beautiful black-sand beach of Playa Negra, are located the more upscale hotels and private residences, all set in lush, tropical gardens, while at the village center, where the beach mixes rocky stretches with sand, is the main concentration of budget *cabinas*, often run by friendly local families. Playa Cahuita, the jungle-backed white beach at the southeastern end, is part of the national park.

Rasta rules Life in Cahuita veers from hot Caribbean nocturnal rhythms to long, slow, steamy days punctuated by sudden downpours. Bars, restaurants, and tourist shops are plentiful, reggae music is everywhere, the English-speaking Afro-Caribbeans are outgoing, and Rasta style is part of Cahuita's image. However, this happy scene also includes a major problem—drugs—which has led to petty thefts and muggings. Occasionally the crime has been more serious. When an American tourist was murdered in 1994, local tourism temporarily fell by half. The shooting took place 9 miles to the north and, perhaps unjustly, Cahuita got the blame. No one is denying that the town does suffer from drug-related crime. Problems stem from Cahuita's role as a transshipment point from Colombia, and from a semi-permanent population of young travelers who have developed a taste for narcotic highs. Crack is the number one merchandise, and local police feel singularly ill-equipped to deal with it. Only three Guardia Rural officers patrol a coastal area stretching over 12 miles, and they have no motorized transportation. New measures were subsequently announced in San José, so the situation

Playa Negra has safe swimming, black sand, hammocks, and a string of cabinas

may improve. In the meantime, you should be extra-alert here, particularly after dark, and take sensible precautions.

Telephones and tours Telephone lines are limited and many hotels and restaurants use extensions, although this may change in the near future. Cahuita Tours (tel: 758-1515 ext 232, fax: 798-0652), on the main street, has a public phone, cashes travelers' checks, organizes snorkeling and glass-bottom boat tours of the reef, and runs tours to Tortuguero and the Bribrí reserve as well as renting bikes. Not far away, next to the Guardia Rural, is Moray's (tel: 758-1515 ext 216), which offers a similar range of services plus fishing trips and horse-trekking.

National park From the park ranger station at Playa Cahuita (*Open*: 8–4. *Admission charge* expensive), a 4-mile trail leads around the headland to Puerto Vargas, a lovely long beach that is good for snorkeling and has a campground near the second park entrance/exit. Winding in and out of the jungle and across Río Perezoso (Sloth River), the trail takes in a string of scenic and secluded beaches alive with fiddler and land crabs, where snorkeling means close encounters with over 120 species of tropical fish.

Inland, a wealth of palms and dense vegetation shelters raccoons, howler and white-faced monkeys, opossums, sloths, agoutis, armadillos, and porcupines, and the birdlife includes tricolored herons, magnificent frigatebirds, green ibises, and green kingfishers. Unfortunately, the 1991 earthquake caused extensive damage, toppling tall trees and destroying parts of the 1,500-acre coral reef, already suffering from agricultural pollutants, sedimentation, and illegal fishing activities.

135

Breadfruit tree
A typical tree of this region is the breadfruit (*Artocarpus incisus*), a descendant of southeast Asia's jackfruit. It was introduced to the West Indies from the Pacific in 1793 by Captain Bligh. From Jamaica, this tree came with early settlers to the province of Limón, and it now flourishes throughout the coastal region. The 65-foot evergreen has dark green, shiny lobed leaves that can reach 3 feet in length. Its large fruits, covered in a bumpy yellowish skin, contain a fibrous flesh that is fried, roasted, or boiled, and is high in carbohydrates.

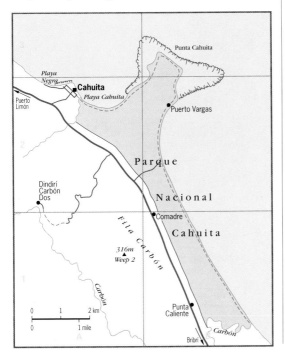

Punta Cahuita

Playa
Negra
■ **Cahuita**
Playa Cahuita

Puerto
Limón

Puerto Vargas

P a r q u e

Dindiri
Carbón
Dos

N a c i o n a l

●Comadre

C a h u i t a

Fila Carbón

316m
▲
Weep 2

Carbón

Punta
Caliente

0   1   2 km
0   1 mile

Carbón

Bribri

Local names
Limón province's cosmopolitan past is clearly demonstrated by names of small villages—some more imaginative than others. Within a 20-mile radius of Puerto Limón you can visit such cultural highlights as Venecia (Venice), Stratford, Bristol, Boston, Cuatro Millas (Four Miles), Westfalia, Bolivia, Beverly (not quite Hills), Larga Distancia (Long Distance), and, not least, Liverpool—the European port that welcomed Costa Rica's first coffee exports in 1843.

Commerce thrives in downtown Limón

Tourist help
Helennik Souvenirs Shop, Calle 8/Avenida 3 & 5 (tel: 758-2086) is an agent for budget tours to Tortuguero, and will help with other local information. Odysses Tours (tel: 758-1940, fax: 758-0824) organizes budget Tortuguero day trips.

► **Manzanillo** 131E1

The road south along Costa Rica's Atlantic coast ends just before Panama at the headlands of Punta Manzanillo and Punta Mona (Monkey Point). Just before lies the village of Manzanillo, not much in itself, but close to a number of imaginative beach hotels and at the heart of the **Refugio Nacional de Vida Silvestre Gandoca Manzanillo (Gandoca-Manzanillo Wildlife Refuge)►►**. Sea, coastline, marshes, and tropical rain forest come within its boundaries, but above all this is where you will find wild, remote white-sand beaches with sculptural, bleached driftwood, and hermit crabs your only companions, except from February to July, when leatherback turtles come to lay eggs. Coral reefs are only 200 yards from the shore, whose gentle slope and calm waters makes it ideal for swimming and snorkeling. In the southeast part of the refuge is the mangrove-lined Gandoca Estuary, home to crocodiles and oysters. There are no facilities in the refuge, which is reached by a 7-mile gravel road from Puerto Viejo. The best way to visit is by bike, taking in restaurant and beach stops, and allowing time to watch toucans, parakeets, and turkey vultures along the way.

► **Puerto Limón** 131D2

The decaying capital of the province of Limón is an ethnic melting pot, with a population of Jamaican, Antillais, European, Chinese, Tico, and indigenous descent. Many of their forebears came to Puerto Limón (usually shortened to Limón) in the 1870s to work on the railroad and later in the banana plantations of the United Fruit Company. Today, the port activities have been updated with new docks, and the local economy diversified by an electricity plant and large oil refinery. In typical tropical port tradition, Puerto Limón has a dual nature: rough and dangerous or colorfully exotic and extrovert, characteristics that peak during the carnival week in October. The brightly painted backstreet hovels may appear picturesque, but at all times visitors to Limón should be extra-streetwise, leave rented cars in hotel parking lots and avoid nocturnal strolls.

Crumbling glories The central grid of streets abuts a solid sea wall with, at its farthest point, the lovely Parque Vargas, a fading relic of Limón's heyday. Tropical shrubs, huge royal palms, and banyans encircle a leprous, ornately stuccoed old kiosk, all overlooked by brightly painted clapboard hotels and shops. From here you can take a breezy walk north beside the sea wall or head three blocks west to the Mercado Municipal, a vast, decrepit building whose

vendors and merchandise spill onto the streets. On the southwestern corner stands the old Correos (post office) resplendent with ice-cream-toned pink and green stucco.

The **Museo Etnohistórico de Limón**► (Avenida 1 & 2/Calle 2, tel: 758-2130/3903. *Open* Mon–Thur 2–5. *Admission charge* inexpensive) covers local indigenous and Afro-Caribbean culture, the history of the railroad, the port, and the arrival of Christopher Columbus. A different aspect of Limón's culture can be seen on the western outskirts of town, by the railway, at Collina China, a hillside cemetery blanketed with horseshoe-shaped Chinese tombs—decorative reminders of the burgeoning Chinese community.

Afro-Caribbean culture: a mural in the Parque Vargas, and inspired stucco decoration

Out and about Christopher Columbus's first steps on Costa Rican soil were made at Isla Uvita►►, a tiny uninhabited island that is situated about half a mile east of the port. It can be visited by rented boat. To the northwest of Limón toward Moín is **Playa Bonita**►, site of Limón's better hotels but badly polluted by the oil refinery. Less developed is neighboring **Playa Portete**►►, a pretty cove with clear, calm waters that invite swimming and snorkeling. Near the docks at the Paradero de Moín is an attractive tract of wild jungle.

Although the jungle train no longer functions, it is still possible to take a ride on its extension, the **banana freight train**►►, which runs south past Penshurst to the Valle de la Estrella. There are twice-daily departures from Limón station (Calle 8/Avenida 1 & 2) and the whole trip takes 1½ hours. It makes an unusual, sometimes monotonous ride through flat plantations and some forest, but entertainment in plenty is provided by village stops and encounters with local passengers who are keen to chat with visitors.

The muggy stillness
"The sky would suddenly get dark, the clouds thunder, the wind blow loudly, shaking the mountain, the howler monkeys would roar... and a minute later we'd be shoveling yellow mush and shivering from the cold... Then the sun fell on our backs again, drying out our clothes ... and again the muggy stillness and the suffocation of the sweat... then water again... then more sun. And that's how it went until noon almost every day."
Carlos Luis Fallas, *In the Shadow of the Banana Tree* (1941)

■ **Costa Rica's Afro-Caribbean community is concentrated along the Talamanca coast stretching south from Puerto Limón. After over a century of geographical and cultural isolation when Afro-Caribbeans were denied citizenship or any rights, they are now confronting the mitigated benefits of tourism.** ■

While fishing and farming still occupy some young Talamancans, many have acquired tastes from visitors— including the passion for surfing

138

Wh'appen man? Such is the leisurely greeting of Limón's Afro-Caribbeans, occasionally alternating with *How de morning*? or, more succinctly, *OK*? as they saunter past in their inimitably relaxed style. Costa Rican's minority black population, barely 5 percent of the country's total and under a third of Limón's inhabitants, cling proudly to their traditions and speak English-based Creole at home before learning Spanish in school. For over a century they have preserved their strong identity, partly because of the lack of any road down their coast and, before the 1949 Constitution, as a result of overt discrimination from the central government. Rasta-style beaded hair, a gregarious *carnaval*, Protestant churches, breadfruit, *pan bon,* and games of checkers are all part of the lifestyle in this still isolated corner of Central America.

Survival techniques The first Afro-Caribbean immigrants sailed to Costa Rica's shores in the early 19th century from Nicaragua's Miskito Coast and from Panama. Seasonal turtle-hunting and lobster- and crab-fishing drew them here but some eventually settled down to farm and trade with the Indians. Later that century a much larger influx from Jamaica and Barbados arrived to construct the Atlantic railroad and subsequently work on the flourishing banana plantations: their natural resilience was recognized and exploited. Others eked out an existence fishing from their dug-out canoes, selling tortoiseshell to European traders in Puerto Limón or cultivating root crops, breadfruit, mangoes and limes that they had brought from their Caribbean islands. Coconut palms shot up the length of the lush coast, providing essential food and oil, and cacao later became an important crop, although in the 1970s the *monilia* fungus destroyed most cacao plantations.

Today, many educated Afro-Caribbeans have left the province for San José or further afield in search of more profitable, professional activities. Those that remain have entered the fray of tourism, which has taken off since the coast road was completed in 1979.

Tumbledown houses
"A trip on a bus took them past tumbledown houses whose porches were filled with black youngsters of all sizes, their naked bellies sporting their navels like misplaced buttons. They waved their arms wildly, greeting the driver. Watching the bus go by was probably one of their favorite diversions and helped them forget the hunger pangs that racked their young bodies. You could see the misery in the houses that were falling apart, in the people dressed in rags, and in the haggard faces of the old folks with their dark stooped bodies."
Julieta Pinto, *The Blue Fish* (1963)

Callaloo and rundown Along with Caribbean island agriculture, these newcomers brought with them culinary traditions, animist beliefs about nature and life, Creole English and customs adopted from the British colonists. English-language bibles are still used, and the older generation remember playing cricket, dancing the quadrille and even performing Shakespeare in their coastal villages. The names of respected women are preceded by Miss. Miss Edith in Cahuita, Miss Sam in Puerto Viejo, Miss Junie in Tortuguero, and Miss Marva in Manzanillo are the magicians behind local gastronomy, whipping up cassava dishes, callaloo soup, or rundown, a fish or meat stew with yams, plantains, breadfruit, peppers, and spices boiled in rich coconut milk. Johnny cakes (originally "journey cakes"), *pan bon* (from the English word "bun" or possibly from the French for "good bread", *pain bon*), ginger biscuits, plantain tarts, and *patti* (a spicy meat pie) are eaten washed down with herbal teas made from wild peppermint, soursop or lime leaves, lemongrass, or ginger.

African heritage
Before the days of books, radios, and TV, which is still rare on the Talamanca coast, local inhabitants would amuse their families by storytelling—a custom that had been passed on down the generations since their ancestors left Africa, but is far from common now. One of the most popular protagonists was Anansi the spider, a narrative vehicle used to explain the mysteries of the world and human behavior in whimsical fashion. His activities changed in tune with society: 20th-century versions feature Anansi scheming for the riches of a white landowner.

Carnaval! Every October 12 (*El Día de la Raza*, "the People's Day") Limón's Afro-Caribbeans abandon their daily routine for one memorable week, to sway to calypso sounds in a riotous carnival. Unlike their West Indian and Brazilian counterparts, they are celebrating not Lent but the anniversary of Columbus's first steps on Costa Rican soil, near Puerto Limón. This annual celebration that started in 1949 reaches a high point when a glittering, brilliantly colored parade of floats and dance-groups staggers along the streets to the irresistible sounds of steel bands, whistles, maracas, and even recycled kitchen pans. Dancing, singing, drinking, eating, and smoking grass are the characteristics of the carnival, but violence and pickpocketing are now equally common. Attitudes are changing as there is an increase in the number of foreigners, lifestyles far from the upfront friendliness of *Wh'appen*?

Over the border
An increasingly popular destination lies over the Panamanian border near Puerto Viejo, in the beautiful archipelago surrounding Bocas del Toro. Crystalline water, unspoilt beaches, jungle, an English-speaking Afro-Caribbean culture, atmospheric old hotels, and above all world-class scuba-diving and snorkeling await you in this peaceful backwater. You can get there by taking the bus to the border at Sixaola, then a Panamanian bus to Changuinola, where a 10-minute flight wings you to Bocas. Alternatively continue to the port of Almirante where there is a cheap water-taxi service. Organize your visa in advance in San José.

Locals offer basic sportfishing and snorkeling trips

▶▶▶ **Puerto Viejo**   *131D1*

Strung along the shore for several miles is the burgeoning beach community of Puerto Viejo, originally a tiny fishing village. Relaxed and friendly, supremely tropical with luxuriant vegetation, croaking nocturnal frogs and scuttling blue land crabs, Puerto Viejo successfully blends low-key western services with a high-profile Afro-Caribbean culture. Although not as threatening as Cahuita or Puerto Limón, it does have theft problems so, again, take precautions and be alert.

Slow genesis As with Cahuita, the access road here was not completed until 1979, electricity was not widely available until 1988, and phones are still scarce and unreliable. Many of the inhabitants have transformed their village homes into *cabinas*, while an imaginative range of more upscale accommodations, often foreign-owned, spreads 6 miles eastward along the gravel road, past blissful Playa Cocles, Playa Chiquita and **Punta Uva▶▶▶** towards **Manzanillo▶** (see page 136). Here, tall coconut palms edge white sands scattered with driftwood, and there are coral colonies in the turquoise waters offshore. Surfers ride *La Salsa Brava* at the point, especially from December to April, but other, more protected areas with gentle slopes offer good swimming and snorkeling, particularly outside those months. Immediately west of Puerto Viejo, along the main road (with a bridge that occasionally collapses in heavy rain), is a long black-sand beach, safe for swimming and backed by a few hotels.

Local initiative A helpful and efficient source of information here is the office of ATEC (Asociación Talamanqueña de Ecoturismo y Conservación, tel/fax: 798-4244), a non-profit-making grassroots organization aiming to promote ecologically sound tourism and small, local businesses. This dynamic group plays an essential community role and organizes nature walks, visits to the nearby Kéköldi Indian reserve, rain forest hikes, horse-trekking, snorkeling and fishing trips, and Tortuguero tours, all accompanied by local guides and reasonably priced. Their office on the main east–west street of Puerto Viejo, opposite Soda Tamara, provides a public phone service and sells publications related to the Talamanca coastal area. The other public phone is at Hotel Maritza near the bus stop.

Next door to ATEC, a private house rents bikes, the best way to get around, and a couple of blocks inland from the bright green church is the *panadería*, where you can stock up on delicious local pastries for the beach. Puerto Viejo has several good restaurants, bars and *sodas*, one early

morning spot (6AM) being a nameless hole-in-the-wall opposite the bus stop on the harbor. Discos and bars are still limited, but many larger hotels outside the village have extensive facilities.

Limpid light after the rain brings out Puerto Viejo's fishermen

▶▶ Reserva Biológica Hitoy Cerere   *130C1*

The name of this remote 22,000-acre reserve derives from Bribrí words meaning respectively "woolly" (referring to moss that blankets the river boulders) and "clear water." Water is the main feature of this underexplored reserve that rises into the Talamanca mountains from the Valle de la Estrella. Very moist rain forest laden with epiphytes, towering trees rising to 160 feet, ferns, numerous rivers, waterfalls, and extremely high humidity greet the few visitors who penetrate it. The 115 (at least) species of bird here include toucans, owls, kingfishers, cuckoos, turkey vultures, and the Montezuma oropendola, whose pendulous nests are common sights. Other inhabitants include tapirs, jaguars, sloths, opossums, howler and white-faced monkeys, and a large variety of frogs, snakes and butterflies. If possible, visit with a guide, as trails are virtually nonexistent. The ranger's station, camping facilities, and entrance lie about 6 miles southwest of Pandora. Access requires four-wheel drive, though taxis can be hired.

▶ Río Estrella   *130C2*

After flowing down the foothills of the Matama range, the Estrella river irrigates the banana plantations of the Valle de la Estrella before reaching the ocean near Penshurst, 5 miles north of Cahuita. The dense network of navigable channels and lagoons is home to over 280 bird species, above all waterfowl, and there is a 240-acre private wildlife sanctuary, **Aviarios del Caribe▶▶**, with accommodations, located right on the estuary. Caymans, crocodiles, sloths, and howler monkeys also inhabit the area.

Getting to Puerto Viejo
The bumpy coastal road from Limón to Sixaola on the Panamanian border was badly damaged by the 1991 earthquake, and its bridges still suffer from the torrential rains that rarely let up in this region. Bus travellers can reach Puerto Viejo directly from Limón, with six daily departures and a trip that takes roughly 1½ hours, depending on the number of passengers. This same bus serves Cahuita and Bribrí or Manzanillo. There are also three daily direct buses from San José to Sixaola (leaving from Calle Central/Avenida 11) but these only stop at the turning (*el cruce*) to Puerto Viejo on the main road, a 3-mile hike from the village. One daily bus links San José directly with Puerto Viejo, a four-hour trip.

Rain, rain, rain
It never seems to stop raining in Tortuguero, and lodges are all well prepared with rain-ponchos and boots. Torrential annual rainfall approaches 240 inches, with 85–90 percent humidity during the so-called "dry season" and 95–99 percent in the wet season, making average temperatures of 78°F seem far higher. In September and October alone, rainfall is equivalent to the entire annual rainfall of Cartago or of Santa Rosa national park. The rain can last for several days on end, though it subsides in March.

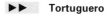

▶▶ **Tortuguero** 130B4

Turtles, birds, and cruising through jungle-lined waterways are the temptations of Tortuguero, a name that refers to a river, a village, a hill, and a national park. Most people come to this isolated region by organized tour from San José, either by bus and boat or directly by small plane, and stay in comfortable lodges along the main canal. However, it is possible to visit Tortuguero on a low-budget tour from Puerto Limón, Cahuita or Puerto Viejo, and stay in simple *cabinas* in the main village. Arriving here independently requires negotiating boat rates at Moín, which may be expensive unless you are in a group.

Water, water... The park covers nearly 47,000 acres of swamps, lagoons, waterways, and rain forest bordering a long, wild, straight beach where three species of turtles come periodically to nest. One main canal runs 43 miles south of Tortuguero through Parismina to Moín and continues 22 miles north of the park to Barra del Colorado. It is crisscrossed by numerous rivers, tributaries and minor canals, and all these together create the local community's only transportation system. Before the canals were developed in the 1970s, Tortuguero's few residents had to walk down the beach or paddle along circuitous rivers to reach Puerto Limón. Today the canals are the region's lifeline, with dug-out canoes, barges, and motorboats hauling livestock, construction materials, gasoline, food—and tourists.

Village interest Most points of interest, the airstrip and accommodations are located in or near the village of Tortuguero, at the base of a skinny spit of land that creates a secondary waterway. Hotels on this side (Mawamba Lodge, Laguna Lodge and village *cabinas*) have the advantage of direct access to the beach for turtle-watching, though dangerous currents make swimming impossible. Village facilities include a handful of souvenir shops and *sodas*, and the Centro Social Turistico La Culebra, which rents canoes and organizes boat journeys. A guide and ticket are necessary for nocturnal turtle-watching in season: ask at the information kiosk near the football field.

At the village center, the **Tortuguero Natural History Museum** (tel: 710-0547. *Open* daily 10–noon, 2–5:30. *Admission charge* inexpensive) provides an excellent introduction to green turtles, and has displays on local flora and fauna, related publications, and a short video. It is run by the pioneering CCC (Caribbean Conservation Corporation), founded in 1954 by an American biologist, Dr. Archie Carr, who lobbied for 20 years to have the park

Count on a deluge in Tortuguero: lodges are designed for them

and vital turtle protection established. Turtle research continues at a new, full-time station, although the original Casa Verde has been dismantled to build a local school.

Forest The main entrance to the **Parque Nacional Tortuguero** (*Open* 8–4 daily. *Admission charge* expensive) lies at the southern end of the village. Park rangers are particularly helpful to independent visitors, as most tourist groups arrive with their own guide. Trails lead from here through swamp forest where you may encounter a deadly, 6-foot-long fer-de-lance, white-tailed deer, white-collared peccaries, racoons, tapirs, anteaters, otters, or three species of monkeys. Glass-frogs, red-eyed tree frogs, and Jesus-Christ lizards, so-called because they walk on water, are relatively common.

More rain forest can be visited at the **Caño Palma biological station**, a 15-minute boat ride from the village. This Canadian conservation organization offers short but informative accompanied hikes through secondary growth rain forest (*Admission charge* donation). Longer treks can be organized with village guides into very humid tropical rain forest around the modestly scaled, 1,020-foot Lomas de Sierpe, or to Cerro Tortuguero (390 feet), a few miles north of the village.

Whitewater rafting
The torrential Río Pacuare rushes down the slopes of the Cordillera Central before coursing through the swamps of Tortuguero and finally ending in the Caribbean. It is attracting increasing numbers of whitewater enthusiasts, who revel in fast currents and rapids offering Class III and IV rides. Aventuras Naturales (tel: 225-3939, fax: 221-8686) organizes rafting excursions combined with accommodation in a beautiful jungle lodge, also a good spot for birdwatching.

The jungle-lined waterways attract flocks of bird-watchers

Birds Tortuguero has more than 300 species, including migratory birds from North America. Hawks, falcons, flycatchers, and ospreys join great green macaws, curassows, trogons, kingfishers, and oropendolas, and numerous waterbirds such as herons, egrets, and cormorants. Any boat trip through the narrow channels, lined with huge clumps of multi-stemmed raffia palms, is accompanied by a melodious soundtrack of jungle cries, and rich bird watching opportunities.

■ **Underwater in Costa Rica means not only exploring the aquamarine depths by scuba-diving or snorkeling, but also juggling with giant snook, blue marlin, and sailfish from a sportfishing boat in ecologically correct "catch and release" style. Business is definitely booming out there in the deep blue sea.** ■

Coral etiquette

Coral is a living organism made up of millions of tiny coral polyps, cup-shaped creatures consisting of a ring of tentacles surrounding a mouth. Many corals resemble plants but they are in fact carnivorous animals, feeding on plankton that float in the sea and are caught with tentacles charged with stinging cells. These organisms are extremely fragile and one break can set off a destructive chain reaction that may affect a whole reef. Do not collect coral from the seabed, and make sure your diving operator anchors outside the reef.

Fishing permits

Fishing licenses are necessary to fish in Costa Rica, and freshwater fishing is subject to strict seasons. Sportfishing operators will carry out the necessary formalities for deep-sea fishing, but anglers heading for inland rivers need to obtain permits in San José and to be able to present them, together with their passport, to any wildlife rangers. A good source of information about seasons and permits is the San José fishing-tackle shop, Desportes Keko, Calle 20/ Avenida 4 & 6, tel: 223-4142.

In a country with more than 600 miles of coastline, squeezed between two great oceans, marine activities understandably play a large role. Coral reefs once edged most of the coastline, but natural disasters such as earthquakes and the Niño phenomenon have combined with man-made destruction to reduce their area drastically. Sportfishers, on the other hand, find themselves riding the waves of one of the world's best arenas, although commercial overfishing is taking its toll here too.

Top corals Number one destination for seasoned scuba-divers is the pristine aquatic universe of the remote Isla del Coco, lying off the Pacific coast. Crustaceans and molluscs join 18 species of coral and 200 fish species, including white-tipped sharks, giant hammerhead sharks, tuna, parrotfish, mantarays, and crevalle jacks. If your budget does not stretch to such exotic depths, then the next best destination is the Caribbean. Plunge into the waters off Cahuita's national park, and enter a world where 35 species of coral form a captivating backdrop to about 123 types of brilliantly patterned tropical fish, as well as sea urchins, lobsters, turtles, eels and sharks. This reef has, however, suffered from sedimentation caused by banana plantations.

Caribbean Less damaged but also off a less accessible coast are the 1,200 acres of coral reef that edge the Gandoca-Manzanillo refuge; the coral colonies off Puerto Viejo also make good snorkeling destinations. For the moment Costa Rica's Caribbean coast has limited diving facilities: Viajes Tropicales Laura (tel/fax: 758-2410) is the local operation in Puerto Limón, and Cahuita has Cahuita Tours (tel: 758-1515 ext 232). Sportfishing is, in contrast, well catered for, at the lodges of Barra del Colorado, where enthusiasts indulge in magnificent tarpon and snook fishing (said to be the world's best), above all from January to June, when these determined creatures start their 120 mile haul up the Río Colorado to reach Lake Nicaragua. At the beach resorts to the south, this sport becomes a case of "catch a local fisherman" first, as there are no specialist operators and visitors must organize their own equipment. Small wooden boats are launched by being rolled down the beach on logs, a far cry from the sophisticated, often American-operated vessels of the Pacific.

Pacific highlights On the more developed Pacific coast, scuba diving is much higher on the agenda, with numerous dive-shops operating out of large hotels at the main beaches of the Península de Nicoya, and at Bahía Drake, Manuel Antonio, Puntarenas, and Dominical. Spectacular tropical fish are guaranteed on this side around the Isla del Caño and also around the protected islands of Manuel Antonio and Marino Ballena, although reefs are limited. This, too, is where deep-sea sportfishing enjoys year-long popularity thanks to the plentiful snapper, tuna, wahoo, rooster, shark, snook, dorado, sailfish, and marlin, though they peak in abundance between May and August. Costa Rica's first sportfishing operators concentrated on the Golfo de Papagayo, where hefty 110-pound sailfish indulge in fantastic acrobatics, but countless individuals and agencies now offer their services at other Guanacaste beach resorts, above all around Flamingo, Nosara and Sámara, as well as farther south at Quepos, Golfito, and Playa Zancudo.

Top: queen angel fish
Above: Sally Lightfoot crab

Fresh water Fishing is not confined to the oceans. *Guapote* (rainbow bass), *bobo* (mullet), and *machacha* (*Brycon guatemalensis*) flourish in Costa Rica's mineral-rich rivers, while mountain streams at higher altitudes, such as those at San Gerardo de Dota, are rich in rainbow trout. Although initially introduced, trout have since bred naturally. The most popular spot for freshwater fishing is Laguna de Arenal, as this is where challenging *guapote* reach up to 13 pounds. Gaining in popularity too are the lagoons and rivers of Caño Negro, offering a combination of freshwater fish and huge migrating tarpon and snook fresh from the Caribbean.

THE SOUTH

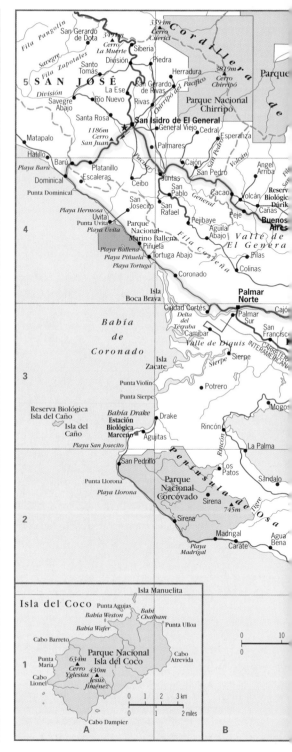

Previous page: Golfito's water-village, squeezed between rain forest and the Golfo Dulce

Map labels

Teliré
Shiroles
Suretka
Margarita
Sixaola
Valle de Talamanca
Coén
San José Cabécar
Coroma
Bratsi
Katsi
Teliré
2435m
Cerro Puiñbeta
Fila Dúrika
LIMÓN
Internacional
3280m
Cerro Dúrika
Lari
Uyén
3078m
Cerro Utyum
La Amistad
3549m
Cerro Kámuk
Ujarrás
Talamanca
3122m
Cerro Nai
2558m
Cerro Aká
PA
Cabagra
Mosca
Heléchales
Brujo
Cabagra
érraba
Paso Real
Potrero Grande
oruca
General
3162m
Cerro Echandi
Zona
Protectora
Las Tablas
Curré
Valle de Coto Brus
Coto Brus
Cotón
Alturas
2486m
Cerro Pando
érraba
Vueltas
Coto Brus
Santa Elena
Chánguena
Jabillo
Sabanilla
Gutiérrez Braun
NTARENAS
Fila
Brisas
Venecia
Limóncito
San Vito
Sabalito
hacanta
1707m
Cerro Anguciana
Limón
Linda Vista
La Navidad
Piedras Blancas
Esquinas
Guaria
Wilson Botanical Gardens
Costeña
Briceño
Agua Buena
Cañas Gordas
Parque Nacional Las Equinas
Gamba
Refugio Nacional de Fauna Silvestre Golfito
Río Claro
Caracol
Ciudad Neily
laya ativo
san Josecito
Golfito
Playa Cacao
Unión
Coto
47
Coloradito
Golfo Dulce
Zancudo
Colorado
Pueblo Nuevo
Colorado
Paso Canoas
Playa Platanares
Puerto iménez
Playa Zancudo
Sábalos
Pavones
Valle de Coto Colorado
La Cuesta
Playa Tamales
Bahía de Pavón
Laurel
Conte
Vaca
Playa Sombrero
Puerto González Víquez
Cabo Matapalo
Punta Banco
Higo
Nicaragua
20   30 km
10   20 miles
Bahía de Charco Azul
See drive pages 174–175
Península de Burica
C
Punta Burica
Isla Burica   D

The back-packing naturalist

If you have the luxury of an extended vacation, then opt for at least one back-packing trek into hill country. Always bear in mind the increased strain caused by altitude and remember to drink plenty of nonalcoholic fluid. Naturalists should make the best possible use of the mornings since low cloud and fog often form by midday, making wildlife observation difficult, if not impossible. Arguably the single best piece of advice for a backpacker in Costa Rica is always to stuff your socks into your shoes at night, as scorpions and large spiders have an uncanny way of finding their way into these seemingly safe refuges!

149

THE SOUTH

Rancho life
As you head south you enter the land of the *rancho* (hut), a typical indigenous construction that is also seen in the Península de Nicoya and in the Bribrí reserve on the Caribbean side. Although every Indian community has its variation, the basic structure consists of wooden poles joined by bamboo and rattan, with a palm-leaf thatch. The thatch can last up to 30 years if a fire is kept lit inside: the wood smoke forms a protective layer that prevents it from rotting during the rainy season. A common feature inside used to be a termites' nest, sections of which were spooned onto the fire to produce a fragrant white smoke that kept insects at bay.

A view of the mountain town of San Vito and the surrounding coffee plantations

The South Costa Rica's south encompasses some of the wildest, and also poorest, areas of the entire country. It possesses the most acreage of protected areas, the highest mountain, longest river, largest delta, most biologically diverse of the nation's rain forests—and an immense amount of rain. Its western coast borders the cobalt blue Pacific, but compared with other zones the south remains undeveloped for tourism. Those travelers that do come here revel in the experience.

Contrasts run deep From San José to Paso Canoas on the Panamanian border it is only 220 miles. However, the contrast between the two is enormous, and on the way from one to the other you could take in the biologically vital international park of La Amistad, go through dense and sometimes dangerous jungle in Corcovado, plunge underwater at Marino Ballena, swim with dolphins around the magical Isla del Caño, explore the Wilson Botanical Gardens, or kayak the gentle waters of the beautiful Golfo Dulce. Sybarites and surfers should head for Dominical, a community that is slowly expanding thanks to the recent completion of the *costanera sur,* the road down the southwest coast that links Quepos with Palmar Norte, or venture farther south to Playa Zancudo and tiny coves dotted around the gulf northwest of Golfito.

Adventure package Jungle, mountain, and beachfront lodges are scattered across this region. They are often isolated, usually blighted (or blessed?) by terrible roads and nearly all claim to be environmentally concerned. Some possess large private reserves, making for convenient birdwatching or hiking. Many lodges offer

package deals from San José, including access by small plane rather than road, so taking the sweat out of the journey. This is ideal for visitors with limited time but it does mean that you miss out on the sense of adventure and odd encounters that highlight a trip by bumpy road. Telephone systems are still backward down here, and many places rely on radio communication. A number of hotels and ecotourism centers use Selva Mar (tel/fax: 771 1903) as a central booking agency, while others have agents in local towns.

Civilization? The main towns in this region are San Isidro, the gateway to the south; Golfito, the old United Fruit Company banana town, now frequented by Ticos for its duty-free status; Palmar Norte/Sur, home to pre-Columbian stone spheres; and, for tourists and gold-panners, the tiny port of Puerto Jiménez. Add to these the prosperous modern coffee-town of San Vito and you have the limited selection. Between these scattered outposts lie vast plantations of pineapples, bananas, and oil palms, and huge tracts of forest, on the slopes of the imposing Talamanca range that forms the southern backbone, on hills towering high above the Pacific, and in the sweltering, low-lying Península de Osa.

Wilderness High up in the enormous Reserva de la Biósfera La Amistad (La Amistad Biosphere Reserve), you may encounter only tiny Indian villages, and beyond these, nothing. Wildlife relishes this vast, untouched and unpopulated region, and scientists are moving in to study it, recognizing this as Central America's greatest biological laboratory. Visitors can catch a glimpse of this wildlife wealth by trekking to the summit of Chirripó, but the park of La Amistad itself is still difficult to access. In contrast, Corcovado has good facilities, and it is now rivaled by its former annex, the recently created national park of Las Esquinas, just north of Golfito.

Indigenous life The south is where Costa Rica's largest concentrations of indigenous people live, mostly in loosely defined reserves. Boruca Indians make a living from handicrafts along with subsistence farming, and are quite happy to show off their crafts to visitors, although the latter should behave sensitively. Indigenous peoples are regaining confidence in their cultural traditions, which for generations have been repressed, by design or default. The Chirripó region is home to the Cabécar, while the Guaymi are scattered between Coto Brus valley, the Panamanian border and the Península de Osa.

151

Bushmaster snake

Sir Francis Drake
In March 1579, Sir Francis Drake pulled into Playa Colorada (at the northern end of Bahía Drake) to overhaul his ship, the *Golden Hind*, before resuming his circumnavigation of the globe. Depending on one's viewpoint, Drake was either a pirate or a great explorer, but the Costa Rican government saw fit to erect a plaque in his honor in Agujitas, 400 years after he landed there.

▶▶▶ **Bahía Drake**   148A3

This sweeping bay on the Pacific side of the Península de Osa has become a popular base for trekking into the Parque Nacional Corcovado (see pages 162–163), and for bird-watching, horse riding, sportfishing, sailing, snorkeling, and diving or swimming in transparent waters off exquisite untouched beaches. This is one of Costa Rica's jewels, discovered over 400 years ago by Sir Francis Drake on his circumnavigation of the globe. Access to the bay is by a two- to three-hour boat-ride along the Río Sierpe from Sierpe itself, and the negotiation of powerful waves and currents where the river hits the ocean can be an adrenalin-raising experience.

The small town of Drake lies at the northern end, but it is around Agujitas at the southern headland that most accommodations are concentrated, including the pioneering Drake Bay Wilderness Camp, the luxury Aguila de Osa Inn, and some more affordable places near the tiny village. Just beyond the point lies **Estación Biológica Marenco (Marenco Biological Reserve)**, where 1,200 acres of rain forest, edging superb beaches and the Río Claro, are now devoted to efficiently run ecotourism. All lodges in this area arrange day trips to the Isla del Caño (see page 156), visible on the horizon, and most have biologist guides who accompany treks into Corcovado. The only limit to the scope of outdoor activities is your budget, so come prepared. Wildlife is omnipresent, from unpleasant no-see-ums (sand fleas) on some of the beaches to scarlet macaws and toucans that swoop around the lodges (plus the mosquitoes and a spider or two that enhance your cabin).

▶ **Boruca**   149C4

The isolated home of the Boruca Indian community (see pages 158–159) lies high up in the dry hills above Palmar Norte. Access is either from the south by a rough 5 mile-road (requiring four-wheel drive) or by a marginally more manageable road, used by buses, which branches off the Interamerican Highway at Brujo. This sprawling village is the source of most of the Borucan baskets and weavings sold around the country, and local women will happily demonstrate their craft, particularly if you buy something. Men apply themselves to carving spears, gourds, and balsa wood masks, when not tending their corn and beans. A small thatched building houses the Museo Indigena de Boruca (*Open* any time. *Admission charge* inexpensive) and also sells some handicrafts. There is one very basic *cabina* and daily bus connections with Buenos Aires, which has a bus link with San Isidro (see page 170).

▶▶ Dominical   148A4

This tropical beachside community seems poised for development now that the *costanera sur* (coast road) from Quepos has been improved. Foreigners are snapping up tracts of hillside of an enchanting area called Escaleras that rises abruptly—with breathtaking views—from the coast. Some interesting hotels are developing here, but access requires four-wheel drive. The future of this idyllic spot is thus decidedly in the balance, but it still offers a relaxed setting at the mouth of the lazy Río Barú, with decent, mainly low-budget facilities, a couple of low-low-key nightclubs, and small hotels scattered several miles south. Telephones are scarce so most residents rely on radio communication, but one of the advantages of being in an overwhelmingly foreign community is that there is a strong sense of cooperation —if you need information, ask around. The notice board at the San Clemente restaurant is also a good source.

Activities Best for swimming is the sheltered, though rocky Playa Dominicalito, 2 miles south or, for a small fee, the large pool of the landscaped Río Mar hotel. Meanwhile, surfers slalom the waves on Dominical's main beach. Other potential includes diving and snorkeling trips to the Marino Ballena reserve (see page 164) with Dominical Dive Center (tel: 771-1903), water-taxis to Bahía Drake, river-kayaking (contact Albergue Willdale), biking and boogie-boarding, as well as horse riding through superb rain forest to the double Nauyaca waterfall and its huge swimming hole (Centro Turistico Nauyaca, tel: 771-4468/3187). North of the river lies the pioneering Hacienda Barú (tel: 771-1903), an American-owned ecotourism center that offers accommodations and trekking.

Hacienda Barú

This pioneering private reserve was set up in the early 1970s by Jack and Diane Ewing, who now work with a new partner, Steve Shroud. The 790 acres of land encompass an immense ecological variety, from primary tropical wet forest to regenerated forest, mangroves, fruit orchards, scrub, beach, and cacao plantations. The numerous attractions include night-hikes, camping in the jungle, horseback tours, rain forest trekking, and, a recent innovation, a platform 115 feet up in the jungle canopy. An ongoing dream is to create an ecological corridor linking Corcovado, Barú and Cerro La Muerte.

153

Dominical—idyllic, but for how much longer?

Typical frame-houses in the Zona Americana

▶▶ **Golfito** 149C2

A strange destiny awaited this languishing banana port when in 1990 it was declared a duty-free zone. Ticos now flock here to stock up on their quota of duty-free goods, especially electro-domestic appliances, at the huge warehouses of the Depósito Libre, and as a result the town has been regenerated. Golfito occupies a superb site on a narrow strip of land between sheer forested mountains and the calm waters of an almost enclosed bay opening onto the Golfo Dulce. Much of the surrounding land is protected as a wildlife refuge, where tall hardwoods laden with epiphytes and 146 bird species are encouraged by Golfito's abundant rain. Remember that when it rains in Golfito it can average 27 inches in a month, October being the worst.

Dual centers From the airstrip and duty-free complex at the northern end, Golfito's only road enters the sprucer Zona Americana. This was the headquarters of the United Fruit Company, which from 1938 until 1985 (when union troubles led to closure) dominated the area's economy, and where executives lived in elegant frame houses surrounded by lawns. Many of these have now been converted to guest houses aimed at the big shoppers. South of the Hotel del Cerro, which fronts the old banana company wharf (*muelle bananero*), is Golfito's other persona, the Pueblo Civil. This is the livelier side of town, characterized by a typically decrepit tropical port atmosphere, boatyards, bars and a water-village tumbling into the gulf. At the southern end are some upscale hotels and restaurants with lovely gulf views.

Rent a boat Swinging round the southern end of the bay is the Golfito peninsula, home to the Jungle Club, an essential watering and feeding hole for yachters, while the Sanbar Marina, also at this end, is where foreign yachts dock and sportfishing can be arranged. More practically, water-taxis can whizz you across the water to Puerto Jiménez or south to Playa Zancudo and Pavones: contact the Asociación de Boteros (tel: 775-0712) at the *muelle bananero* for rates and bookings. There is a 24-hour guarded parking lot, so car drivers can take long excursions without worrying. Any boat trip may include

Duty-free
Ticos are allowed to invest in $400 worth of duty-free goods twice a year if they first spend 24 hours in Golfito, a law that on some weekends can make the town nightmarish. Specially chartered "shopping" buses descend on the port, *cabinas* fill up, and hordes of shopping families, laden with kitchen appliances or TVs, monopolize the taxis. Foreigners can make purchases at the Depósito Libre, but imported items are still heavily taxed, and so not necessarily a bargain.

sightings of dolphins, flying fish, or splashing manta rays. For swimmers, clean, palm-fringed Playa Cacao on Golfito's northern headland is the closest beach, accessible by a rough road from the duty-free zone, or by a five-minute boat-ride. Several reasonably priced hotels and *cabinas* are here, including the legendary Shipwreck Hotel, founded some 40 years ago by the late, one-legged Captain Tom.

Sausage tree

Water-babies The coast northwest of Golfito is lined with secluded, jungle-backed beaches and lush, forested headlands, obvious targets for ecotourism projects. The only means of access is by boat, but a 30-minute ride can bring you to paradisical spots such as Punta Encanto, with its rustic lodge, nature trails, waterfall and sublime sunsets. Next stop up the coast on Playa San Josecito is **Casa de Orquidéa** (*Open* Sun–Thu 7–10AM), a well-established private botanical garden with an inspiring collection of bromeliads, heliconia, cycads (also-called "living fossils"), palms, and orchids. Farther on is Playa Cativo, where a decidedly upscale lodge occupies a 1,000-acre private reserve. Strangest of all, however, is Dolphin Quest, a New Age project run by Calfornian maritime spiritualists. If you want to communicate telepathically with dolphins, meditate beneath a waterfall, or have your child born on a raft in mid-ocean, this is where to go.

Save the forest A road north from Golfito's duty-free zone leads to Gamba and a remarkable ecotourism project conceived by the Austrian violinist Michael Schnitzler in 1991. It has since raised over $600,000 to help the Costa Rican government purchase 3,950 acres of tropical rain forest, now known as the Parque Nacional Las Esquinas. An attractive rain forest lodge that obeys every possible precept of ecotourism has been constructed, as well as a biological research station. Local farmers and former loggers at Gamba have cooperated extensively with the entire project.

Sausages that grow on trees
Heard the one about the tree that grows sausages? One of Costa Rica's few specimens stands in a garden of Golfito's Zona Americana. The lofty, wide-spreading tree, *Kigelia africana*, grows sausage-shaped fruits, weighing up to 13 pounds and measuring some 20 inches long, that dangle on cordlike strings from the branches for several months, getting larger and softer with age. These curious gray fruits are not edible, but are used for external medicinal purposes in Africa.

155

The Golfo Dulce

▶▶ **Isla del Caño** 148A3

This magical little island lies 12 miles west of Bahía Drake and has been protected since 1978 as a biological reserve. Deep turquoise waters and low coral reefs attract divers and snorkelers to explore a rich aquatic world, full of giant conches, limpets, mollusks, lobsters, and sea urchins. Polychromatic shoals of tropical fish flit through the rocks while dolphins play in the waves. Diving is best off the northwest corner but snorkelers can plunge in from the beautiful main beach, also ideal for swimming. Unfortunately, much of the reef has been destroyed by the periodic Niño phenomenon (a mass of abnormally warm water that rises to the surface of the Pacific, creating freak weather patterns).

One of the baffling stone spheres peculiar to the Isla del Caño and the Palmar area

Deep past The 500-acre island has produced a wealth of artifacts, giving rise to various theories about its past, one being that it was a pre-Columbian cemetery, although it is known to have been inhabited about 500 years ago. Gold votive offerings, tombs with stone statues and puzzling stone spheres were unearthed in the middle of the island, most of which were taken to San José's museums. Today, only a few minor artifacts are displayed and even these are disappearing thanks to some light fingers.

Tree milk A one-hour trail to the site leads from the beach-front ranger's hut (*Open* 8–4. *Admission charge* moderate) up the steep slopes to a high plateau thick with shady fig, locust and rubber trees, wild cacao and the cow tree. The cow tree, the *Brosimum utile,* is thought to have been planted by Indians for its high-protein white latex, once used as milk for new-born babies and for pregnant women, though this is now prohibited. Although there is little other wildlife, Caño has a wide variety of snakes (boa constrictors, grass snakes, chunk-headed snakes, and the poisonous sea snake), as well as a phenomenal variety of epiphytic plants, above all giant philodendrons, bromeliads, and monkey-ladder lianas.

Mystery spheres
The people of Palmar (see opposite page) are justly proud of their mysterious inheritance and, in the early 1980s, when the San José administration tried to sequester two examples (now in Palmar's Colegio) for the capital's Plaza de La Cultura, student demonstrations stopped the scheme. San José's Museo Nacional has other examples on display.

▶▶▶ **Isla del Coco** 148A1

Only those with generous budgets will reach this legendary paradise island, flung into the Pacific 330 miles southwest of Costa Rica. Considered a natural ecological laboratory due to its isolation, Coco's rugged topography, virgin rain forest, and thundering waterfalls flourish under an annual rainfall of 200–300 inches. Some 70 species of plants are said to be endemic, as well as certain birds and insects, but this isolated ecosystem is threatened, bizarrely, by rooting pigs whose ancestors

Red-footed booby

were introduced in 1793. Access to the island is only by luxury diving tours that periodically explore the surrounding coral reefs, or by private boat.

Lusting for booty Part of Coco's fascination lies in its colorful history. It was discovered in 1526 by Juan Cabezas and soon figured on Spanish maritime charts as the Isla del Cocos. During the 17th and 18th centuries it became a haven for pirates and privateers, who used it as a base for forays along the Pacific coast of Spanish America and gave its bays names such as Chatham, Wafer, and Weston. Above all it was a hiding place for treasure, including the Lima booty, a fantastic haul of gold and silver ingots, sheets of gold from church domes, and sacred ornaments. English pirate William Davies and Portuguese Benito "Bloody Sword" Bonito added to the island's hoards, titillating imaginations and partly inspiring Robert Louis Stevenson's *Treasure Island,* as well as more than 500 treasure-hunting expeditions over the last century. Coco was also the inspiration for *Jurassic Park*'s fictitious Isla Nebular, and aerial views were used in the film.

▶ **Palmar Norte/Palmar Sur** *148B3*
The adjoining villages of Palmar Norte and Palmar Sur lie on either bank of the Río Térraba, in a valley once inhabited by the Diquí Indians. Palmar's only interest lies in the mysterious, almost perfect stone spheres (*esferas*), up to 6 feet in diameter, that have been excavated solely in the region of Palmar and on the Isla del Caño. The significance of their function and their fabrication—accurate to within 0.07 inch—continues to puzzle archaeologists. Two large versions are displayed on lawns by the road through Palmar Sur, and another, more perfect, pair may be seen in the grounds of the Colegio in Palmar Norte (see panel opposite).

Foiled again
Illustrious visitors to the Isla del Coco have included Franklin D. Roosevelt and Erroll Flynn, their names cut for posterity in rocks on the main landing beaches. A few years ago the South African-born actress Moira Lister invested a minor fortune in seeking the Lima booty, which she had first heard about as a child from her uncle, who had old charts of the island.

A typical clapboard church in Palmar Sur

■ **Three main indigenous groups have retreated to mountainous, inaccessible areas of the country, and the largest concentration is in the Talamanca range. After years of keeping a low profile, Costa Rica's Indians are gaining a new self-assertiveness, which is helping them to counter persistent threats to their land.** ■

Chicha

Chicha, a fermented drink made from corn, pejibaye, banana, or yucca, is liberally consumed on special occasions by all indigenous groups, men, women, and children alike. It is made by parboiling the chosen ingredient, then making a dough to which water is added. This is left to stand for a couple of days before sugar is added and then allowed another day or two's fermentation, during which the alcohol content rises dramatically. Yucca *chicha* has an added attraction: the parboiled tuber is chewed by a young woman who spits it into a calabash before the dough is made. Another typical Indian beverage is cocoa, drunk by the Cabécar, Bribrí, and Guaymi.

Women and children make use of the Uatsi river

Descendants of Costa Rica's pre-Columbian Chorotega, Huetar, Bribrí, Cabécar, and Diqui indigenous tribes now number barely more than 15,000 people—a sharp decline from the population that inhabited the country when Columbus arrived. After the Indigenous Law was passed, in 1977, a concerted effort was made to help protect their traditions, beliefs, and land, within the boundaries of 23 reserves. However, a new dynamism has become necessary to defend these areas against commercial operations such as logging, mineral and oil companies, and hydro-electric dams, as well as non-indigenous squatters.

Talamanca groups About 7,000 Bribrí and Cabécar Indians are scattered across a vast, 521,000-acre area rising from the Valle de Talamanca, near Bribrí, high into the mountains of La Amistad Biosphere Reserve. Belief in a harmonious coexistence with nature is deeply rooted, and medicinal plants and shamans are still part of their culture. Traditionally they live in individual homes far apart from one another, using the virgin forest for hunting, fishing and the shifting cultivation of corn, beans, or *pejibaye* (palm fruit), as well as for building materials. Fine string baskets of natural fibers and carved gourds are their main crafts. Reforestation projects and organic farming methods are now being taught near Shiroles at the Finca Educativa Indigena, the result of coordination between over 20 NGOs and indigenous councils. At the tiny Bribrí Kékóldi reserve, just inland from Puerto Viejo, an experimental project is under way to raise green iguanas, an endangered species.

The Bribrí form Costa Rica's largest indigenous group, and are the more integrated of the two, whereas the Cabécar are less tolerant of outside influences: permits are necessary if you wish to visit any of the latter's remote communities, and these are accessible only on horseback or on foot. There is, however, growing

A typical Bribrí home

recognition of the economic potential of tourism, and inroads are slowly being made with carefully controlled, guided groups.

Boruca Fewer than 3,000 Boruca and Térraba Indians inhabit a 79,000-acre reserve centered around the village of Boruca, high above the Térraba valley in southern Costa Rica. Descended from the Diquis, the creators of most of the gold ornaments exhibited at San José's Museo de Oro (see page 116), they were given an artificial ethnic unity in 1649, when Franciscan missionaries brought them together under one name. Conversion to Christianity and their relatively accessible location has allowed a greater penetration by the Tico way of life, although a new sense of identity will certainly emerge following the recent introduction of the Boruca language at the local school. Apart from cultivating rice, corn, and beans, the Boruca are known for their handweaving, and, for woodcarving that mostly takes the form of masks for their three-day festival, *Los Diablitos* (the little demons), a reenactment of the struggle between Indians and Spaniards. In this version, the white man is vanquished.

Guaymi Costa Rica's 5,000 Guaymi immigrated from Panama in the early 1940s and still maintain close links with their 100,000 or so counterparts there. They are scattered between Coto Brus, north of San Vito, Montezuma, east of Ciudad Neily, and the heart of the Península de Osa. Despite this, traditions remain strong. No other group so closely resembles Amazonian Indians: women wear brilliantly colored, appliquéd dresses and paint their faces for ceremonies, and teeth-filing is still practiced. Spanish comes second to their own Guaymi language, and customs are deeply entrenched. In 1995, Costa Rica's first crowning in over 60 years of an Indian *cacique* (chief) took place at the Guaymi village of Montezuma. His role is essentially a moral and spiritual one to complement that of the political leaders, who participate in the community's Development Association.

Sibu is God
Bribrí and Cabécar Indians believe that Sibu was the creator of all things on earth, and that every object or plant has a supernatural guardian. These protectors allow humans to kill animals and use forest products for subsistence, but otherwise the Bribrí and Cabécar maintain great respect for their natural environment. In the words of a Talamanca shaman: "This land is alive, it is not dead! It lives everywhere in the Talamanca range, in its headwaters... Sibu left this source so it could nourish all the cultures."

Indigenous languages are taught at some schools

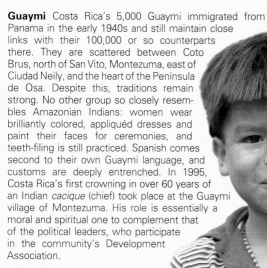

The immense sweep of La Amistad contains unique and still untapped biological wealth

To the paramo
The varying altitudes of La Amistad's untouched terrain perfectly illustrate natural graduations in vegetation. Lowland humid tropical forest is characterized by high forests (up to 135 feet tall) wreathed in epiphytes and lianas, and thick with palms, tree ferns and bamboo stands. Next stage, at about 6,500 feet, comes the cloud forest, rich in oaks, laurels, and shrubs laden with lichen. This is the transition to paramo, a more exposed terrain of stunted, gnarled trees, where temperatures have dropped radically and cold winds blow. At about 11,000 feet even these trees thin out and above that level only grasses survive.

▶▶ **Parque Internacional La Amistad** *149C5*

Open: 8–4. Admission charge: expensive

The vast, often inaccessible area of La Amistad, Costa Rica's largest wilderness area, makes it a boon for scientists and a challenge for keen hikers. Nearly 500,000 acres of the Cordillera de Talamanca are incorporated into the park, considered to be one of the world's largest unaltered tropical forests. In 1982 the park and an area around it was declared a Biosphere Reserve by UNESCO, and then named a World Heritage Site. Now cooperation with Panama has joined it to an equivalent area over the border, so making it an international park. La Amistad's great biodiversity (seven life habitats and six transitional zones) comes from an immense variation in altitude, climate and topography. Vegetation changes from very moist forest and rain forest to cloud forest and paramo (high, exposed land with stunted trees) as the territory climbs from 500 feet on the Caribbean side and 2,700 feet on the Pacific side to the highest points at Cerro Kámuk (11,788 feet) and Cerro Dúrika (10,758 feet).

Natural abundance Wildlife in this large, isolated area is extremely rich and includes endangered species such as the jaguar, cougar, jaguarundi, and ocelot, as well as the largest concentration of tapirs in the country and over 260 species of amphibians and reptiles. Ornithologists revel in some 400 bird species, including the resplendent quetzal, harpy and solitary eagles, orange-breasted falcons and sulfur-winged parakeets. Park headquarters are at Potrero Grande, but for the moment there are no public facilities and visitors must rely on services provided by a handful of lodges nearby. See also Reserva Biológica Dúrika, page 169.

▶▶ **Parque Nacional Chirripó** *148B5*

Costa Rica's highest peak rises over 12,400 feet above the Cordillera de Talamanca, at the heart of a 125,000-acre park that starts at a height of 4,600 feet. Despite its size, magnificent landscapes and cool mountain environment, few tourists visit Chirripó. Those that do encounter striking contrasts between cloud forest and lichen-draped dwarf forest, lakes of glacial origin, rushing rivers, and windswept paramo—as well as cold. Chirripó is part of La Amistad Biosphere Reserve and World Heritage Site but, although its mountain wildlife is as rich as that of the neighboring Parque Internacional La Amistad, vegetation remains within the montane category.

Preparations The base for visiting Chirripó is at the modest mountain village of San Gerardo de Rivas, where park headquarters are located together with simple accommodations. As the steep, 12-mile climb to the summit requires a minimum of two days, trekkers should book dormitory space in a mountain shelter well in advance. Even those making day-hikes need to book their entrance as visitor quotas are limited. This should be done through the Servicio de Parques Nacionales in San José. A useful porterage service is offered by villagers who will take your gear on horseback to the huts; guides, horses, sleeping-bags, and gas stoves can all be rented through lodgings in San Gerardo. Remember that night temperatures on the mountain hover just above freezing point, rains are frequent, and you need to take all your own food and water as well as a gas stove (it is illegal to gather firewood here). Be prepared for intense, cold winds and strong sun, and dream of a recuperating soak in the hot springs at nearby Herradura on your return.

Straight up The overnight shelter is situated 9 miles from the park entrance along a clearly marked though strenuous trail that can take anything from 8 to over 11 hours. You will need to start the trek before dawn to avoid the afternoon rain. A short distance before the huts are the spectacular Los Crestones, a ridge of sculptural, jagged rocks that stand on a stark, exposed ridge where icy winds reach over 40mph. There are numerous spectacular hikes to be made from the huts, including those to the summit (barely two hours away), some beautiful glacial lakes and Cerro Ventisqueros. Alternative routes back to San Gerardo are possible, but make sure you have planned for them.

Jaguar power
Once roaming the forests of the Americas from Oklahoma to Argentina, the jaguar is now a rare sight throughout the continent. Your best chance of seeing one in Costa Rica is at La Amistad. This king of the forest was held in great awe by the indigenous peoples due to its unique method of killing its prey by crushing the skull with one snap of its jaws. The Mayas' most powerful hieroglyph was a fanged jaguar head, and the animal figured in all Indian pantheons. Until the advent of the rifle, it was virtually invulnerable, but today, figures high on the list of endangered species.

161

San Gerardo de Rivas, the base for Chirripó

Gold fever

Fortune-seeking gold-diggers (*oreros*) flooded into the park in the early 1980s, and were able to pan undisturbed in rivers high up in remote areas. Their activities created extensive damage by silting up rivers and the central lagoon. Park boundaries are a hazy affair in the thick of the rain forest and patrols are quite insufficient, but in 1986 a concerted effort was made to evict the gold-seekers. Many were desperate unemployed farmers, and so the government now allows them to work just outside (theoretically) the park boundaries. You can visit a typical gold-digging settlement at El Tigre, west of Puerto Jiménez.

▶▶▶ **Parque Nacional Corcovado**   148B2

Open: 8–4. Admission charge: expensive

Nearly 135,000 acres of the steamy Península de Osa are protected as a national park that was established in 1975, and that offers an unparalleled abundance of tropical rain forest flora and fauna. Rainfall exceeds an annual 200 inches, nurturing some 500 species of trees (25 percent of Costa Rica's total), numerous mammals and birds, and 48 species of frogs and toads. Herds of white-lipped peccaries thunder through the undergrowth, while all four of Costa Rica's monkey species swing from the branches and scarlet macaws wing through the skies. This fascinating destination is well organized for trekkers and it is possible to spend a few hours or several days here.

Ups and downs Corcovado's undulating forest is bordered to the west by a string of deserted, palm-fringed white beaches. A trail follows the entire coastline, with a few inland detours, from Playa San Josecito in the north though Playa Sirena to Playa Madrigal in the south, a tempting proposition for swimming but dangerous due to currents and sharks. A lesser drawback are the clouds of no-see-ums (sand fleas) that infest most of the beaches and are seemingly immune to insect repellents. Inland trails lead past rivers (often full of reptiles) and cooling waterfalls, and basic shelters are conveniently located.

Snake drill Local guides are easily available and will help you understand Corcovado's rich ecosystem as well as its sometimes tricky geography, but make sure you are well prepared with essential trekking gear, and know your snake drill. Thirteen species of poisonous snake inhabit the Península de Osa. Local advice, always delivered in a calm, resigned fashion, is to look at the shape of the head. Poisonous snakes have triangular heads due to their extra venom-filled glands. They tend to wait before

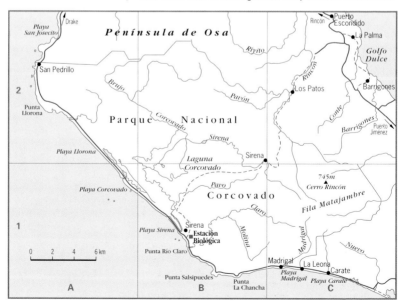

attacking, giving you time to move slowly backwards before fleeing into the undergrowth. Watch out, too, for pythons lurking on branches—not easily visible but not venomous. Snake-serum is carried by most naturalist guides in Corcovado, but if you brush with a poisonous sea snake, there is no antidote.

Hit the trail Three entrances lead into the park. San Pedrillo, in the north, is accessible only by boat from Sierpe or from the lodges around Bahía Drake (see page 152). From here there is a circular day-trippers' trail as well as the main beach route, which, at Playa Llorona, branches northeast to limited facilities at Los Planes, or cuts across the center to the second, eastern entrance, Los Patos, where there is a shelter. The nearby village of La Palma has a few *cabinas*. Another trail leads southwest from Los Patos to the research station at Sirena, where visitor services rise to the sophistication of a dormitory (advance booking necessary) and an airstrip (for charter flights from Puerto Jiménez). This flat area is known for wildlife sightings, and the five-hour beach trail around the point to La Leona, the southern park entrance, combines mangroves with sandy and rocky shores. La Leona is located on the long and wild Playa Madrigal, a 40-minute walk west of Carate.

Carate This small village offers reasonable accommodations, is relatively easily accessible by chartered plane or by daily truck from Puerto Jiménez, and, not least, is the animated social point for local gold diggers, most of whom work legally outside the park. This is part of a typically Costa Rican compromise that is intended to allow poor farmers to try their luck at panning for gold, while at the same time protecting a sensitive environment. For years the gold diggers have sold their nuggets at the Pulpería Morales, run by a fascinating character who also offers camping facilities. Far more comfortable, however, are the elevated tents of the Corcovado Lodge in their own rain forest reserve, a short distance west of Carate.

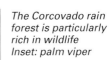

The Corcovado rain forest is particularly rich in wildlife
Inset: palm viper

Marino Ballena is best appreciated from a boat or, even better, underwater

►► Parque Nacional Marino Ballena 148A4

Open: at all times. Admission free

At first sight there is nothing special about the sparsely vegetated beaches of this park, although they do offer safe swimming. Marino Ballena's main glories lie underwater, in a 13,300-acre reserve created in 1990 to protect a marine habitat that is one of the last survivors on Costa Rica's Pacific coast. Coral and rock reefs edge the tiny island of Isla Ballena and the main headland of Punta Uvita, which is actually an island joined to the mainland by a rocky tombolo (see panel, page 103). At the point are sponges, sea anemones, corals, mollusks and crabs. To the south, Isla Ballena and Las Tres Hermanas are the tips of a submerged rock arch that extends from Punta Uvita to Punta Piñuela, and are roosting sites for magnificent frigate birds, brown boobies, pelicans, and ibises. Back on the shore are the sheltered, gray-sand beaches of Uvita (see page 171) and Ballena►►, with Hermosa north of the point and Piñuela►► several miles to the south.

Windows on the world
Boat trips around Marino Ballena often continue a good distance south to a striking geological phenomenon at Playa Ventanas. This consists of a string of caves (*las ventanas* means 'windows') stretching along the rocky shore, including a perfect rock arch that can be entered by boat at low tide. Time your trip carefully to catch another of this park's natural jewels—sunset, a captivating sight in glorious color behind the foreground of sculptural, rocky pinnacles.

Spot a whale In the water, apart from catfish, flying fish, snappers, Caribbean snook, jewfish, and dolphins, you may spot a humpbacked whale. These endangered mammals, measuring up to 50 feet, migrate to tropical waters from North America during the winter season, and this area is thought to be their southernmost destination. November to March is their visiting period at Marino Ballena. Boats can be hired through the ranger's station or from fishermen on the beach (ask for Captain Jenkin), but the best way to visit the marine park is through diving centers in Dominical (see pages 152–153).

Paso Canoas   *149D2*

Fly-blown, dirty, teeming with money-changers and bus-travelers, Paso Canoas is also where you must cross the border if you want to go to Panama on the Interamerican Highway. It is full of low-cost clothes stalls aimed at Panamanian shoppers, and shops selling luxury items from Panama at bargain prices for Ticos. There are banks, a run-down ICT office beside the bus terminal, numerous malfunctioning phone booths, and several cheap *cabinas*. Treat this town as a transit place only.

►   Pavones   *149C2*

This surfers' mecca is reputed by those in the know to have the longest wave in the world, above all during the rainy season. Low-budget lodgings are aimed essentially at surfers' modest needs, though there is also a luxury jungle lodge to the south at Punta Banco. Access from Playa Zancudo to Pavones requires several grueling hours by four-wheel drive or, far better, an hour by boat. Such isolation has brought problems. In the 1980s Pavones hit the headlines when it was revealed that it was the site for major international drug-trafficking operations. Although the main protagonist is now imprisoned (see page 24), the repercussions continue in a complex and embittered battle between U.S. landowners, local squatters and the Costa Rican government, which expropriated large portions of the land involved.

►   Playa Zancudo   *149C2*

About 8 miles south of Golfito is the Golfo Dulce's main beach development, still a very low-key affair. It can be reached in about two hours by car via a debilitating and circuitous route from Golfito or in 30 minutes by boat. Playa Zancudo's facilities are scattered along 4 miles of gray-sand beach, on a skinny spit of land created by the mangrove-edged Río Sabalo.

Surfers and swimmers enjoy the tranquil atmosphere here, using their own hotels for any social action. Zancudo Boat Tours, next door to Cabinas Sol y Mar, provides transport to Golfito and to points of interest north of there, as well as nature-tours along the Río Coto, where otters, crocodiles, monkeys, and birds are abundant. Some hotels organize boat and nature-tours, and sportfishing is available through Golfito Sportfishing (tel: 775-0353) or Roy's Fishing Lodge (tel: 775-0515). There are plans to build a marina, but that may never happen. Do not miss a visit to the charming old lady who sells homemade fudge and coconut oil from her kitchen, signposted on the road.

A free national park?
Marino Ballena is the only national park in Costa Rica to have no entrance fee. The reason is that many local people and fishermen still live within the park boundaries, between the estuary of the Río Morete on Playa Hermosa and Playa Uvita. By Costa Rican law, you cannot charge some people and not others. So, in this case, tourists are on a much-appreciated freebie. The park was originally set up on the initiative of local inhabitants, to protect the area from lobster catchers who came from further afield to fish intensively around the coral reefs.

165

Playa Piñuela, an often-deserted beach at Marino Ballena

Tropical rain forest

■ **Enter a tropical rain forest and you observe a system that has remained unchanged for millennia. Camouflage, symbiosis, dependence, and mutualism are just some of the games that this multifarious host of trees and plants play in an ongoing battle for survival. ■**

The *Ceiba* tree
On rare occasions the legendary *Ceiba* tree rises to 200 feet., making it one of the tallest trees in tropical America. It is also a fast grower, shooting up as much as 13 feet. in a year. The tree's structural majesty—a huge, thick trunk with perpendicular branches forming a vast umbrella—made it sacred for the Mayas, who perceived it as the tree of life. Glossy, dark green clusters of leaves produce creamy white flowers that are eventually replaced by black seed pods. Inside the pods is a white floss used for stuffing cushions and mattresses, which has given the tree its alternative English names—the kapok or silk cotton tree.

The majestic Ceiba

Tropical rain forest is one of the 12 life zones to be found in Costa Rica, defined according to elevation, latitude, average annual rainfall, and temperatures. It is the archetypal jungle, where tangles of ropelike lianas, huge buttress trunks, gigantic ferns and exuberant bromeliads create a dense, impenetrable universe. Impenetrable is the key word, as 75 percent of the estimated 2,000 species of rainforest plants and trees remain unknown and unstudied, let alone the thousands of reptiles, mammals, amphibians, insects and birds. In the words of Dr. Donald Perry, inventor of the Rainforest Aerial Tram (see page 71). "This is the largest genetic reservoir on the planet—a library from the earliest times of evolution."

Three-story structure In any given acre of tropical rain forest there is a staggering diversity of about 90 tree species—a far cry from the repetitive forests of more temperate European and North American climes. There are also three strata of forest: the main canopy, composed of trees reaching 100–130 feet; the sub-canopy, which includes palms from 30–90 feet high; and the understory, where familiar houseplants attain gigantic sizes. Capping them all are what are termed "emergents," a handful of species rising to over 150 feet, including the magnificent *Ceiba* (see panel)

Beneath the canopy, sunlight is so rare that seedlings wait years for a gap to appear before starting the sprint to the top. The rate of canopy replacement is estimated at about 1 percent per year. Among the scores of competitors for available light is the fast-growing and hence weak-limbed cecropia, whose ridged trunk resembles bamboo. In a perfect example of co-evolution, or mutualism, the cecropia's partly hollow trunk serves as an ideal nesting site for Azteca ants, which, in return, defend the tree against encroaching vines or epiphytes that would break the fragile limbs. Cecropia leaves are also the favorite food of three-toed sloths, which seem unmoved by the giant ants.

Epiphytes Two thirds of the plant species grow high in the more luminous canopy: the more there are, the more ecologically rich the forest. Generally categorized as epiphytes, they include the bromeliad family, of which 170 species have been catalogued in Costa Rica. These self-sufficient, leafy clusters seeded by birds, bats or the wind, store water and nutrients that in their turn support an incredible number of insects, frogs and spiders—biologists have identified 250 species living in bromeliad "tanks." A more flamboyant epiphyte is the dazzling orchid

Plants familiar to many visitors as houseplants take on quite different proportions in the rain forests

Hardest workers
Walking along a trail, you may be bemused to see a line of fresh green leaves moving rapidly in front of you. This is not a rain forest hallucination, nor a new species. It is a column of leaf-cutter ants that systematically strip the tropical forest of about 15 percent of its total leaf production. *Atta* workers cut and collect foliage that they transport over distances of up to 200 yards back to their nest. At the nest, home to up to 5 million ants, they carefully clean and chew the leaves before adding them to a sticky mulch deep inside. This nurtures a unique fungus, the leaf-cutter ants' favorite food.

family, whose 1,200 species, like bromeliads, only use their host tree for mechanical support. In contrast, a true parasite, the strangler fig, roots itself in its chosen victim then wraps it in an ever-tightening and all-encompassing grip...finally killing its host.

Undergrowth At ground level, vines, ferns, mosses, and philodendrons proliferate, although they are less dense in the shady understory of primary rain forest than in the lighter secondary forest. Woody, twisted lianas drape themselves from tree to tree in the form of chains or ladders. Younger vines resemble ivies and some, like the passion flower, produce flowers or seeds that are used for food and medicine.

Palm species include the ivory palm, so called because of its hard nuts that were once used as substitutes for ivory and carved into buttons. Tall, solitary fishtail palms contrast with tree ferns, front-runners in the race for light, and the very common *Welfia georgii* with its bright-orange young leaves that are devoured by monkeys and agoutis, which then disperse the seeds. Equally common is the *Socratea exorrhiza*, a palm that stands high on a pyramidal root structure and is dubbed the "walking palm." Rain forest trekkers should watch out for the tree fern with a spiny trunk—it hurts!

The strangler fig spells a slow death to its victims

The shopkeepers of Puerto Jiménez sell machetes to gold-panners and bus tickets to visitors

►► **Puerto Jiménez** 149C2

Facing Golfito across the Golfo Dulce is Osa's main town, Puerto Jiménez. This friendly, slow-paced place consists of a handful of streets with essential facilities such as an airstrip, bank, clinic, post office, laundry, hardware store, and general stores catering for *oreros* (gold-diggers) and trekkers, and a reasonable number of *cabinas* and restaurants. A growing American community is livening up the town and its environs, and it is an essential stopover on the route south to Corcovado. It has water sports too.

Organization Puerto Jiménez surrounds a small bay, with the main center to the west and the Pueblo Nuevo, airstrip and deserted **Playa Platanares**►► to the east. The two sides are connected by a bridge below the central playing field, or by a backstreet from the center. All tourist information is located along the main street. At the geographical and social hub is Restaurant Carolina, base for Escondido Trex (tel/fax: 735-5210), which offers kayaking, hiking, birdwatching, mountain-biking, and camping treks. Tienda Dylana (tel: 735-5024) sells tickets for the twice-daily truck to Carate; Tienda Recor rents bikes; Souvenir Corcovado & Activity Centre (tel/fax: 735-5005) organizes horse riding, boat trips, and rain forest tours, and makes hotel reservations by radio; Cabinas Puerto Jiménez (tel: 735-5152) doubles up as the local taxi service; and Transporte Acuatico Laura Carolina (tel: 735-5195) offers water sports activities. Anyone intending to overnight in Corcovado should make arrangements at the Corcovado national park office (tel/fax: 735-5036), located next to the bank parallel to the main street.

To the cape The rough road south to Cabo Matapalo is practicable with two-wheel drive only in the dry season. After traversing farmlands the road heads into forest with

One tree down
Few entrepreneurs can claim to have equalled the achievement of John and Karen Lewis when constructing their rain forest lodge of Lapa Ríos: only one tree was felled. This is typical of an approach that gives ecotourism an active role, in which responsibility is the key concept. Apart from protecting endangered rain forest and obeying strict ecological precepts, the owners of Lapa Ríos have contributed to the building of a community school (previously there was none), and are now organizing a local chamber of tourism to promote ecotourism, with sustainable development as the main goal.

occasional glimpses of the gulf. This beautiful cape has attracted several upmarket lodges, all environmentally conscious and set in huge tracts of rainforest. The most impressive in scope and dedication is the American-owned Lapa Ríos, about 12 miles south of Puerto Jiménez (see panel opposite), well worth a visit for a drink or lunch. The eccentrically creative Tierra de Los Milagros is New Age in style, and simple accommodations are available.

Heart of the gulf North of Puerto Jiménez, the road reveals the disastrous effects of deforestation, with denuded hillsides and patchy forests before denser vegetation takes over beyond Rincón. Accommodations take a nosedive in price and comfort, with a few *cabinas* only at La Palma or at Rincón, the latter in a lovely corner overlooking the gulf. La Palma is also home to the Asociación Femenina de La Palma (tel/fax: 735-5116), an enterprising group of local women who offer refreshments, tourist information, and some handicrafts in a thatched *rancho*. From here a 7-mile track leads inland across countless rivers to Corcovado's Los Patos entrance. It is practicable —just—with a two-wheel-drive vehicle as far the Reserva Indigena Guaymi de Osa, signposted from the road, where colorfully dressed Guaymi women hover around one tiny grocery and handicrafts shop.

▶▶ Reserva Biológica Dúrika   *148B4*

Apartado 9, Buenos Aires, tel: 730-0153, fax: 730-0003
For those frustrated by the lack of visitor services at Parque Internacional La Amistad (La Amistad International Park; see page 160), this private biological reserve is the solution. It is situated high in the rugged Talamanca mountains northeast of the village of Buenos Aires, inside La Amistad Biosphere Reserve, and is centered on the self-sufficient farming community of Finca Anael. This was set up in 1991 by a group of idealistic Costa Ricans in search of a back-to-nature existence and, since 1992, has been open to like-minded visitors. Among the reasonably priced facilities are rustic cabins, organic vegetarian meals and a choice of activities: yoga; bird-watching with a naturalist guide to help you spot eagles, parrots, toucans, and trogons; hikes to local villages, including the Cabécar Indian community of Ujarrás; and climbing the peak of Cerro Dúrika. Access is by taxi from Buenos Aires, then a one- or two-hour hike or horse ride.

Paddling round the gulf
Kayaking in the mellow Golfo Dulce is an unbeatable experience, particularly at sunset, when the coastal rain forest comes alive with roosting birds, dolphins arrive to feed in the calm bays, and the gulf glows with photoluminescent microbes. Daytime kayaking along mangrove-fringed estuaries brings sightings of parrots, eagles, hawks, numerous waterbirds and brilliantly colored scarlet macaws, while white-faced and howler monkeys are never far away.

Ferry to Puerto Jiménez
Public passenger boats ply the gulf daily, leaving Golfito at 11:30 and Puerto Jiménez at 6AM, and taking 1½ hours. Invest in a water-taxi and the trip takes only 30 minutes.

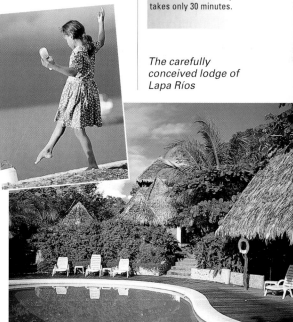

The carefully conceived lodge of Lapa Ríos

Sierpe, the starting-point for trips down crocodile rivers to the Pacific and Bahía Drake

▶ **San Isidro de El General** 148A5

Theoretically, San Isidro lies in the province of San José, but in practice it is the gateway to the south, situated in a fertile tropical valley 22 miles south of the formidable Cerro La Muerte (see page 94). As the road winds down from the pass, it reveals hillsides of orange groves, while beyond San Isidro it enters the **Valle de El General▶▶**. The uninspiring town of San Isidro itself is an unavoidable crossroads for travelers from all directions, including the beach resort of Dominical (see pages 152–153), 20 miles to the southwest. Of the several bus stations, those serving San José are located to the north of the Parque Central and the Dominical terminus immediately to the south. Hotel Chirripó's terrace, on the south side of the square, offers good meals. A small museum, **Museo Regional del Sur** (*Open* weekdays 9–noon, 1–5. *Admission free*), located in the Complejo Cultural Peréz Zeledón (Avenida 1/Calle 2), has artifacts related to the Talamancan indigenous groups, with a neighboring souvenir and crafts shop.

▶ **San Vito** 149D3

From the crossroads town of Ciudad Neily a magnificent road twists precipitously north through the **Cordillera Brunqueña▶▶**, up to the mountain town of San Vito. This stretch was, like the Interamerican Highway, built by the U.S. in 1945 for strategic purposes related to the Panama Canal. Today the higher slopes are blanketed with coffee plantations and fruit orchards, whose products are marketed at San Vito. You can stock up here with Coto Brus coffee (the name Coto Brus applies to the northern valley), which is one of Costa Rica's finest. San Vito was founded in the 1950s by Italian immigrants, and is now the center of a large Italian community. They have integrated and absorbed the Tico spirit to the point of being indistinguishable, though there are a couple of Italian restaurants in the town.

The cool mountain air, lovely views, good accommodation and proximity to the Wilson Botanical Gardens (see page 176) make it a welcome contrast to the humid and less prosperous towns of the hot plains. The protected rain forest of Las Tablas lies 22 miles to the north, while a mile south, at Linda Vista, is the **Finca**

Cantaros▶ (tel: 773-3760), a project masterminded by Gail Hewson de Gomez, associate director of the Wilson Botanical Gardens. Catering as much for the community as for tourists, it consists of a lakeside park and an excellent roadside handicrafts shop—painted an unmistakable saffron yellow.

▶ **Sierpe**   148B3

At the end of a vast area of banana plantations to the south of Palmar Sur lies this small river port and the main jetty for boats to Bahía Drake (see page 152). Sierpe lies at the center of the extensive and little-visited **Delta del Térraba▶▶**, Costa Rica's largest river basin. The 30,000 acres of mangrove swamps nurture nearly 400 species of birds and over 200 of mammals, reptiles, and amphibians. This network of channels is used daily by small boats linking tiny villages and farms with the main port of Sierpe. Both the Río Térraba and the Río Sierpe can be navigated for over 12 miles upstream. Tours of the delta that usually include good crocodile sightings are available through Estero Azul Lodge (tel: 233-2578, fax: 222-0297) or the small, Canadian-owned Hotel Pargo Rojo (tel/fax:788-8032), located by Sierpe's main jetty.

▶ **Uvita**   148A4

The interest of this one-telephone coastal village is its location in the Parque Nacional Marino Ballena (see page 164). Several beach hotels offer good facilities and there are a few budget *cabinas*. An alternative to Uvita's marine delights is a family-run biological reserve, **Oro Verde▶▶** (c/o Selva Mar, tel/fax: 771-1903), located in the mountain village of San Josecito. This 370-acre tract of virgin rain forest with fabulous coastal views has been conserved by a Tico family since the early 1960s, and is now seeing the return of species such as the spider monkey; howler monkeys, sloths, agoutis, and armadillos are also common

Volunteer patrols
Costa Rica's growing consciousness of its natural riches has inspired some private initiatives, not least in Uvita. After lobbying for the national marine park, local inhabitants have now turned to patrolling the tropical forests that clad the mountains rising precipitously inland. Three volunteer forest guards are on call 24 hours a day to ward off hunters and to defend the area against fires and logging. This is the result of a local association formed specifically to preserve what it can of the Fila Tinomastes, a 12,000 acre mountainous area of primary and secondary forest.

171

Handhewn wooden canoes are still the norm for inhabitants of the Delta del Térraba

■ **Costa Rica's wildlife may be enticing but it is also disappearing. Certain species are now on the brink of extinction, due to hunters, poachers, or the disapearance of their natural habitat. Although the government is waking up to this threat and private initiatives are helping, in some cases it may be too late.** ■

Green iguana
This enormous but herbivorous lizard was once a common sight in Costa Rican lowlands, including the dry tropical forest of Guanacaste. Adults reach 6 feet in length and love sunning themselves on riverbanks. Their tender white flesh is much appreciated on the dinner table, and so the green iguana is one of the nation's endangered species. However, in 1985, a German biologist set up a project to breed iguanas for legalized sale and for reintroduction into the wild. Some 80,000 were released in the first five years, and the rest sold as exotic pets or for food. Cattle farmers may well convert, as iguanas yield 10 times more meat per acre than cattle and relish forested environments. Investigate Iguana Park at Coopebarre near Orotina, about 20 miles west of San José (tel: 240-6712. *Open* 8–4 daily. *Admission charge* expensive), and have a light iguana lunch.

Three-toed sloth

Buying a wild animal or bird as a pet is now forbidden in Costa Rica. Since the Wildlife Conservation Law of 1992 it has become illegal to keep captive wildlife, especially endangered species, and permits are required for special circumstances. This is one small step towards dealing with the problem of the dramatic loss of biodiversity, a direct result of deforestation, development, and poaching. Another is to create "corridors" linking the national parks, and a greater step would be to extend these throughout Central America to create the projected *Paseo Pantera*. If realized, this would provide uninterrupted natural forest for larger mammals, which experience genetic decay when isolated within parks. Wildlife breeding centers and a few, rare rehabilitation centers are the other protagonists in the struggle to preserve numerous extraordinary species.

Big game For decades Costa Rica's wild cats have been hunted for their much-prized pelts, and this, combined with their territorial requirements (each adult jaguar needs at least 40 square miles as a hunting ground), has been their downfall. Jaguars used to be common in elevations of up to 3,000 feet, but their conspicuous tracks make them easy targets for poachers. Not the most sociable of mammals, they live off peccaries, monkeys, agoutis, deer, and alligators.

Pumas, ocelots, and margays, in descending order of appetite, are also suffering from the conversion of their natural habitat into plantations or cattle pasture. White-collared peccaries that once roamed in aggressive groups of over 100 now team up with only 20–30 comrades—though this does not stop them from attacking and even devouring humans. With tapirs the situation is different. Their vegetarian diet has given their meat a reputation as a delicacy, so they are prized hunting targets.

In the branches Where branches used to rustle with activity, today there may be only silence. Costa Rica's only endemic monkey, the gregarious squirrel monkey, is now close to extinction and is only very rarely spotted, in Manuel Antonio national park and around Golfito. Similarly threatened is the acrobatic spider monkey, which propels itself in the company of two or three comrades through the tallest forest

trees, using its curling tail as a fifth grip.

At the opposite end of the metabolism scale are the sloths, extra-terrestrial-looking crea-tures that spend their 40-year-long existences hanging upside-down from branches, occa-sionally scooping leaves s-l-o-w-l-y 173into their mouths, and descending once a week to defe-cate. Both two-toed and three-toed species exist, the former at higher elevations, and both are under threat, mainly due to habitat loss or degra-dation. Even the verdant town squares of Puerto Limón and Alajuela have seen their resident sloths disappear.

Left to right: scarlet macaw, ocelot kittens, peccaries, iguana, orange-chinned parakeet, puma. Inset: quetzal

Sanctuaries

Private initiatives are valiantly dealing with members of endangered species that have been captured by hunters, confiscated by airport customs controls, or rescued from misguided owners. Lily Hagnauer's sanctuary, Las Pumas, located near Cañas (see page 42) is devoted to cats —jaguars, pumas, ocelots, and margays—for the most part confiscated from illegal hunters by MIRENEM, the national parks administration. However, once the cats have lived in captivity, it is virtually impossible to release them into the wild. In contrast, Dario Castelfranco's Jardín Gaia (see page 109) concentrates on rehabili-tating confiscated animals and birds and reintro-ducing them into their natural habitats.

173

Airborne Resplendent quetzals, scarlet macaws, harpy eagles, yellow-napped parrots, and great curassows are among the numerous bird species that are in danger of extinction within Costa Rica's boundaries. The 16 species of the parrot family range from the tiny barred parakeet to the exuberant scarlet macaw. All are favorites on the pet market and need to be protected. The chestnut-mandibled toucan (*Ramphastos swainsonii*), Central America's largest, is also threatened.

Waterlogged Thanks to campaigning, the plight of turtles is well known (see pages 56–57). Less advertised is the predicament of caymans and crocodiles, which are suffering from chemical pollution of their watery habitats and from hunters after their skins. The cayman is a comparatively non-aggressive Latin-American crocodilian, measuring up to 3 feet, that lives in lagoons and canals. Its much larger and more dangerous big brother, the American crocodile, is literally a prehistoric sight. How much longer will they be around?

American crocodile

Drive From Pacific to pineapples

See map on pages 148–149.

This circuit follows a spectacular stretch of the Pacific coast before turning inland along a river valley and circling north to San Isidro. It requires at least one night en route if you want to appreciate the rich natural offerings and recover from some dire roads.

To the beach From San Isidro de El General take the road southwest towards Dominical. This twists up to a pass near the peak of San Juan (3,890 feet) before descending through a beautiful, often misty valley. In the rainy season it is neither a comfortable nor an easy ride. After the village of Platanillo you can stop at Centro Turistico Nauyaca, a small private rain forest reserve with trails and horse riding to the impressive Nauyaca waterfalls. From Barú the road follows the Río Barú down to the coast, where it forks left to the lively beach resort of **Dominical**►► (see pages 153-154). To the right, more rain forest activities and a fuel-stop are available near Hacienda Barú. If hunger bites, stop at Cabinas Punta Dominical, located on a promontory ending Dominical's main beach, where surf crashes on both sides. Continue along the *costanera sur* (southern coast road) through lush tropical vegetation, with steep forested hills rising to your left. After 10 miles you reach **Uvita**► (see page 171) and the national

marine park of **Marino Ballena**►► (see page 164), a must for a swim, snorkel, and, if you have time, a boat tour round the offshore reefs and islets.

Spheres and mangroves Farther south, at the embryonic beach resort of Playa Tortuga, a newly completed stretch of gravel road veers inland. After 12 miles it passes Ciudad Cortés to reach Palmar Norte through altogether flatter, less inspiring landscapes. At **Palmar Norte**► (see page 157) don't miss the perfect stone spheres on display. Nature enthusiasts should make a detour from here through seemingly endless banana plantations to tour the mangrove swamps surrounding **Sierpe**► (see page 171).

River valley Back at Palmar Norte, follow the road (this is now, amazingly, the Interamerican Highway) going east on its circuitous way to Buenos Aires. You immediately enter the broad, majestic Térraba valley, which for 25 miles marks the course of the meandering river, its gently sloping hills alternating with sheer rock cliffs on the opposite bank. At the end of the dry season water levels are very low, sometimes nonexistent. Stands selling *pipa fría* (cold, fresh coconut milk), soursops, and seasonal avocados dot the roadside in front of tiny farms. Evidence of slash and burn methods, used by tropical farmers all over the world, is sometimes visible.

Handicrafts Just before Curré, a dirt-road branches off to the left and will take you along a high mountain ridge to **Boruca**► (see page 152), but four-wheel drive is essential. If you make this

detour, you can continue north and cut back onto the Interamerican Highway at Brujo. At Curré, stop to buy Borucan handicrafts sold at derisory prices. A few miles farther at Paso Real you pass a turning to **La Amistad▶▶** (see page 160) and **San Vito▶** (see pages 170–171), offering further detours requiring overnight stays. For years this route involved crossing the Térraba by car-ferry, but in 1994 a bridge was finally completed.

Canned pineapples From Paso Real the road leaves the stifling lowland temperatures and starts climbing up through a wild, deserted valley, backed in the east by the dramatic Talamanca range. It follows the Río

The landscape around San Vito, on a detour from the main drive

General as far as Brujo, from where it ascends more sleeply to reach the high plateau of the Valle de El General around Buenos Aires. This village lies just off the road and offers little other than a food and fuel stop.

Between here and the village of Volcán, huge swathes of tilled terra-cotta soil alternate with vast pineapple plantations belonging to the canned fruit company Del Monte. In the distance, orange splashes of flame trees emerge from the silhouette of the Talamancan foothills. San Isidro de El General is 29 miles farther.

Botanical perfection: pristine specimens at the Wilson Botanical Gardens

Primary and secondary
The view from the gardens' lookout point west across the valley clearly shows the difference between primary and secondary rain forest. Looking from left to right, to the far left is agricultural land, followed by a patch of forest (in the middle) with even textures and varying colors. This is secondary forest—that is, the land has been logged and what you see is regrowth. To the right, the primary forest canopy reaches heights of 135 feet in a dense mass of uneven texture somewhat resembling broccoli.
Below the canopy, two or more additional levels are formed by trees, palms and ferns.

▶▶▶ **Wilson Botanical Gardens/Jardín Botánico Robert y Catherine Wilson/ Las Cruces** 149D3

Las Cruces, San Vito, tel/fax: 773-3278
Open: Tue–Sun 8–4. Admission charge: moderate
This internationally renowned collection of tropical plants extends over 25 acres beside a further 360 acres of forest reserve in the Brunqueña mountains. Established in 1963 by Robert and Catherine Wilson, it was transferred to the OTS (Organization for Tropical Studies) for tropical biological research in 1973. Ten years later it was declared part of UNESCO's Reserva de la Biósfera La Amistad (La Amistad Biosphere Reserve) and serves as an important buffer zone to the international park. Day-visitors are welcome, and students, researchers and tourists can lodge in dormitory-style cabins in the garden.

Garden of Eden Heavy annual rainfall has helped develop about 2,000 species of tropical plants, including bromeliads, orchids, marantas, heliconias, bamboos, begonias, palms, tree ferns, rhododendrons, and cycads, ancient plants that evolved over 100 million years ago. Paths wind around undulating, superbly landscaped grounds, with detours signposted to wilder areas of rain forest. Greenhouses and an experimental garden can also be visited, and an insectarium is planned for the future. Two hours are the minimum needed for exploring the main garden; longer walks can be taken downhill to the river, where there is excellent birdwatching. Altogether, some 330 avian species have been recorded around Las Cruces, and one researcher reported sighting a third of them in a single day. The numerous flowers also attract over 3,000 types of butterflies and moths.

Catastrophe In 1994 catastrophe struck when the main research building of the OTS burned down. This accidental fire caused untold loss through the destruction of many years' research documents, reports, and slides, quite apart from the material loss of laboratories and facilities. A new research center is now being built, but funds are short so generous visitors are especially welcome.

Arriving

By air This is the way most visitors arrive in Costa Rica and all flights land at Juan Santamaría airport (24-hour information tel: 441-0744), near the capital, San José.

Most international flights transit via Miami, Houston, or Dallas. Europeans will find that KLM (via Curaçao), Iberia, British Airways, Continental, and American Airlines offer the most convenient connections, with waits of varying duration. Count on anything between 16 and 19 hours' traveling time from Europe. **Aero Costa Rica** (tel: 296-1111 or 232-2025) and Lacsa (tel: 231-0033 or 221-9414, fax: 255-2176), Costa Rica's own international airlines, fly daily from Miami either direct or via Managua in Nicaragua.

Transatlantic passengers arrive in the evening when exchange offices (*Open* Mon–Sat 9–4) are closed, but there are plenty of unofficial money-changers, and taxis accept U.S. dollars. The airport terminal has car-rental offices and tourist information, and taxis are readily available to whisk you the 11 miles (costing about $10) to the center. Budget travelers can use the Alajuela–San José bus, which passes frequently in front of the airport.

Liberia airport, in Guanacaste, is due for promotion to international status in 1996, but flights arriving here will be mainly package charters.

The influence of the United States even extends to secondhand clothes shops

By sea Apart from private yachts, the only passenger boats to Costa Rica are cruise ships. These stop at Caldera, near Puntarenas on the Pacific coast, or at Moín, near Puerto Limón on the Caribbean, and allow rapid visits: inquire at your local travel agent about itineraries and companies. Freighters sometimes have passenger accommodations.

By bus Budget travelers can reach Costa Rica by long-distance bus from Managua, in Nicaragua, via Peñas Blancas; from Panama City via Paso Canoas or from Changuinola on Panama's Caribbean side via Sixaola. These routes can take anything from 9 to 14 hours depending on border delays and road conditions. Buses arrive in San José at their respective company offices: **Sirca**, Avenida 6 & 8/Calle 7 (tel: 222-5541), **Ticabus**, Avenida 4/Calle 9 & 11 (tel: 221-8954), **Tracopa**, Avenida 18/Calle 2 & 4 (tel: 221-4214).

By car Tourists arriving by car must pay a road tax (currently $10), buy an insurance stamp, and receive a car entry permit at the border. Cars are also obligatorily fumigated for a small fee. Make sure your insurance covers you as comprehensively as possible for driving around Costa Rica.

Customs regulations

Incoming passengers can bring in 200 cigarettes or 500g of tobacco, 2 liters of liquor or wine and up to six rolls of film. There are no restrictions on amounts of currency taken in or out of the country. Sporadic customs checks are made, particularly at land borders.

Travel insurance

Take out a reliable travel insurance policy before leaving home. Most travel agents supply these, which should cover theft, illness and repatriation. If you are considering some of Costa Rica's wilder activities (bungee-jumping, whitewater rafting), read the small print carefully. Check also the benefits attached to your credit card as some companies offer partial travel insurance cover.

Entry requirements

Current requirements should be checked before departure. A valid passport is required, except for U.S. and Canadian citizens visiting for less than 30 days, who can enter with an original birth certificate and two other IDs. Citizens of the United States, Canada, and the United Kingdom do not need visas for stays of up to 90 days. Citizens of Australia and New Zealand are permitted visa-free stays of up to 30 days. For an extension of 30 days, obtain an exit visa through a travel agent at least three working days before your scheduled departure. Alternatively, make a 72-hour exit over the border. When you arrive in Costa Rica, an immigration card is stamped and attached to your pass-

One of Costa Rica's main draws is her charismatic people

port: keep this document for leaving the country. Visitors arriving by bus or air should have a return ticket or other ticket out of Costa Rica.

Departing

An airport tax is charged on departure (currently US$10). This can be paid in dollars or *colones* at a travel agent when confirming your return ticket, or at the airport check-in. Seats on all international flights must be confirmed with the airline 72 hours before departure.

Do not let any photographic film go through the X-ray security machines; they are not film-safe.

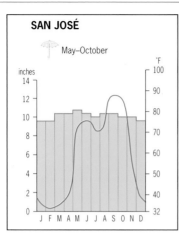

SAN JOSÉ

May–October

Climate
Costa Rica has a hot, dry season (which Ticos call summer) from December to April, and a rainy or "green" season (known as winter), from May to November. Transitional months can bring surprises, and the rainy season is not constantly wet: July invariably brings a temporary abatement and, in general, mornings are clear. There are plenty of micro-climates, too, with temperatures descending as altitudes rise.

In the dry season, San José and other Central Valley towns enjoy a fresh, breezy, springlike climate requiring a jacket or sweater in the evenings, while Guanacaste's arid interior endures stifling tempera-tures. Rain still occurs in high mountainous areas and, above all, in the Caribbean lowlands, where downpours can last for days—or break into brilliant sunshine after a couple of hours. When the "green" season starts, it is the southern zone around the Golfo Dulce that gets the most rain.

All year round, the sun rises dutifully at about 6 AM and sets about 12 hours later.

National holidays
- **New Year's Day**
  January 1
- **Feast of San José** (patron saint of the capital)
  March 19
- **Juan Santamaría Day**
  April 11
- **Easter**
  March/April, from preceding Thursday to Easter Sunday
- **Labor Day**
  May 1
- **Corpus Christi**
  June (movable)
- **St. Peter and St. Paul**
  June 29
- **Guanacaste Day**
  July 25
- **Feast of the Virgin of Los Angeles**
  August 2
- **Assumption and Mother's Day**
  August 15
- **Independence Day**
  September 15
- **Columbus Day (Limón carnival)**
  October 12
- **Immaculate Conception**
  December 8
- **Christmas Eve**
  December 24
- **Christmas Day**
  December 25

When to go
The favorite period for vacationers is December–January, when hotel rooms tend to fill up. Aim for late March and you will have the advantage of the dry season, plus slightly lower hotel rates. If you do not mind downpours, the green season (May to November) offers a more refreshing climate, a wide choice of accommodations, and substantially lower prices.

Time differences.
Costa Rica time is the same as US. Central Standard Time, one hour behind Eastern Standard Time.

Opening times
Stores generally open Monday to Saturday from 8 or 9 to 6 or 7. Some close for lunch any time between 11:30 and 2. Government offices are theoretically open weekdays 8–4 but assiduity slows considerably in the afternoon. Banks are open weekdays 9–3, with some San José banks opening at 8 AM.

Addresses
Most residents have a numbered post office box (Apartado, shortened

to Apdo) for receiving mail. Main towns have a grid layout of avenues cut across by streets. These are numbered starting from the center, with odd numbers on one side and even numbers on the other (see map of San José on pages 116–117). Addresses are given as intersections between an avenue and a street, or two streets (for example, Avenida 1 & 3/Calle 2 means on Calle 2 between Avenida 1 and Avenida 3). In suburbs and small towns, directions are given in relation to a local landmark: see page 116.

Money matters
Local currency is the *colón* (*colones* in the plural, written as ¢). It is divided into 100 *centimos*, but these are practically obsolete. Coins range from 1¢ to 100¢, and banknotes from 50¢ to 10,000¢. The *colón* is floated (steadily dropping about 20 percent yearly since 1990) against the U.S. dollar, which is the only currency worth bringing. Bills and traveler's checks can easily be changed at banks with your passport. Most banks have a special counter for foreign exchange (*cambio*): go early to avoid queues. San José's Banco Mercantil (Avenida 2/Calle Central) has an outlet specifically for foreign exchange.

Itinerant money-changers abound in the streets of San José near the Banco de Costa Rica (Avenida 2/Calle 4) but their tricks are many, so only use them if you are desperate. Large hotels change travelers' checks and cash at slightly lower rates than banks.

Credit cards are accepted in more expensive establishments, and by car-rental and tour agencies, but not by small *cabinas*, hotels or local restaurants. Cash dispensers for VISA are found at branches of the Banco Popular y Desarollo and for MasterCard at Credomatic branches, but these are rare outside San José. For credit card inquiries, or to report loss or theft, contact:
VISA tel: 223-2211;
MasterCard tel: 253-2155;
American Express tel: 233-0044 or 223-0116.

U.S. dollars are accepted in most large hotels but change sufficient amounts into *colones* before heading out into the countryside. Many small towns and resorts have no money-exchange facilities.

Tipping
Tourist hotels and restaurants automatically add on a tax and service charge amounting to around 25 percent, so tipping is not essential. Taxi-drivers appreciate having their modest fares rounded up, and tour guides generally expect a few dollars' tip.

Tico families take to the beaches between December and April

By car

Car rental Car-rental agencies are numerous in San José and rates follow the tourist season—rising between December and March. Expect to pay $200–550 per week with unlimited mileage, depending on whether you want four-wheel drive and/or air-conditioning. Rates should include comprehensive insurance (not always offered, so check carefully) which accounts for about $12–15 per day. Special deals crop up during leaner periods, so check the local press (*Tico Times*, *Costa Rica Today*) on arrival. Cars can also be booked in advance from your home country through international companies, but rates may be marginally higher than in Costa Rica.

Car-rental agencies require a valid driver's licence (international licences are not necessary), passport and a major credit card. Few will rent cars to drivers aged under 25. Before signing the rental agreement, check all existing dents on the car and make sure they are noted on the contract. Any car using Costa Rican roads takes a real beating, so make a trial run and check everything before heading out into the wilds. Ask your car-rental agency for contact numbers in case of breakdown. Flat tires can be fixed at petrol stations.

Rental cars have special licence plates, making them easy targets for break-ins. Never leave them parked with your belongings inside (even in the trunk) unless well guarded. San José car-rental offices include:

- **Adobe** Avenida 8 & 10/Calle 7 (tel: 221-5425, fax: 221-9286)
- **Avis** Avenida Los Americas/Calle 427 (tel: 232-9922)
- **Budget** Paseo Colón/Calle 36 (tel: 223-3284, fax: 255-4966)
- **Elegante** Avenida 13 & 15/Calle 10 (tel: 221-0066, fax: 221-5761)
- **Hertz** Paseo Colón/Calle 38 (tel: 221-1818/223-5959, fax: 233-7254)
- **National** Avenida 7/Calle 36 (tel: 233-4044, fax: 233-2186)
- **Tico** Plaza de la Cultura (tel: 222-8920/223-9642, fax: 222-1765)

Speed limits Speed limits are 100kph (62 mph) on highways and 40–80kph (25–50 mph) elsewhere: watch for signs and stick to the limits as radar checks are common. In more remote areas where roads have gravel or dirt surfaces, speeds are automatically reduced to around 20kph, and in the rainy season these can become impassable even with four-wheel drive. Always ask about the feasibility of your desired route.

Driving tips San José's complex one-way systems and traffic-jams do not make driving fun. Taxis are cheap, so keep your car for exploring outside the capital. Once you are on the rural roads, Costa Rican potholes, streams, landslides, switchbacks, torrential downpours, and unpaved

Driving may well be an adventure in itself

surfaces make for some exciting off-road-style driving but also require constant alertness. Cowboys, straying cattle and cyclists are occasional obstacles, and the infamous Cerro La Muerte pass can be shrouded in thick fog, reducing visibility to a few feet. Road signs become a rarity once you are off the main roads, so learn your Spanish and have a good map for asking directions. Rivers are often better signposted than villages, and make useful landmarks. Driving at night is not recommended, partly for security reasons, and partly because of badly marked roads and invisible hazards. Fuel costs are reasonable but gas stations may be rare: fill up whenever you see one.

Police Traffic police sometimes attempt to extract on-the-spot fines for speeding or other reasons: this is now illegal and fines should only be paid at police stations, where receipts are issued. Armed *guardia rural* manning road blocks near the Nicaraguan and Panamanian borders sometimes make spot-checks, so make sure you have your passport and all car documents with you.

Accidents In the case of an accident, do not move anything, vehicles included, until the police have arrived. Call the traffic police (tel: 222-9330 or 222-9245) if there is no local police station. Insurance claims need to be filed within five days; this should be done by your car-rental agency. Tow trucks monitor police radios and so will appear without your asking. Rental cars should always be towed back to the agency.

Public transport
Bus Costa Rica's long-distance bus services radiate from different termini in San José to towns all over the country. This is a budget way to travel (costing about $1 per hour) and buses will drop you at intermediary points on request. However, it means you are limited to visiting only major centers, missing out on less accessible parks, reserves, beaches, or ecotourism projects. Connections can be tricky, as private bus companies operate from different parts of town, and may involve a long walk or taxi ride and inter-mediary waits. Buses can be packed to the gills but they normally respect their timetables. Luggage is stored in side-lockers—no receipts are given, so keep your eye on it at stops.

The ICT office in San José has current bus timetables and points of departure. If using San José's Coca Cola bus station, be especially aware of pickpockets and watch your luggage carefully.

Tourist bus Two private tourist bus companies offer a fast and comfortable alternative to public buses. **Pura Natura** (tel: 233-9709 or 233-9469) covers six daily routes, leaving from various hotels in San José and taking you directly to specific destinations in air-conditioned comfort. **Saragundi Specialty Tours** (tel: 255-0011) operates a similar system, connecting 70 hotels throughout the country. Both offer a pass system valid for two weeks' travel.

A traffic (transito) policeman

Internal flights are readily available and relatively inexpensive, but seats should always be booked well ahead

Plane Two companies, **Sansa** (tel: 233-3258 or 233-2714, fax: 255-2176) and **Travelair** (tel: 220-3054, fax: 220-0413), operate small planes to Barra del Colorado, Tortuguero, Golfito, Puerto Jiménez, Palmar Sur, Quepos, Tambor, Sámara, Nosara, Tamarindo, and Liberia. Luggage is limited to 12kg (26 lb) and demand for seats is often high, so book well in advance. Travelair is slightly more expensive than Sansa but offers a more reliable service with fewer delays and canceled flights. Travelair flights leave from the small Tobias Bolaños airport, 3 miles from the center of San José, while Sansa operates from the domestic terminal of Juan Santamaría airport.

Planes can also be chartered to any airstrip in the country, averaging a price of about $250 per hour for a six-seater, which is economical for a group as no destination in Costa Rica is over an hour's flight away. Check the Yellow Pages under *Taxis aereos* for the numerous air-taxi companies that are located at the Tobias Bolaños airport.

An interesting alternative is to charter a sea-plane that can alight on land or water. This new service is operated by **Alas Anfibias** (tel: 232-9108, fax: 232-9567) with rates averaging $300 per hour.

Rail Costa Rica's railroad lines shrink yearly. After the closure of the Atlantic railway and the Puntarenas line in 1995, it was the turn of two of the three Central Valley commuter trains, leaving only the San José–Heredia service functioning. This departs Monday to Saturday from the Atlantic railway station at 5:45 AM, and from San Pedro at noon and 5:15 PM. Word is out that the Siguerres-to-Puerto Limón stretch may reopen after repairs, and that the Puntarenas line may run a special service, so check with the ICT on arrival for the latest developments. In the Caribbean region, the banana freight train (see page 137) offers a short ride.

Taxi Costa Rican taxis are inexpensive and taxi-drivers are mostly honest, though there are exceptions. By law they should use a meter (*maria*) for town trips, but many don't. In this case, negotiate a reasonable fare or change taxis. Many try to charge a surcharge for waiting outside hotels: this is illegal and you should refuse to pay it. Payment for any trip over 12km (7.4 miles) should be negotiated before starting: count on around $50 per day.

Radio taxis operate in San José and are useful for nocturnal excursions, rainstorms or early morning airport trips:
● **Coopetaxi** tel: 235-9966
● **Coopetico** tel: 221-2552
● **Coopeuno** tel: 254-6667
● **Coopeirazú** tel: 254-3211

Ferries There are several ferry routes to the Península de Nicoya. The Río Tempisque car-ferry has hourly departures 6 AM–6 PM but avoid Christmas, Easter and Sunday evenings when three-hour waits are common. Puntarenas–Playa Naranjo has five daily car-ferry departures in both directions and Puntarenas-Paquera four, with an extra passenger-only ferry. **Simba** (tel: 661-0344) is a motor-yacht service carrying passengers (December to August) between Puntarenas and Montezuma, with an optional stop at Tambor. Departure from Montezuma is at 7 AM and from the Bar Bananas in Puntarenas at 1 PM. In the south, the Arco Iris passenger ferry runs daily between Golfito and Puerto Jiménez, and water-taxis can be rented through the Asociación de Boteros (tel: 775 0712).

Student and youth travel
Discounts are available on international flights to Costa Rica if you have an International Student Identity Card. Some small hotels are affiliated to the International Youth Hostel Federation: check in your home country or contact the Hostel Toruma, Avenida Central/Calle 29 & 31, San José, for information.

Cheap restaurants and sodas *are a bonus for backpackers*

Media

The most intellectual of Costa Rica's daily newspapers is *La República*, closely followed by the more popular *La Nación*. Both contain freely expressed news and opinions. The official government mouthpiece is the weekly *La Gazette*. English-speaking visitors can rely on the weekly *Tico Times* (Fridays) for a synopsis of events, as well as cultural listings, tourist information, a garrulous letter column, and classi-fied ads, sometimes useful for rented accommodations, private car rentals, or local services. *Costa Rica Today* is a free color information newspaper (out on Thursdays), distributed at large hotels and other tourist establishments.

There are six local TV stations and numerous local radio stations. Canal 19, Master and Supercanal are Costa Rican cable TV stations which transmit 24-hour TV from the United States. Most upmarket hotels receive satellite TV, including CNN.

Post offices

San José's elegant old central post office (Correo Central, Avenida 1 & 3/Calle 2, *Open* weekdays 7–6, Sat 7–noon) offers the fastest service for international mail: one to two weeks to North America and Europe, about the same time as the inefficient internal mail service. Poste restante can be addressed to you at Lista de Correos, Correo Central, San José. Receiving parcels entails complicated customs procedures and duty that are best avoided. Packages can be sent abroad reasonably reliably (although avoid sending valuables), but postal rates are high. Outside San José, post offices are usually signposted as CORTEL and offer mail and telephone services; postal delivery time is considerably longer.

Telephones and fax

In San José there are two efficient international phone/fax offices: **Telecom**, Avenida 2/Calle 1 & 3 (fax: 257-2272 or 2273. *Open* Mon–Thu 7 AM–10 PM, Fri–Sun 7 AM–midnight)
Radiográfica Costarricense, Avenida 5/Calle 1 & 3 (fax: 223-1609 or 7932. *Open* 7 AM–10 PM).

Pay-phone booths (using 5¢, 10¢ or 20¢ coins) exist in most large towns but those that work generally have long queues. Most rural villages have a public phone run by a local opera-tor, often in a *pulpería* (grocery store) and signposted from the road. Many parts of Costa Rica outside the Central Valley have no telephone lines, and radio is the only means of communication for local hotels. Even so, Costa Rica has the highest number of telephones per capita in Latin America.

● International calls via operator: 116 (for reverse charge calls—*una llamada a cobrar*—or if using an inter-national phone-card)
● Telegrams/faxes by phone: 123
● International information: 124
● Costa Rica directory: 113
● International call: prefix 00

All phone numbers in Costa Rica have seven digits and there are no area codes. To call Costa Rica from abroad, dial country code 506 before the number.

Language

English is spoken in all the pricier hotels, but elsewhere some basic Spanish is essential. Ticos are extremely courteous and pepper their conversation with little phrases such as *con mucho gusto* (with pleasure) and *con permiso* (with your permission), both worth repeating. They also, notoriously, use diminutives such as *ahorita* (in a while) instead of *ahora* (now).

Pronunciation

Every letter is sounded, except h. The letter c is hard, as in "cat," except before e or i when it is soft, as in "cell." Accents show where to stress a word. If there is no accent, stress the second-to-last syllable of words ending in a vowel, n, or s, and the last syllable of other words.

¡hola!	hello
buenos días	good morning
buenas tardes	good afternoon
buenas noches	good evening/night
adiós	goodbye (definitively), also used for hello
hasta luego	goodbye/see you later
por favor	please
(muchas) gracias	thank you (very much)
perdone	excuse me/sorry
si/non	yes/no
¿cómo está?	how are you?
muy bién gracias	very well thanks
no entiendo	I don't understand
¿habla inglés?	do you speak English?
¿dónde está/están...?	where is/are...?
el banco	the bank
el parque central	the main square
la gasolinera/ bomba	the gas station
los sanitarios/servicios/baños	the toilets
la parada de autobuses	the bus stop
a la derecha	to the right
a la izquierda	to the left
todo derecho	straight on
¿hay campo...?	is there space/a seat?
¿cuanto vale esto?	how much is this?
la cuenta por favor	the bill please
¿tiene...?	do you have...?
un cuarto sencillo/doble	a single/double room
con dos camas	with two beds
con cama matrimonial	with a double bed
con aire acondicionado	with air conditioning
con ventilador	with fan
con baño privado	with private bathroom
¿puede hacer un descuento?	can you do a discount?
¿cuando/a qué hora?	when/at what time?
pura vida	"good life," used as a greeting or to mean great, fantastic

Crime and police

In the last decade crime has become a serious problem, especially in San José and the province of Limón. Tourists should not walk in badly lit side-streets or city parks at night, nor attract attention by flaunting jewelry or cameras. Always be alert, especially in markets, crowded bus stations or on packed buses. Beware of over friendly approaches from either sex, particularly at night—con men and con women abound. Report any theft or assault to the Recepcion de Denuncias at the Judicial Police (OIJ) at Avenida 6/Calle 19 & 21, in the court complex, or call 255-0122. You need to file a report to make an insurance claim, so try to find a good Spanish-speaker to accompany you.

In some situations tourist cameras may be a temptation: in crowded places always keep a careful eye on your possessions

Some corrupt police may try to extract bribes, particularly traffic police. Only pay fines at police stations and demand a receipt. You can file a complaint at the Ministry of Public Works and Transport (Avenida 22/Calle 9, tel: 227-2188) if you have the officer's name and number. By law you must carry your passport (or a photocopy of it) on you.

Emergency phone numbers
- All emergencies: 911.
- Police: 117.
- Fire: 118.
- Red Cross: 128.
- Red Cross ambulance: 221-5818
- Hospital San Juan de Dios: 257-6282
- Traffic police: 222-9330 or 222 9245

Embassies and consulates
USA Carreteras Pavas, Rohrmoser (tel: 220-3939 weekdays 8–4:30; 220-3127 outside these hours)
Canada Edificio Cronos, Avenida Central & 1/Calle 3, San José (tel: 255-3522)
United Kingdom Edificio Centro Colón, Paseo Colón/Calle 38 & 40, San José (tel: 221-5566)

Lost property
Report the loss of passports, traveler's checks or credit cards to the police immediately, and to your embassy and the issuing bank. It helps to have photocopies of your passport and airline tickets, and a note of traveler's check and credit-card numbers (keep these separately from the originals). Report other losses to a local police station for insurance claims (good Spanish will be needed). If lost items are returned, it is common courtesy to give a token reward to the finder.

Health
Hygiene standards are high and medical services excellent. San José's tap water is drinkable, though elsewhere it is advisable to stick to bottled mineral water—easily available. Uncooked fruit and vegetables should be washed, but most restaurants prepare food hygienically.

Standards of hygiene are good, but it's always safer to stick to bottled water

prescription medicines alleviate the symptoms. Malaria may not be a risk (see above), but parts of Guanacaste and Puntarenas have recently had outbreaks of dengue fever, another debilitating disease carried by mosquitoes. Always use mosquito repellent at dusk and light anti-mosquito spirals (*espirales*, available at all grocery stores) at night.

Pujarras (no-see-ums or sand-fleas) are intensely annoying insects whose itchy bites can become infected if scratched. The humid tropical climate does not help healing and any infected bite or cut should be cleaned with antiseptic cream. Sulfur powder, also a good insect repellent, helps to dry out and disinfect wounds. Snake-bites are not common, but if hiking, be informed of venomous species to watch out for.

Two constant hazards are dehydration and sunburn, both very easy to acquire in this climate. Bring total sun block from home and stock up on high-protection-factor lotions in San José: they are difficult to find outside major resorts. Always drink lots of water (carry it with you on treks) and other non-alcoholic liquids, wear a hat during the midday hours of strong sunshine, and avoid spending long periods in the sun.

Medical treatment
For minor illnesses, prescription drugs, and emergency first aid, pharmacies are generally very competent, but bring from home any medication you usually take, and a copy of the prescription or a doctor's note.

Anything more serious can be treated at a local health center or one of San José's social security hospitals. Costa Rica's public health service is among the world's best, and a profusion of private clinics offer inexpensive dental and cosmetic surgery.

There are no vaccination requirements for visitors entering Costa Rica, but bus travelers from Nicaragua are sometimes asked to show anti-malarial treatment and/or cholera inoculations (although the latter are now recognized as less effective than being careful over food and water). However, the World Health Organization predicts that cholera will spread again through Central America in coming years, so risks may rise. Check with your doctor or travel health clinic before being vaccinated, but malaria tablets and yellow fever inoculations are advised, despite claims that malaria has virtually been eliminated. Costa Rica does not pose a high risk of contracting hepatitis, but some of its neighbors do. An inoculation called HAVRIX does not use human blood agents with their risk of HIV infection.

Hazards
If the change in diet causes diarrhea, drink plenty of (reliable) water. Non-

189

Camping

The few campgrounds with facilities are located inside certain national parks: for further information contact the Servicio de Parques Nacionales (MIRENEM) in San José, Avenida 8 & 10/Calle 25 (tel: 257-0922, fax: 223-6963). Some farms and hotels also allow camping on their land. Camping equipment can be bought or rented at the Centro de Aventuras, Avenida 2 & 4/Calle 32, San José.

Clothing

Dressing in layers is the best way of dealing with Costa Rica's constantly changing elevations and climate. Cotton T-shirts, long-sleeved shirts, cotton trousers, and a sweater are the essential basics. A waterproof such as a rain poncho is needed for higher altitudes, and beachwear for the coast. If you envisage trekking in rain forest, bring sturdy walking-shoes, preferably of canvas with thick rubber soles as they dry out easily, and sprinkle your socks with sulphur powder to deter errant insects. Monteverde's cloud-forest reserves and Tortuguero's lodges all rent or supply rubber boots and rain ponchos. San José's cooler climate requires a jacket or sweater in the evenings and, if you are traveling during or near the rainy season, a collapsible umbrella is always useful.

Electricity

110 volts, 60 cycles AC using flat-pin U.S. plugs. Europeans will need to bring adaptors.

Church of Las Mercedes, Grecia

Etiquette

Ticos are warm, friendly people who also have a clear sense of etiquette. When introduced to someone, shake hands and address them by name if you know it. It is considered impolite to enter someone's house unless you have been invited in, even if the door is wide open—if you are looking for someone, call out *Upe!* first. Avoid wearing beach clothes in towns and never attempt nude sunbathing.

Green Pass

This should be purchased from the Servicio de Parques Nacionales (see **Camping**, above) in San José. At the current rate of $29, it offers entrance to four national parks of your choice, plus one extra assigned by the Parks Office. This represents a saving of over 50 percent on paying entrance fees at individual parks.

Photography

Film is expensive, so bring all you can with you. Officially the limit is six rolls but this is often overlooked. Color-print film is easily available, but stock up in San José on color-slide or black and white film. Do check expiration dates. Rain and cloud forests need fast film, so take 400ASA or, better still, 1,000ASA. Take extra batteries, as these run out fast in warm, humid conditions. 24-hour processing is available in San José but the quality is poor. Do not allow any exposed or unexposed film through the X-ray machines at Juan Santamaría airport.

Places of worship

Protestant services in English
● Episcopal Church of the Good Shepherd, Avenida 4/Calle 3 & 5, San José (tel: 225-1560)
● Union Church, Moravia (tel: 235-6709)
● International Baptist Church, San Pedro (tel: 253-7911)
● Escazú Christian Fellowship, Escazú (tel: 231-4159)
● Victory Christian Center, Santa Ana (tel: 282-7720)
● Berean Baptist Church, San Antonio (tel: 236-1987)
Roman Catholic mass in English
● San Rafael de Escazú Church (tel: 289-7530)

Jewish
- B'Nai Israel (Reform Jewish community) San José (tel: 257-1785/ 231-5243)
- Chabad Lubavitch of Costa Rica, Centro Colón, San José (tel: 231-5745)

Toilets

Public toilets are found in bus stations (not the most salubrious), airports, museums, restaurants, and most *sodas*. Ask for *servicios*, *sanitarios* or *baños*.Tico plumbing is not elaborate, so used paper is thrown into a waste-paper basket.

Visitors with disabilities

Extreme difficulty of access must be expected, even in towns, where such pavements as do exist are often in bad condition and buildings have no ramps. That said, taxis are cheap, internal flights may be an option, and spacious four-wheel-drive vehicles can be rented (at a price). A few hotels have been designed for wheelchairs, such as San José's Holiday Inn (see page 200); Hotel Fiesta de la Playa, El Roble, Puntarenas (tel: 663-0808, fax: 663-1516); and Hotel Herredura (Sheraton), San Antonio de Belén (near Juan Santamaría airport; tel: 239-0033, fax: 239-2292). For further information contact the Consejo Nacional de Rehabilitación y Educacion Especial, Apdo 72 170-1000 San José, or at Avenida 6/Calle 21 & 25 (tel: 287-8055).

Women travelers

Costa Rica is as safe for women as it is for men. Thefts and assaults are not generally sexist: just follow normal precautions. Avoid walking on deserted urban streets at night and be careful about choosing budget hotels in large towns and ports. The odd comment or hiss from a macho Tico is no more annoying than in any other country, but some Ticos also see *gringas* (foreign women) as easy game, so their gambits should be treated with a large pinch of salt. Otherwise, Costa Rica's extensive tourism infrastructure makes it an unusually relaxing destination for women, either alone or in groups.

CONVERSION CHARTS

FROM	TO	MULTIPLY BY
Inches	Centimeters	2.54
Centimeters	Inches	0.3937
Feet	Meters	0.3048
Meters	Feet	3.2810
Yards	Meters	0.9144
Meters	Yards	1.0940
Miles	Kilometers	1.6090
Kilometers	Miles	0.6214
Acres	Hectares	0.4047
Hectares	Acres	2.4710
Gallons	Liters	4.5460
Liters	Gallons	0.2200
Ounces	Grams	28.35
Grams	Ounces	0.0353
Pounds	Grams	453.6
Grams	Pounds	0.0022
Pounds	Kilograms	0.4536
Kilograms	Pounds	2.205
Tons	Tonnes	0.9057
Tonnes	Tons	1.104

MEN'S SUITS							
US	36	38	40	42	44	46	48
UK	36	38	40	42	44	46	48
Rest of Europe	46	48	50	52	54	56	58

DRESS SIZES						
US	6	8	10	12	14	16
UK	8	10	12	14	16	18
France	36	38	40	42	44	46
Italy	38	40	42	44	46	48
Rest of Europe	34	36	38	40	42	44

MEN'S SHIRTS						
US	14	14.5	15	15.5	16	16.5	17
UK	14	14.5	15	15.5	16	16.5	17
Rest of Europe	36	37	38	39/40	41	42	43

MEN'S SHOES						
US	8	8.5	9.5	10.5	11.5	12
UK	7	7.5	8.5	9.5	10.5	11
Rest of Europe	41	42	43	44	45	46

WOMEN'S SHOES						
US	6	6.5	7	7.5	8	8.5
UK	4.5	5	5.5	6	6.5	7
Rest of Europe	38	38	39	39	40	41

Outside Costa Rica
● **USA** tel: 1-800-343-6332
Elsewhere, contact your Costa Rican embassy or consulate.

Inside Costa Rica
● **San José:** ICT (Instituto Costarricense de Turismo), Plaza de La Cultura/ Calle 5 (tel: 222-1090)
● **Caldera** ICT, Puerto Caldera (tel: 634-4067)
● **Golfito** ICT, Deposito Libre Comercial de Golfito (tel: 775-0496)
● **Heredia** ICT, Avenida 4/Calle 5 & 7 (tel: 223-1733)
● **Liberia** ICT, Casa de La Cultura (tel/fax: 666-1606)
● **Paso Canoas** ICT, Edifico de Aduana (tel/fax: 732-2035)
● **Peñas Blancas** ICT, Edifico de Aduana (tel/fax: 679-9269)
Telephone information is available for **Monteverde** (tel: 645-5010 fax: 645-5180) and for **Limón** (tel: 758-4691).

Selected tour agencies
● **Adventureland** Avenida 1/Calle 1 & 3 (tel: 222-3866, fax: 222-3724). Useful for ballooning, car rental, horse riding, surfing, biking, camping, rafting, bungee-jumping, and the like. Regular tours include the Caribbean banana train.
● **Aventuras Naturales** San Pedro (tel: 224-0505, fax: 253-6934). Mountain-bike tours, kayaking, and whitewater rafting.
● **Costa Rica Expeditions** Dept 235,

PO Box 025216, Miami, FL33102-5216 (San José tel: 257-0766, fax: 257-1665). American-owned tour agency, one of Costa Rica's largest. Birdwatching tours to Monteverde, Tortuguero and Corcovado, and a pioneer of rafting trips.
● **Diving Safaris** (tel/fax: 670-0012). Guanacaste-based agency offering diving trips off Playa Ocotal, the Islas Murciélagos and to Isla del Coco.
● **Dos Montañas Tours** (tel: 233-6455, fax: 255-4354). Scuba-diving, mountain-biking, whitewater rafting, kayaking, and bungee-jumping.
● **Escenarios Tropicales** (tel: 224-2555, fax: 234-1554). Luxury 10-day diving trips to Isla del Coco.
● **Geoventuras** (tel: 221-2053, fax: 282-3333). Unusual 'humanitarian tours' that visit the other Costa Rica, e.g., orphanages, a women's prison, and an indigenous reserve.
● **Guanacaste Tours** Apdo 55, 5000 Liberia (tel: 666-0306, fax: 666-0307). Horseback tours of Guanacaste's national parks (Santa Rosa, Rincón de la Vieja, Palo Verde), Arenal, and Tamarindo.
● **Horizontes** Apdo 1780, 1002 San José (tel: 222-2022, fax: 255-4513). Highly reputable tour agency with emphasis on environmental concerns. Nature and adventure tours; tailor-made tours for individuals.

Hotels exuding old-world charm may not be the most comfortable

HOTELS AND RESTAURANTS

HOTELS AND RESTAURANTS
ACCOMMODATIONS

Costa Rica's hotels range from basic *cabinas* (literally "cabins" but more often a row of simple, family-owned rooms) to luxury lodges set in vast grounds overlooking the ocean, deep in the rain forest or high in the cloud forest. With a few exceptions, hotels are pleasantly small-scale, and in many places will be your base for adventure tours and activities. Outside the main tourist centers of San José and Manuel Antonio and, to a lesser extent, Guanacaste's and Limón's beach resorts, they are often isolated, requiring private transportation or the hotel's own shuttles, charter planes, boats, or tractors. Prices per double room or *cabina* are grouped here in three categories:

- **budget** (\$) up to \$40
- **moderate** (\$\$) \$45–70
- **expensive** (\$\$\$) \$75 upwards

GUANACASTE
Cañas
Hacienda La Pacífica (\$\$\$) 3 miles north of Cañas (tel: 669-0050 fax: 669-0555). Well-designed wooden cabins with hot water and fans in large private reserve near Corobicí river. Pool, international restaurant, birdwatching and other activities.
Hotel Cañas (\$/\$\$) Calle 2/Avenida 3 (tel/fax: 669-0039). 36-room hotel in town center. Rooms with air conditioning or fan, and hot water. Good restaurant and bar, laundry service.

La Cruz
Amalia's Inn (\$\$) La Cruz (tel/fax: 679-9181). Well indicated from highway, on hilltop in town with sweeping views over bay. Small hotel with comfortable, spacious suites and hot showers. Pool, convenient for beaches.

Liberia
Hotel El Sitio (\$\$\$) Liberia (tel: 666-1211 fax: 666-2059). Well located near main crossroads of Interamerican; under dynamic new German ownership, with spacious grounds, pools, spa, restaurant and bright, modern rooms with phone, cable TV and hot showers. Exemplary recycling operation.
Hotel La Siesta (\$) Calle 4/Avenida 4 & 6 (tel: 666-0678 fax: 666-2532). Quiet location in central Liberia. Simple, clean rooms with hot showers, and fan or air conditioning. Small pool, restaurant, laundry service.

Montezuma
El Ancla de Oro (\$) Cabuya (village tel: 642-0023). Friendly Tico hotel with basic accommodation; shared bathrooms. Tranquil village location, garden. Tours to Malpaís, horse riding, boating, sportfishing.

El Saño Banano (\$\$\$) Montezuma (tel/fax: 642-0272). Beautifully landscaped beach-front grounds about 2 miles east of village. Igloo-style or wooden cabins, all with kitchenette, spring-water showers and terrace. Cheaper rooms, also a three-bedroom apartment. Transport to and from village. Friendly, tranquil atmosphere. Wholefood restaurant (\$) run by same people on Montezuma's main crossroads shows nightly videos.
Hotel Amor de Mar (\$/\$\$) Montezuma (tel/fax: 642-0262). Easy-going atmosphere in old clapboard house at southern end of village right on rocky beach. Simple rooms with shared or private bathrooms, some with hot water, all leading off spacious wooden veranda. Bar/restaurant.
Hotel Celaje (\$/\$\$) Cabuya de Cóbano (tel/fax: 284-7562). On isolated stretch of road to Cabuya, fronting beach. A-frame thatched cabins sleep four, with shower, porch and hammock. Well laid-out grounds with Jacuzzi, pool, restaurant. Italian owners organize kayaking, fishing, boat and horse tours.
Hotel Los Mangos (\$/\$\$) Montezuma (tel: 661-1122 ext 259 fax: 661-2320). Garden hotel surrounded by mango trees overlooking sea at southern end of village. Greek owners. Pleasantly rustic cabins or spacious rooms in old hotel section, sleeping up to four. All with fans and decent cold showers. Pool and verdant, breezy restaurant.
Hotel Montezuma (\$) (tel: 642-0258). Old clapboard hotel right on main beach at heart of nocturnal action. Simple, clean rooms with fan and shower, for up to four people. Upstairs rooms with balconies are cooler. Reasonably priced open-air bar and restaurant.

Nicoya
Hotel Jenny (\$) 50m south of Parque Central (tel: 685-5050 fax: 686-6471). Uninspired modern hotel in center. All rooms air-conditioned with TV, shower and phone. Private parking.

Nosara
Almost Paradise (\$) (tel/fax: 680-0856). German bed and breakfast on hilltop with lovely ocean views. Large garden, pleasant rooms with hot showers, fans, some balconies. Gourmet restaurant. Three minutes' walk to beach.
Casa Pacifico (\$\$) Playa de Garza (cellular tel: 257-8585 fax: 224-5220). Pretty little Dutch-owned *cabinas* right on beach south of Nosara. Four comfortable rooms with hot showers, fan and quirky furnishings. Rustic atmosphere, relaxed beachfront bar and restaurant. Horse riding, reef-snorkeling, hiking.
Hotel Chorotega (\$) (no phone). Simple, friendly *cabinas* on edge of village. Pleasant two-story design around courtyard with rocking chairs. Restaurant in

season. Clean, basic rooms with fans, shared or private showers.

Hotel Playa de Nosara ($$) Apdo 4, Nosara de Nicoya (tel/fax: 680-0495). Extraordinary Mediterreanean-style and -owned hotel rising between Playa Guiones and Playa Nosara. Superb views from pricier rooms with balconies, fans, reading-lights and good bathrooms. Mature garden, pool, and panoramic domed restaurant areas. Greek taverna 100 yards down road near beach.

Villa Taype ($$) Apdo 8, Nosara (tel/fax: 680-0763). About 100 yards from Playa Guiones, a German-owned hotel with 21 rooms surrounding gardens and pool. Air conditioning or fan, some separate bungalows. Turtle tours, sportfishing, tennis, bikes.

Papagayo

Costa Smeralda ($$$) Apdo 12177-1000, San José (tel: 670-0044 fax: 670-0379). Large luxury Italian-owned hotel opened in 1995 in spectacular site overlooking Playa Panamá and Bahía Culebra. 80 well-designed rooms scattered over landscaped hillside, free-form pool, towering rancho bar. Generously scaled restaurant serving international cuisine.

Refugio Natural Papagayo ($$$) c/o Estratur, Apdo 234-1017, San José (tel: 296-5118 fax: 220-3742). The ultimate in back-to-nature luxury. Former US Army tents (MASH-style) with shower-rooms and verandas in jungle setting on narrow Papagayo isthmus between two lovely beaches. Gourmet restaurant, full bar. Four-wheel-drive access through Papagayo development, but conditions may change as resort develops.

Parque Nacional Guanacaste

Hacienda Los Inocentes ($$) Apdo 1370-3000, Heredia (tel: 679-9190 or 265-5484 fax: 265-6431). Characteristic old hacienda on 1,000-acre cattle ranch with lofty rooms, each with private bathroom located across corridor. Verandas with rocking chairs and hammocks for gazing at Volcán Orosí. Some cabins in woods. Pool, restaurant, horse riding tours, dynamic young owners.

Parque Nacional Rincón de la Vieja

Rincón de la Vieja Mountain Lodge ($$) Apdo 114-5000, Liberia (tel: 225-1073 tel/fax: 695-5553). Wooden lodge in beautiful and extensive ranch adjoining national park. Modest rooms with porches and private bathrooms, central meeting and eating area for mainly European clientèle. Horse riding, canopy tours, camping facilities available.

Playa Conchal

Hotel Brasilito ($) Playa Brasilito (tel: 654-4237 fax: 654-4247). Bright yellow wooden house with open-air restaurant on beach near Playa Conchal. Simple rooms with

fans and cold showers. Horse riding, boats, snorkeling, and diving.

Playa del Coco

Cabinas Playa del Coco ($) Apdo 2, Playa del Coco (tel: 670-0110 fax: 670-0167). The first hotel on this popular beach. Funky old wooden structure containing dilapidated rooms with showers, in great position overlooking beach. Lively open-air restaurant and disco, so can be noisy.

Flors de Itabo ($$$) Playa del Coco (tel: 670-0011 fax: 670-0003). Set in gardens on main road leading into resort. Well-equipped rooms with air conditioning, satellite TV. Facilities include pool, excellent Italian restaurant. Horse riding and fishing tours.

Playa Flamingo

Bahía Potrero Resort ($$/$$$) Apdo 45-5051, Santa Cruz (tel: 654-4183 fax: 654-4093). Well-situated beachfront hotel a few miles north of Flamingo. 14 ranch-style rooms with fans and hot showers around large, mature garden with pool. Pricier, more spacious rooms have air conditioning, real baths, and kitchenettes. Restaurant, boutique, safe swimming, horseriding and fishing trips.

Casa Sunset House ($) Playa Potrero (tel/fax: 654-4265). Individual cabins built up hillside, 15 minutes' walk from Playa La Penca. Fresh, simple rooms with double bed and bunks, fan, good showers and verandas. Reductions for longer stays, pick-up from Flamingo. Friendly American family atmosphere.

Flamingo Marina Hotel ($$$) Apdo 321-1002, San José (tel: 654-4141 fax: 654-4035). Large complex overlooking marina. Sports facilities include tennis, boogie-boards, mountain bikes, and snorkeling—all free for guests. Large pool with swim-up bar and Jacuzzi. Well-appointed though unimaginative rooms, suites and condominiums. Adjacent to casino.

Hotel Cielomar ($/$$) Playa La Penca (tel: 654-4194). 11 *cabinas* on pretty white beach north of Flamingo. Simple rooms with air conditioning, fan and showers. Tico owners provide breakfast and dinner on request.

Sugar Beach Hotel ($$$) Playa Pan de Azúcar (tel: 257-4667 or tel/fax: 654-4242 fax: 654-4239). Fabulous headland setting with views south to Flamingo and over rocky offshore islands. Very comfortable rooms or spacious bungalows with air conditioning, fans, hot water, porches, hammocks right on lovely beach with safe swimming. Excellent, breezy bar/restaurant with stunning sunset views. Transport arranged from Tamarindo airport.

Playa Grande

Hotel Las Tortugas ($$$) Apdo 164-5051, Santa Cruz (tel/fax: 680-0765). Even the hotel pool is turtle-shaped on this turtle-obsessed beach. Reasonable rooms with hot showers and fan or air conditioning. Breezy restaurant overlooking beach and plenty of turtle-related activities, canoe-trips, fishing, scuba-diving.

Playa Hermosa

El Velero Hotel ($$) Playa Hermosa (tel: 670-0330 tel/fax: 670-0310). Small-scale, upmarket Canadian-owned hotel fronting pretty beach. Tastefully designed rooms with fans and good bathrooms, around verandas, garden, bar/restaurant and pool. Fishing and sailing tours.
Hotel Playa Hermosa ($) Playa Hermosa (tel/fax: 670-0136). Located down first turn-off to beach in quiet beachfront site. Reasonable rooms with showers, hot water, fans, plus a good Italian restaurant in garden.
Playa Hermosa Inn ($$) Playa Hermosa (tel/fax: 670-0163). Lovely beachfront garden setting. Spacious, bright, fan-cooled rooms with hot showers. One air-conditioned apartment with kitchen. Pool.

Playa Junquillal

Cabinas Junquillal ($) (no phone). A good budget choice at entrance to beach and run by dynamic Tico. Lively bar/restaurant serving Tico dishes, simple but clean rooms with showers and fans.
Hotel Hibiscus ($$) Apdo 163-5150 Santa Cruz (tel: 680-0737). Reasonably priced hotel in jungle garden setting. Tastefully decorated bungalows equipped with fans, porches, hot showers. European restaurant.

Playa Naranjo

Complejo Turistico Playa Naranjo ($) (tel/fax: 661-4148). Convenient location near ferry. Expanding complex of *cabinas*, popular bar, restaurant and pool in small garden. Pleasant family rooms with air conditioning or fan, and private showers.
Hotel Rancho Bahía Gigante ($) (tel/fax: 661-2442). About 5½ miles south of Playa Naranjo, a ranch-style hotel in lovely grounds with rancho restaurant, large pool and very reasonably priced, fan-cooled rooms with showers. Friendly, gregarious American owner. Kayaking around islands in the bay, horse riding, snorkeling. Untouched jungle surroundings.
Oasis del Pacifico ($$) Apdo 200-5400, Puntarenas (tel/fax: 661-1555). Beautiful landscaped grounds bordering wild forest with nature trails. Clean, whitewashed rooms and suites, all with fans, good bathrooms and porches. Two pools, open-air dining, hammocks by bay. Horse riding, tennis, sportfishing.

Playa Ocotal

El Ocotal ($$$) El Coco (tel: 670-0321/0324 fax: 670-0083). Luxurious hotel in spectacular hilltop location. Well-appointed rooms, suites and bungalows with endless amenities, three pools, Jacuzzis, spa, gym, sport-fishing, scuba-diving, sailing, tennis, horse riding.
Villa Casa Blanca ($$) (tel/fax: 670-0448). Canadian-owned, Spanish-style villa with ten well-decorated, fan-cooled or air conditioned rooms in lush garden and pool setting. Two family apartments.

Playa Sámara

Casa del Mar ($$) Playa Sámara (tel/fax: 685-5004). Friendly Québecois-owned 18-room hotel one block from beach. Fresh, fan-cooled rooms with insect screens and good bathrooms. Well-maintained, cheaper rooms with shared bathrooms. Jacuzzi, bar, and breakfasts.
Hotel Giada ($) Playa Samara (tel/fax: 685-5004). New Italian-owned hotel with cheerful modern rooms, bamboo furniture, balconies, fans. Breakfasts.
Hotel Guanamar ($$$) Playa Carrillo (tel: 293-4544 fax: 293-4839). Large resort hotel geared to sportfishers. Bungalows with lovely views scattered over terraced slope overlooking beach. Kitsch interior decoration but all possible amenities and activities—including a casino. Popular with Tico politicians.
Hotel Punta Islita ($$$) Nandayure, San José (tel: 296-3817 fax: 231-0715). Exclusive hideaway accessible by charter plane or four-wheel drive from Sámara. Sensational hilltop location overlooking private beach. Tasteful bungalows and exceptional suites arranged on slope. Lovely pool/ bar and lofty rancho restaurant—reasonably priced with good wine list. Colonial-style atmosphere helped by props from the *1492* film about Christopher Columbus. Jeeps run guests down to the beach for jet-skiing.
Hotel Sámara Beach ($$/$$$) Apdo 001, Sámara (village tel: 680-0445). Attractive, Spanish-owned, two-story hotel overlooking garden and pool. Thatched open-air restaurant and 20 excellent-value, tasteful rooms with real bathtubs and bidets, air conditioning or fan. Fishing, horse riding, diving, boat, and bike rental.

Playa Tamarindo

Hotel Capitan Suizo ($$$) (tel/fax: 680-0853). Beautifully designed, stark white bungalows with beds on raised platforms, teak furniture, huge windows and luxurious bathrooms. Cheaper rooms in main block. Large open-air restaurant/ bar by pool a few steps from beach at southern end of Tamarindo. Swiss-owned.
Hotel Jardín d'Eden ($$$) Apdo 1094-2050, San Pedro (tel: 654-4111 tel/fax: 220-2096). Italian-French ownership. Intelligently terraced and landscaped Mediterranean-style hotel on hillside overlooking beach. Two free-form pools, one with swim-up bar adjoining breezy restaurant with European cuisine. Comfortable though small rooms with air conditioning, terrace, and pretty tiled bathrooms. Copious breakfasts included in rates.

Hotel Zullymar ($) (tel: San José 226-4732). Three room-types around small garden, all with hot showers and fans, some air-conditioned. Simple, spacious porches. Good central location.

Playa Tambor
Hotel Dos Lagartos ($) Playa Tambor (tel/fax: 642-0236). Oldest hotel on beach, in a characteristic clapboard house, now American-owned. 23 small rooms, with or without shower, all with fan. Very clean; breakfasts available.
Playa Tambor Beach Resort ($$) Playa Tambor (tel: 661-1915 fax: 661-2069). Huge, controversial resort owned by Spanish Barceló group geared to package holidays. 402 well-designed rooms with air conditioning, safes, satellite TV, good bathrooms and balconies—all prefabricated in the United States! All rates include buffet meals, pools, water sports, nightly cabarets, entertainment, and shops. Adjoining nature reserve with trails.
Tambor Tropical ($$$) Playa Tambor (tel: 288-0491). Five hexagonal two-story cabins impressively handcrafted in 12 different woods by American owner. Open-plan living/bedroom space and fully equipped kitchen area with bathroom, terrace and veranda. Set in coconut palms by pool overlooking beach. Bar/restaurant, riding, snorkeling, fishing.

Río Tempisque
Hotel Rancho Humo ($$/$$$) Puerto Humo (tel: 255-2463 fax: 255-3573). Superb views from this strategic hotel on banks of Tempisque river within easy striking distance of Palo Verde, Lomas Barbudal and Barra Honda. Thatched cabins with shared bathroom or air conditioned rooms in main lodge. Restaurant, pool, boat tours, horse riding, hiking in private reserve.

Santa Cruz
Hotel La Estancia ($) 100 yards west of Plaza Los Mangos (tel: 680-0476). Relatively new *cabinas*-style hotel in town center. Very clean, comfortable rooms with two fans and cold showers. Good for an emergency stopover.

THE NORTH
Fortuna de San Carlos
Cabinas Grijalba ($) 100 yards west of church on main road (tel: 479-9129). Well-maintained, fan-cooled rooms with hot showers; low prices. Thin walls so check out your neighbors. Friendly Tica owner does laundry.
Cabinas Guacamaya ($) next to school (tel/fax: 479-9087). Tucked away in quiet location south of main square. Air-conditioned rooms with hot showers and fridge, simply decorated. Friendly owner organizes tours.

Cabinas Ribera ($) 300 yards north of main square (tel: 479-9048). Friendly family farm in ultra-quiet riverbank location. Simple, clean rooms with fans, hot showers.

Guápiles
Casa Río Blanco ($$) Apdo 241-7210, Guápiles, (tel/fax: 710-2652). On edge of Braulio Carrillo national park, in relaxing, riverside setting, perfect for birdwatchers. Canopy-level viewing areas. Rooms with fans and hot-water bathrooms. Naturalist tour and breakfast included in rates. Swimming, hiking.
Las Palmas ($) opposite EARTH college, Pocora (tel: 716-5289 fax: 716-5101). A good halfway halt between San José and Limón. Small, clean rooms, most with hot showers and TVs. Adjoining private reserve with trail. Ambitious plans to create a heliconia garden and a waterfall running through hotel. Good restaurant.

Laguna de Arenal
Hotel Tilawa ($$$) Nuevo Arenal (tel: 695-5050 fax: 695-5766). At western end of lake, a large colonnaded hotel with wind-surfing center down dirt road. Restaurant, bar, pool, tennis, and comfortable, spacious rooms, some with kitchenettes. Horses and mountain bikes. Weekly package rates.
La Ceiba ($) Apdo 9, Tilarán (fax: 695-5387). Four comfortable, bright *cabinas* fronted by generous porch with hammocks and chairs in spectacular scenic position high above lake. Extensive, well-tended gardens and organic farm surround the steep access track from lake road. Well signposted from road; owned by two German artists.
Mystica Lake Lodge ($$) near Nuevo Arenal (fax: 695-5387). Six comfortable, spacious rooms with hot-water bathrooms, open onto front veranda with lovely lake views and cooling breezes.

Monteverde/Santa Elena
Arco-Iris Ecolodge ($) Apdo 003-5655, Santa Elena de Monteverde (tel: 645-5067 fax: 645-5022). Scenic, hillside site in center of Santa Elena, run by friendly polyglot Europeans. Attractive wooden cabins with hot showers. Excellent restaurant, laundry, organic garden.
Cloud Forest Lodge ($$) 1.2 miles east of main road (tel: 645-5058 fax: 645-5168). A naturalist's special in spectacular isolated setting between Monteverde and Santa Elena. 18 well-designed laurel-wood cabins and huge open restaurant; sitting area overlooking valley. Canopy and birdwatching tours in own cloud forest. Very environmentally conscious.
El Sapo Dorado ($$$) between Santa Elena and Monteverde (tel/fax: 645-5010). Well-designed and appointed cabins in land-scaped grounds beside main road. Classical music; vegetarian selection.

HOTELS AND RESTAURANTS

Finca Valverde ($$) Santa Elena (tel: 645-5157). Family-run complex of spacious log cabins in forest off road. Good birdwatching trails. Bar is favorite meeting-place for American volunteers.

Hotel Fonda Vela ($$) Apdo 7-0060-1000, San José (tel: 645-5125 fax: 645-5119). At base of hill leading to Monteverde Cloud Forest Reserve. 28 well-designed rooms with porches in landscaped grounds. Restaurant, horse riding and sunset views to Gulf of Nicoya.

Parque Nacional Volcán Poás

La Providencia ($$) (tel: 232-2498 fax: 231-2204). Pleasant rustic cabins on large family farm bordering park. Panoramic views, hiking, horse riding, birdwatching.

Poás Volcano Lodge ($$) near Vara Blanca (tel/fax: 441-9102). Elegant old manorhouse offering upmarket bed and breakfast. Living-room fireplace, personal service.

Puerto Viejo de Sarapiquí

Albergue de Montaña El Gavilán ($) Apdo 445-2010, San José (tel: 234-9507 fax: 253-6556). Pleasant log cabins in lovely peaceful grounds by river. Open-air restaurant, Jacuzzi, small private reserve. Horse riding, boat trips, guided hikes.

Albergue Oroverde ($) Puerto Viejo, Sarapiquí, (tel/fax: 223-7479). A vast 2,500-acre rain forest paradise on Sarapiquí river near Nicaraguan border. Dormitory or basic cabin accommodation. Three-day packages from San José with all-inclusive rates. Local naturalist guides.

Albergue Selva Verde ($$) Chilamate (tel: 766-6077 fax: 766-6011). A long-established rain forest lodge with elaborately designed walkways in superb private reserve, popular with birdwatching groups. 5 miles west of Puerto Viejo, set back from main road. Open-air restaurant, butterfly enclosure, botanic garden, reference library. Well-conceived rooms; some of the bungalows are situated in the forest.

Islas del Rio Lodge ($$) Apdo 979-4050, Alajuela (tel/fax: 710-6898). Log-cabin overlooking Sarapiquí river about 6 miles west of Puerto Viejo. Rooms with private or shared bathrooms, relaxed atmosphere. Rates include three meals. Hiking, boat tours to river islands, rafting available.

Posada Andrea Cristina ($) Apdo 14, Puerto Viejo (tel/fax: 766-6265). Relaxed, friendly family-run *cabinas* in lush garden just west of village. Simple rooms with showers, fan, terrace, excellent breakfast. Boat tours, riding. Very good value. Only four rooms so phone ahead.

Rara Avis ($$/$$$) Sarapiquí (tel/fax: 253-0844). Legendary private reserve founded in 1983 (see page 80). Accommodations either at El Plástico, a rustic research station, or at more luxurious Waterfall Lodge in comfortable rooms. Access by tractor from Las Horquetas, south of Puerto Viejo. All-inclusive rates.

Refugio Nacional Caño Negro

Albergue Caño Negro ($$) Los Chiles (tel: 460-0124 tel/fax: 240-5460). Superb, isolated setting in private reserve 6 miles south of Los Chiles and 4 miles west along a rough track. Four-wheel drive in dry season, tractor in rainy season. Comfortable wooden cabins sleeping five overlooking lagoon by Río Frío. Open rancho restaurant. Riding, fishing, boat-trips, perfect for birdwatchers.

Tilarán

Hotel Yasmine ($) west side of main square (tel: 695-5043 fax: 695-5617). Basic, small rooms with or without shower. Well maintained by American owner who offers plenty of information on area. Laundry, restaurant.

Volcán Arenal

Arenal Lodge ($$$) (tel: 289-6588 fax: 289-6798). Atmospheric lodge 11 miles west of La Fortuna up a steep hill. Comfortable, attractive suites and older rooms are all bright and clean with wicker furniture and good bathrooms. Library with fireplace and pool table, superb glassed-in restaurant and open porch with rocking chairs for musing on the volcano.

Arenal Observatory Lodge ($$) (tel: 257-9489 fax: 2575-4220). About 6 miles south of main road along rough track requiring four-wheel drive. Simple, rustic rooms with bunk beds and hot showers, set among pine and eucalyptus trees with fantastic views of the rumbling monster. Buffet-style restaurant, tours.

Linda Vista del Norte Lodge ($$) El Castillo de La Fortuna (tel/fax: 479-9025 for messages). On a superb hilltop site with close-up of Arenal's fireworks. Simple, spacious *cabinas* with showers and porch—you pay for the volcano, not the trimmings. Good, reasonably priced restaurant, friendly staff. Horse riding, boat-trips, hiking activities. Four-wheel drive advisable.

THE CENTER
Alajuela

Hotel Alajuela ($) Parque Central (tel: 441-1241 fax: 441-7912). Clean, pleasant rooms and apartments in old or new annexes. Showers and baths, fans.

Las Orquídeas ($$$) 2 miles northwest of Alajuela (tel: 433-9346 fax: 433-9740). Convenient for airport (10 minutes away). Reasonably appointed and decorated rooms, some with air conditioning, some with fans. No children, maybe because of their Marilyn Monroe bar?

Cerro La Muerte

Albergue de Montaña Savegre ($$) Apdo 482, Cartago (tel: 771-1732). Three generations of the exceptionally friendly, original family that pioneered the magical valley of San Gerardo de Dota run this popular hotel. Clean *cabinas* with hot baths, large dining area for family-style meals, all-inclusive rates. Apple orchards, trout-fishing, and quetzals.

Trogon Lodge ($$) Apdo 10980-1000, San José (tel: 223-2421 fax: 255-4039). Youngest member of Mawamba group of lodges. Family-run, comfortable, rustic cabins with heating and hot showers by rushing river in beautiful mountain valley of San Gerardo de Dota. Home cooking, trails, quetzals.

Escazú

Amstel ($$) Apdo 4192-1000, San José (tel: 228-1764 fax: 228-0620). Close to center, pleasant small but upscale hotel with lovely garden and pool. Two suites and 14 carpeted rooms with cable TV, phone. Breakfast included in reasonable rates.

Hotel Mirador Pico Blanco Inn ($$) Apdo 900, Escazú (tel: 228-1908 fax: 289-5189). Sprawling British-owned country inn with fabulous views high up in San Antonio. Comfortable, whitewashed rooms and good bathrooms. Reasonably priced restaurant, pool, terraces. Soon to expand.

Tara Resort ($$$) San Antonio de Escazú (tel: 228-6992 fax: 228-9651). Play at Scarlett O'Hara in this Beverly Hills-style fantasy. Porticoed Tara offers—at a price—health and spa treatment, horse riding, pool, plush rooms, international cuisine.

Esterillos

Hotel Delfin ($/$$) Playa Bejuco, Parrita (tel: 779-9246 fax: 257-0014). Aging beach hotel with astonishing grand staircase. Good-sized rooms with sea views, air conditioning, TV, safe, hot water and balconies. Pool, restaurant, bar. Special four-day rates.

Hotel Fleur de Lys ($$) Playa Esterillos Este (tel: 779-9117 fax: 779-9108). Québecois-owned beach hotel in large garden. Spacious, high ceilings, nicely decorated, fans and hot showers. Room 1 is largest. Same rates for two or four people. Restaurant and relaxed cocktail bar.

Heredia

El Pórtico ($$$) San José de la Montaña, Apdo 289-3000, Heredia (tel: 260-6000/1 fax: 260-6002). Costa Rica's first mountain hotel, recently renovated and extended. Attractive wood and brick ranch in pine forests above Heredia. Well-appointed rooms, public areas with fireplaces, pool, sauna, Jacuzzi, bar, Italian restaurant. Horse riding, hiking trails, tours.

Hotel America ($$) Apdo 1740-3000, Heredia (tel: 260-9292 fax: 260-9293). 40-roomed modern hotel with bar and restaurant, located south of Parque Central. Carpeted rooms with hot showers.

Hotel Valladolid ($$$) Calle 7/Avenida 7 (tel: 260-2905 fax: 260-2912). Heredia's latest top hotel, full of local artwork, well worth its reasonable rates. Very comfortable rooms with cable TV, kitchenette and power-showers. Rooftop Jacuzzi with fabulous views over Central Valley, spectacular sunsets from bar. Adjacent restaurant. Helpful tour desk arranges all-inclusive three-day tour packages (tel/fax: 260-6161).

Jacó

Cabinas Las Palmas ($$) (tel: 643-3005). Tucked away in a large, shady garden down quiet side street. Peppermint-green *cabinas* with shower, fan, porch. Safe parking.

Pochote Grande ($$) Apdo 42, Jacó (tel/fax: 220-4979). Very pleasant German-owned hotel, top of middle range. Lush garden, pool, bright modern rooms with high ceilings, fan, balcony, kitchenette and hot shower. Restaurant/bar. Near beach.

Villa Caletas ($$$) Apdo 12358-1000, San José (tel: 257-3653 fax: 222-2059). One of Costa Rica's most extraordinary luxury hotels, perched on a hilltop beween Tárcoles and Jacó. Oozes old-world charm and taste, antique furnishings, superb design, spectacular views. Comfortable, individual villas, each with different decoration. Pool melts into horizon, amphitheater hosts classical and jazz recitals. No air conditioning, no phone, no TV, no radio. French-Tico ownership.Gourmet bar/restaurant ($$).

Parque Nacional Manuel Antonio

Hotel Arboleda ($/$$$) Apdo 211-6350, Quepos (tel: 777-1056 fax: 777-0092). Several acres of forested grounds spill downhill to private beach. Wide price range, from budget rooms with shared bath to comfortable beachfront cabins. Tours, pool, two restaurants, horse riding, sportfishing.

Hotel Casitas Eclipse ($$$) (tel/fax: 777-0408). Fresh, tastefully decorated Mediterranean-style villas in lush tropical garden around pool. Ground-floor air-conditioned suites with kitchenette and good bathrooms or spacious double rooms upstairs with large terraces. Restaurant ($$) with 360-degree panoramic views under construction, serving barbecued seafood and meat, and international cuisine. Gregarious Tico owner.

Hotel La Mariposa ($$$) (tel: 777-0355 fax: 777-0050). Manuel Antonio's exclusive hotel. Accommodation in rooms or villas, rates include breakfast and dinner. Brilliantly colored furnishings, some scenic garden bathrooms. Open-air bar/restaurant commands Manuel Antonio's best ocean views.

La Quinta ($$) (tel: 777-0434). Signposted from coast road up a short track. Charming, peaceful, Hungarian-owned bed and breakfast with five comfortable rooms (hot showers, fans, large balconies) all set in a large garden with pool and superb views.

Makanda-by-the-sea ($$$) Apdo 29, Quepos (tel: 777-0442 fax: 777-1032). Ultra-contemporary tropical-wood villas in extensive jungle overlooking ocean. 10-minute trail to private beach, lovely pool. All villas and studios are fully equipped for rentals. No children under 16. Californian owner.

Vela Bar ($/$$) Playa Espadilla (tel: 777-0413 fax: 777-1071). Well located close to park and main public beach. Wide range of simply furnished, cool rooms with insect screens, showers, some with private verandas. Good restaurant, small garden. Popular.

Parque Nacional Volcán Irazú

Hotel de Montaña ($) Volcán Irazú (tel: 253-0827 fax: 225-9647). Scenic site under the volcano, overlooking valley and football pitch. Rock-bottom rates for basic rooms, all with showers. Pleasant family-run restaurant with crackling fire; fresh cream is a specialty.

Puntarenas

Costa Rica Yacht Club ($/$$) Cocal (tel: 661-0784 fax: 661-2518). Very reasonably priced fan-cooled or air-conditioned rooms and bungalows with phone, hot water. Pool, parking, laundry, restaurant, tours, yacht charters, sportfishing. Book ahead.

Hotel Las Brisas ($$) Paseo de las Turistas/Calle 31 (tel: 661-4040 fax: 661-2120). Comfortable, quiet, air-conditioned rooms facing beach at western end of landspit. Recommended restaurant serves Greek and Italian dishes and fresh lobster. Small pool.

Hotel Portobello ($$) on estuary (tel: 661-1322 fax: 661-0036). Near Yacht Club a few miles east of town center. Charming, atmospheric hotel in lush tropical gardens. Comfortable rooms with bathtub, TV, phone, and air conditioning. Good open-air bar/restaurant, pool, parking, mooring.

Quepos

Cabinas Ceciliano ($) on exit road toward Manuel Antonio (tel: 777-0192). Family-run budget hotel with 20 small but cool, clean rooms for 2–4 people, with cold showers and fans. Laundry.

Hotel Malinche ($) 75 yards west of bus station (tel/fax: 777-0093). Friendly Tico hotel with cheaper fan-cooled rooms in old wing and comfortable carpeted rooms with air conditioning in new wing. Breakfast, laundry.

Hotel Sirena ($$) 50 yards west of Banco Nacional (tel/fax: 777-0528). Pleasant 15-room hotel with very clean, air-conditioned rooms, all with hot showers. Central pool and sundeck, restaurant.

Reserva Biológica Carara

Villa Lapas ($$$) Apdo 419-4005, Ciudad Cariari, San José (tel: 284-1418 fax: 293-4104). Unadulterated nature in heart of a private forest reserve adjoining Carara. 47-room lodge with spacious, gabled rooms, excellent bathrooms, fans, safe. Small pool but interest lies in riverside trail. Open-air restaurant serves international cuisine; bar. A reasonably priced birdwatchers' paradise.

San José

Hotel Aurora Holiday Inn ($$$) Avenida 5/Calle 5 (tel: 233-7233 fax: 255-1036). Towering 200-room block in center. For those who want to play safe on arrival. All usual amenities, good views.

Hotel Bienvenido ($) Avenida 1 & 3/Calle 10 (tel/fax: 221-1872). Spacious, well-maintained hotel near Mercado Central. Reasonably quiet rooms with hot showers. Restaurant. A safe, central, budget address.

Hotel Fleur de Lys ($$$) Avenida 2 & 6/Calle 13 (tel: 223-1206 fax: 257-3637). Central location opposite Museo Nacional. Swiss-owned hotel in old and pretty frame house with terrace bar, interior restaurant, plants and contemporary Tico artwork. Wide range of well-appointed rooms. Helpful staff, travel desk.

Hotel Galilea ($) Avenida Central/Calle 13 (tel: 233-6925 fax: 223-1689). Uninspired frontage but an excellent budget address. Spacious, clean rooms with good hot showers, fan, phone. Some rooms overlook fortress of Museo Nacional. Friendly staff, safety boxes.

Hotel Grano de Oro ($$$) Avenida 2 & 4/Calle 30 (tel: 255-3322 fax: 221-2782). Charming Canadian-owned luxury hotel in intelligently renovated 1920s mansion full of plants and vintage photos. Excellent conservatory restaurant ($$) spilling into small garden. Rooftop jacuzzi. Tasteful rooms and three suites, all non-smoking. Efficient, friendly staff. Popular with North American clientèle so book well ahead.

Hotel L'Ambiance ($$$) Avenida 9 & 11/Calle 13 (tel: 222-1598 fax: 223-0481). Exclusive luxury hotel with plush rooms arranged around central patio full of plants and a fountain. Refined furnishings, close to central museums. Continental restaurant, no credit cards.

Hotel Petit Victoria ($$) Next to Sala Garbo, Paseo Colón (tel: 233-1812/3 fax: 233-1938). Unpretentious hotel in pretty 1920s house. Simple rooms with fan, TV, fridge, hot showers. Relaxed atmosphere, private parking.

Hotel Santo Tomás ($$$) Avenida 7/ Calle 3 & 5 (tel: 255-0448 fax: 222-3950). Centrally located in Barrio Amón in coffee baron's superb 1910 mansion. Spacious, lofty rooms with classical furnishings and all amenities. Small, verdant breakfast patio and bar. Helpful staff, tours.

Pensión Dunn ($$) Avenida 11/Calle 5 (tel: 222-3232 fax: 221-4596). Small hotel in attractive 1900s house with patio bar. Unpretentious, comfortable rooms with TV, fan. Restaurant, safety boxes, tour desk.

San Ramón
Villa Blanca ($$$) 11 miles north of San Ramón (tel: 228-4603 fax: 228-4004). Well-appointed rooms with balconies in charming colonial *casona* or adobe *casitas* with bathrooms, fridge, fireplace, and desks. All sensitively thought out by ex-President Rodrigo Carazo and his wife. Buffet-style meals, bar, hiking, and riding in private cloud-forest reserve.

THE CARIBBEAN
Barra del Colorado
Casamar ($$$) Laguna Dulce (tel/fax: 433-9287). 12 comfortable cabins in luxuriant grounds, open only Sep–Oct and Jan–May. Three-day packages with nature tours and/or fishing.

Río Colorado Lodge ($$$) (tel: 710-6879 or 232-4063 fax: 231-5987). Founded over 20 years ago by Archie Fields for serious sportfishers. Sophisticated boats, experienced guides. Hearty meals, labyrinthine walkways, zoo, gardens. Lively atmosphere. Fishing and nature packages from San José.

Tarponland ($$) near airstrip (tel: 710-6917 or 221-9932). Reasonably priced three-day packages in locally owned cabins. Nature and fishing tours.

Cahuita
Atlántida Lodge ($$) (tel/fax: 755-0013). Comfortable, rustic rooms with insect screens in peaceful garden setting near Playa Negra. Large pool, boutique, laundry, breakfasts, bar, tours, parking.

Cabinas Black Beach ($) (tel: 758-1515 ext 251). Nicely designed two-story *cabinas*, all with cold showers, fans, hammocks. Tours, laundry, restaurant, parking.

Cabinas Jenny ($) central beach (tel: 758-1515 ext. 256). Well-maintained *cabinas* overlooking rocky beach, some with bunk beds, all with decent showers, fans and porch hammocks. Upstairs rooms pricier.

Cabinas Smith ($) 100-yards south & 50-yards east of Guardia Civil (no phone). One of Costa Rica's best and friendliest accommodations. Six impeccably clean rooms, each with two fans, good bathrooms and hot showers; porches around small garden. Run by charming Talamancan, Joyce Smith.

Magellan Inn ($$) Apdo 1132, Puerto Limón (tel/fax: 755-0035). Intimate, upscale hotel at northern end of Cahuita. Elegant rooms with fans, patio and real American hot showers. Gardens with pool, full bar and restaurant. American-French owners.

Puerto Limón
Hotel Acón ($) Avenida 3/Calle 3 (tel: 758-1010 fax: 758-2924). A safe address centrally located near market. Clean rooms with air conditioning, hot shower. Good restaurant and loud disco.

Hotel Matama ($$$) Playa Bonita (tel: 758-1123 fax: 758-4499). Well-appointed air-conditioned rooms on scenic beach north of town. Garden, pool, international restaurant, tours.

Puerto Viejo
Almendras y Corales (Almonds & Coral Lodge Tent Camp) ($$) Punta Uva/Manzanillo (tel: 272-2024 fax: 272-2220). Astonishing tent lodge in jungle with walkways to wild beach. Raised, screened platforms with basic comforts, shared showers. Back-to-nature experience. Restaurant.

Cabinas Grant ($) Puerto Viejo (tel: 758-3844). Popular budget address in village center. Nice rooms with showers and fans. Breakfast included, laundry, tours, and restaurant.

El Pizote Lodge ($$/$$$) Apdo 230-2200, Coronado (tel/fax: 798-1938). Superb, huge grounds and jungle with comfortable, individual cabins or spacious rooms with shared bathrooms in lodge. Harmonious design, lively bar but rather overpriced restaurant. Located halfway along Playa Negra, five minutes' walk from Puerto Viejo. Parking.

Playa Chiquita Lodge ($$) Apdo 7043-1000, San José (tel: 233-6613 fax: 223-7479). Ten tranquil, well-designed *cabinas* nestle in dense vegetation with 50-yard trail to beach. All rooms with hot shower, screens, fan and veranda. Excellent open-air restaurant. Snorkeling, fishing, jungle tours. Owned by Wolf Bissinger, inspired ecologist owner of Oroverde, near Puerto Viejo de Sarapiquí.

Selvyn Brown's Cabinas ($) Punta Uva (no phone). Good budget address with fantastic seafood restaurant (closed Mon–Tue). Basic *cabinas* with private or shared bath in great location close to safe swimming.

Villa Paraiso ($) Playa Chiquita (no phone). Very relaxed Euro-American family-run *cabinas* in small, dense garden. Reasonably priced rooms with mosquito nets, showers. International food, laundry; bike and beach-buggy rental.

Tortuguero
Cabinas Sabina ($) Tortuguero (no phone). At center of village. Turquoise *cabinas* offer basic accommodations with shared or private bathroom. Some with fans, screens and locks. Communal veranda overlooks beach. Meals next door, but local disco-bar can be noisy.

Laguna Lodge ($$) Apdo 10980-1000, San José (tel: 223-2421 fax: 255-4039). Part of Mawamba group, a slightly downbeat version but equally pleasant site further north from village with direct beach access. Friendly staff, good local food.

Mawamba ($$$) Apdo 10980-1000, San José (tel: 223-2421 fax: 255-4039).

HOTELS AND RESTAURANTS

Convenient location a half-mile north of village with grounds backing onto beach. Well-maintained cabins, large communal dining room, luxuriant gardens, pool. Pleasant staff and good guide service. Two- or three-day packages from San José.
Miss Junie ($) Tortuguero (no phone). New *cabinas* on main path through village. Private showers, fans, though rooms are small. Adjoining restaurant.

THE SOUTH
Bahía Drake
Cecilia's Lodge ($) Agujitas (no phone). Dormitory accommodations and camping with full board, run by friendly family. Horse riding, boat trips, and transport to Corcovado.
Drake Bay Wilderness Camp ($$) Apdo 98-8150, Palmar Norte (tel/fax: 771-2436). Cabins and tents of varying sizes in lush jungly headland at southern end of Bahía Drake. Canoes, kayaks, sportfishing, horse riding, scuba diving. Bar/restaurant. Relaxed atmosphere.
Reserva Biológica Marenco ($$) Apdo 4025-1000, San José (tel: 221-1594 fax: 255-1340). 500-acre reserve bordering Corcovado, owned by Tico family, once a research station. Comfortable wooden cabins in pristine lush jungle with ocean views to Isla del Caño. Good restaurant, guided hikes to Corcovado, beach, snorkeling, and boat trips. Friendly staff, all-inclusive packages from San José via Sierpe.

Dominical
Albergue Willdale ($) (c/o Selvamar tel/fax: 771-1903; USA tel/fax: 804/973-3723). Long-established riverside *cabinas* run by two of Costa Rica's warmest Americans. Basic rooms sleeping three, with fan, shower, porch and own spring water. Kayaks and dinghy for rent. Also comfortable house ($$) sleeping up to six in La Escalera with sweeping ocean views.
Cabinas Diu Wak ($) (tel/fax: 223-8195). On beach crossroads in garden with pool and Jacuzzi. Clean, simple *cabinas* with decent bathrooms, fan and porch. Family suites also available.
Cabinas San Clemente ($) (no phone). Located at northern end of main beach. Attractive, spacious rooms with cross-ventilation, screens, fans and hot showers. Owned by Californian surfer-owner of popular restaurant of same name.
Escaleras Inn ($$$) Las Escaleras (tel: 771-5247). Appears like a mirage in stunning, isolated spot overlooking Pacific, 400 yards above Dominical. Californian owners have accomplished building miracles. Very comfortable, tasteful rooms, pricier cabins under construction. Pool, gourmet restaurant, tours.
Hacienda Barú ($$) north of Dominical (c/o Selvamar tel/fax: 771-1903). Six family cabins near beach in private reserve (see

panel page 153). Each with one single and two double bedrooms, kitchenette, living room, bathroom and veranda. Good Italian meals at neighboring Manigordo restaurant ($).
Villas Río Mar ($$$) Hotel Villas Río Mar, Playa Dominical (tel: 771-2664 fax: 253-1980). Ambitious Dutch-owned hotel in beautifully landscaped grounds near river. 40 well-appointed thatched bungalows with generous curtained verandas but undersized bedrooms. Large pool and swim-up bar, rancho restaurant, tennis, gym, bike-rental.

Golfito
Bungalows Las Palmas ($) Playa Cacao, Apdo 98, Golfito (messages tel: 775-0357 fax: 775-0373). Nice rustic beach cabins, no electricity, basic comforts. Pretty, tranquil location.
Cabinas y Restaurant Mar y Luna ($) Golfito (tel: 775-0192). Next to Las Gaviotas. Clean, new, fan-cooled rooms sleeping three, with shower. Good value, friendly. Excellent seafood restaurant ($) with views over gulf.
Esquinas Rainforest Lodge ($$$) La Gamba (tel: 775-0849/0131 fax: 775-0849). Exceptional ecotourism project in depths of rain forest (see page 155). Ten comfortable, rustic cabins in gardens with pool. Well-designed restaurant, all-inclusive rates. Trails and numerous excursions.
Hotel del Cerro ($) (tel: 775-0006). An ageing beauty opposite old banana dock, with breezy reception area. Front rooms can be noisy. All sleep up to five, with hot showers, fans. Parking, laundry.
Las Gaviotas Hotel ($$) Apdo 12-8201, Golfito (tel: 775-0062 fax: 775-0544). At southern end of town on waterfront. Large garden with 21 comfortable rooms, good bathrooms, porches. Air conditioning or fans. Stylish open-air restaurant, pool, private jetty. Fishing, kayaking, riding.
Rainbow Adventures Lodge ($$$) Playa Cativo (tel/fax: 775-0220). Vast jungle reserve with trails, fantastic birdwatching, superbly furnished cabins and rooms in main house. Package rates from Golfito airport, fishing, snorkeling.

Parque Internacional La Amistad
Finca Anael ($) Reserva Biológica Dúrika (tel: 730-0153 fax: 730-0003). Rustic cabins high in remote Talamanca mountains. Exceptional ecological farm project (see page 169), excellent-value all-inclusive prices from Buenos Aires.
La Amistad Lodge ($$$) Reserva Las Tablas (tel: 233-8228 fax: 255-4636). Lovely old home in private reserve bordering La Amistad. Comfortable rooms, fireplace in sitting area, family atmosphere. Guided hiking, birdwatching, and riding. Four-day packages from San José.

Parque Nacional Chirripó
Posada del Descanso ($) San Gerardo de Rivas (village phone: 771-0433 ext 106). Budget accommodations with shared bathroom, hearty meals, horses, and guides available.

Parque Nacional Corcovado
Corcovado Tent Lodge Camp ($$$) Playa Madrigal. Contact: Costa Rica Expeditions, San José (tel: 222-0333 fax: 257-1665). Screened tents on raised platforms in jungle clearing on beach near park entrance. Shared bathrooms, restaurant, boat- trips, guided hikes. An adventure experience. Two- or three-day packages by charter plane.

Pavones
Pavones Surf Camp ($/$$) Pavones (tel: 225-0786). Cabins with private or shared bathrooms on rocky surfing beach. All-inclusive rates.

Tiskita Lodge ($$$) Bahía Pavones (tel: 233-6890 fax: 255-4410). Last stop in the deep south, located on Punta Banco south of Pavones. Packages from San José by charter plane. Ten rustic cabins overlooking unspoiled beach, experimental fruit farm, private reserve with trails, great birdwatching.

Playa Zancudo
Cabinas La Vista/Bar Arena Alta ($) Apdo 152, Golfito (no phone). Furthest south on beach along good surfing stretch. Six simple, pleasant *cabinas* with shared washing facilities, verandas and hammocks. Rustic bar and restaurant, friendly, eccentric owners. Rainer's hammock tower is a landmark.

Cabinas Sol y Mar ($) Apdo 87, Golfito (tel/fax: 775-0353). Well-designed German-owned hotel right on beach. Four comfortable rooms with fans, hot showers, screens and verandas. Good restaurant, boat tours, safe swimming.

Puerto Jiménez
Agua y Luna ($$) Puerto Jiménez (tel: 735-5034/5033). Across bridge below Parque Central. Clean, spacious rooms with TV and unexpectedly luxurious bathrooms (with tub) overlooking mangroves. Air-conditioning only, porch with hammocks. Excellent open-air restaurant ($) closer to bridge.

Albergue Lapa Ríos ($$$) Apdo 100, Puerto Jiménez (tel: 735-5130 fax: 735-5179). 14 well-designed thatched bungalows with garden showers and screened walls. Huge rain forest reserve with trails, spectacular restaurant with lookout point, nature tours, boat trips. A tropical paradise (see panel on page 168).

Bosque del Cabo ($$$) Cabo Matapalo (tel: 735-5206). High above cape in large private reserve, with trails and lawns dotted with shrubs rolling down to sea. Tranquil spot

with six aesthetically designed cabins, all with garden showers, screens, large deck and hammocks. Full board, riding, kayaking, sportfishing, birdwatching.

Cabinas Puerto Jiménez ($) Puerto Jiménez (tel: 735-5090/5152). On western corner of Parque Central next to El Rancho disco. Three simple, clean and reasonably sized rooms with cold showers and fans. Excellent value, owned by charming taxi-driver, Oscar.

Playa Preciosa ($$) Playa Platanares, c/o Souvenir Corcovado Shop (tel/fax: 735-5005). Play at Robinson Crusoe in 12 cleverly designed thatched cabins with good bathrooms, porches with hammocks. Isolated beachfront location 4 miles from town, extensive gardens, orchards, fresh spring water, lookout point, restaurant, horse riding, kayaking, scuba-diving. Run by idealistic Germans.

San Isidro de El General
Hotel del Sur ($$) (tel: 771-3033 fax: 771-0527). Large hotel complex on Interamerican just south of San Isidro. Family-oriented sports facilities, pool, restaurant, bar. Well-appointed rooms, reasonable rates.

San Vito
Hotel El Ceibo ($) (tel/fax: 773-3025). Large, modern hotel with popular restaurant by central crossroads. Nice, well-furnished rooms with hot showers at back of main block overlooking forest. Cheaper *cabinas* with cold water are popular with early-rising truck drivers. Good restaurant.

Paolo's Guest House ($) (tel: 773-3407). Just outside town in rain forest setting. Beautifully designed, airy house with fireplaces and balconies. Three comfortable bedrooms.

Sierpe
Estero Azul Lodge ($/$$) Apdo 1419-1000, San José (tel: 233-2578 fax: 222-0297). Weekend packages from San José or reasonable drop-in rate. Huge cabins with hot showers and fans, in garden just north of Sierpe. Bird watching trips to mangrove swamps and along Río Estero Azul.

Hotel Pargo Rojo ($) Sierpe de Osa (tel/fax: 788-8032). Canadian-owned hotel beside embarkation point on Río Sierpe. Ten rooms with hot showers, fan or air conditioning. Open-air restaurant, tours to Isla del Caño, Corcovado and mangrove swamps.

Uvita
Hotel El Chamán ($/$$) Uvita (fax: 771-4441). Isolated location on beach a mile south of Uvita. Large garden with hammocks, pool, and 11 cabins with shared or private bathrooms. German-owned. Good open-air restaurant, pleasant atmosphere.

RESTAURANTS

Outside San José, most of the better restaurants are attached to mid-range or upscale hotels, listed on pages 194–203. Otherwise, budget *sodas* are the classic haunts of Ticos all over the country.

The restaurants recommended below are divided into three price categories:
- budget ($)
- moderate ($$)
- expensive ($$$)

Food is generally cheap; even $$$ rarely exceeds $25–30 per person.

GUANACASTE
Liberia
Pizzeria da Beppe ($) Avenida Central/Calle 10 (no phone). A Liberia institution in verdant setting. Great pizza with wide choice of toppings cooked in traditional wood oven.

Parque Nacional Guanacaste
Restaurante Ehecatl ($) Interamerican Highway, La Cruz (tel: 679-9104). Situated 4 miles south of main entrance to park by Río Tempisquito. Breezy open-air restaurant with views of volcanoes. Excellent seafood or meat dishes efficient, friendly service. In La Cruz, hilltop restaurant with same name and same owners has fabulous views.

Playa Naranjo
Hotel El Paso ($$) (tel: 661-2610). Ranch-style hotel with highly reputed seafood restaurant. Plenty of meat dishes and salads too. Enthusiastic owner-manager.

Playa Tamarindo
Sunrise Café ($) village center (no phone). Popular open-air bar/restaurant overlooking beach. Fresh seafood and meat dishes, haphazard service.

THE NORTH
Fortuna de San Carlos
Choza de Laurel ($) (tel: 479-9077). Rustic open-air restaurant at western end of main road. Copious Tico *casados* and some international dishes. Efficient, friendly service.

Puerto Viejo de Sarapiquí
Rancho Leona ($) La Virgen (tel/fax: 761-1019). About 7 miles west of Puerto Viejo. Friendly family restaurant with varied menu including vegetarian dishes. Lodging and kayaking available.

THE CENTER
Escazú
Café El Sol ($$) 300-yards east of Escazú church (tel/fax: 228-1645). Pasta, fish and meat dishes, salads and cocktails in old, pretty house in garden. Sunday brunches are popular with local expatriates. Increasingly geared to groups. Closed Mon.

Manuel Antonio/Quepos
Barba Roja ($$) Apdo 35-6350, Quepos (tel: 777-0331). Open-air terrace restaurant and art gallery with lovely ocean views. Open early for breakfasts and late for dinner.

El Gran Escape ($$) seafront (no phone). Favorite gringo sportfishers' haunt with lively bar. Good seafood, slow service, nautical ambience. Closed Tue.

Jiuberth's ($$) Boca Vieja, Quepos (no phone). Popular taverna-style seafood restaurant on estuary. Charming family set-up but slow service.

Salon Miramar ($) (tel: 777-0332). Popular Tico and gringo bar on seafront road with live music Wed–Sun nights.

San José
Bijahua ($$) Calle 13, opposite Galeria Miro, San Pedro (tel: 225-0613). New, trendsetting restaurant serving Tico nouvelle cuisine. Delectable, unusual mixtures (closed Sun).

El Cuartel de la Boca del Monte ($/$$) Avenida 1/ Calle 21 & 23 (tel: 221-0327). Relaxed, popular bar/restaurant in ranch style. Typical *bocas* and main dishes, cocktails. Fills up later and service slows.

Restaurant Le Chandelier ($$$) 100 yards west and 100 yards south of ICE building in San Pedro (tel: 225-3980 fax: 253-8984). San José's top restaurant, in elegant suburb. Favored by politicians and diplomats for its private rooms, art and antiques.

Restaurant Shakti ($) Avenida 8/Calle 13 (tel: 222-4475). Popular lunchtime spot (open till 8PM); excellent-value macrobiotic food, salads, hamburgers, juices, ice cream.

Taberna y Restaurante Poás ($) Avenida 7/Calle 3 & 5 (tel: 221-7802). Lively jungle-style bar/restaurant with dancing, popular with locals and tourists alike.

THE CARIBBEAN
Cahuita
Restaurante Cahuita Tipico (tel: 758-1515 ext 224). Friendly restaurant in high-foliage décor open all day. Sandwiches, *casados*, prawns, lobster, cocktails. Set back and well signposted from main street.

Puerto Viejo
La Palapa ($) Playa Cocles (tel: 221-9592). About a mile east of Puerto Viejo. Lush garden fronting beach with excellent, reasonably priced seafood.

The Garden ($$) (no phone). At back of village bordering football pitch. Flowery surroundings and decoration. Popular open-air spot serving international, Asian, and Caribbean dishes.

THE SOUTH
Dominical
Soda Laura ($) (no phone). A local institution. Generous portions of fruit salads and typical Tico dishes in simple setting at heart of village.

Index

INDEX

INDEX

Publisher's Acknowledgments

The Automobile Association would like to thank the following photographers, libraries and associations for their assistance.

CLIVE SAWYER (AA PHOTO LIBRARY) took all the pictures in this book except those listed below.

ASSOCIATED PRESS 13a. **BRUCE COLEMAN COLLECTION** 151, 173e. **COSTA RICA EMBASSY** 12, 13b. **F DUNLOP** 19a, 22b, 43, 45, 46b, 62, 131, 141, 148, 155a, 158b, 166b, 167b, 192, 193. **MARY EVANS PICTURE LIBRARY** 25a, 28/9, 28, 31b, 32. **THE NATIONAL MARITIME MUSEUM** 29a, 30, 31a, 31c. **NATIONAL MUSEUM OF COSTA RICA** 25b, 26b, 27a. **NATURE PHOTOGRAPHERS LTD** 16a, 16b, 17a (P R Sterry), 24a (B Burbidge), 48a, 48b, 48c, 49a, 49b, 49c, 49d (P R Sterry), 56a (J Sutherland), 57 (A J Watson), 58a, 58b (P R Sterry), 60a (S C Bisserot), 80 (K Carlson), 82a (A J Cleave), 91a (S C Bisserot), 109 (P R Sterry), 143b, 144/5, 145a, 145b, 157a (P R Sterry), 161a (E A Janes), 163a, 166a (P R Sterry), 172a, 172b (K Carlson), 172c (P R Sterry), 173a (K Carlson), 173c (S C Bisserot), 173d, 173f (E A Janes). **TOPHAM PICTUREPOINT** 35a, 35b.

The Automobile Association would also like to thank Journey Latin America, 14–16 Devonshire Road, Chiswick, London (tel 0181 747 8315) for their help.

Author's Acknowledgments

The author, Fiona Dunlop, would like to thank the following for assisting her in the preparation of this book: Janina Rovinski at the Costa Rican Embassy, Paris; Alfredo Oporta & Susana Orozco at ICT; inspired driver, Jorge Chacon; equally inspired botanist, René Menjivar; the efficient staff of Horizontes Tours; dedicated environmentalist, Dario Castelfranco; hotel manager *extraordinaire*, Loic Dervieu; sloth-sleuth, Jessica Johnson; and countless well-disposed and helpful inhabitants of Costa Rica.

Photographer's Acknowledgments

The photographer, Clive Sawyer, would like to thank the following for their assistance and help in making the photography of Costa Rica a great experience: Ines Trejos at the Embassy of Costa Rica, London; Fernando Chavarria of Costa Rica Top Tours, San José; Eric Maze, guide, San José; Christian Fassler and Pascale Berchmaear of Switzerland, who helped carry bags, mend cars and navigate through the wilds of Costa Rica.

Contributors

Joint series editor: Josephine Perry   **Copy editor**: Susi Bailey
Designer: Design 23   **Verifier**: Alison Baines   **Indexer**: Marie Lorimer